D1634149

THE ART OF SMUGGLING

THE ART OF SMUGGLING

THE GENTLEMAN DRUG TRAFFICKER
WHO TURNED BRITAIN ON

FRANCIS MORLAND

WITH JO BOOTHBY

Milo Books Ltd

Published in November 2015 by Milo Books

Hardback: ISBN 978-1-908479-85-3
Paperback: ISBN 978-1-908479-88-4

Typeset by Zenhancer Technologies Pvt. Ltd.
www.zenhancer.com

Printed in Great Britain by CPI Group (UK) Ltd, Croydon, CR0 4YY

MILO BOOKS LTD
www.milobooks.com

Notes About Boats

Boats are referred to by their maker followed by their length in feet, e.g. a Hillyard 42 is a boat designed by David Hillyard which is forty-two feet long.

Very approximately:

The volume (capacity) of a particular design of boat is proportional to its length cubed.

The weight of a particular design of a boat is proportional to its length squared.

The weight a boat can carry in addition to its own is usually less than one third.

A catamaran is two hulls without keels connected by spars.

A trimaran is one hull without keel with floats connected by spars on either side.

A ketch is a yacht with two masts.

The keel of a yacht is a weighted extension underwater which keeps it upright.

The draught of a yacht is the depth at which its keel touches ground.

Catamarans and trimarans gain their stability from the width of the float elements from each other, have very shallow draughts, and stand upright on a beach.

There is practically no tide in the Mediterranean.

The tidal range on the Atlantic is considerable, and many harbours and rivers are only navigable in the hours before and after high tide.

Contents

PART ONE 1970–71   7

  1   A Knock on the Door   9

  2   Crossing the Atlantic   29

  3   New York   56

PART TWO 1934–71   77

  4   The Morlands   79

  5   Skier   95

  6   Business and Pleasure   111

  7   New Generation   133

  8   Smuggler   141

PART THREE 1971–2015   165

  9   Lewisburg   167

 10 Back to Work   183

 11 Sailor Ted   195

 12 A Family Affair   211

 13 The East Ender   233

 14 One Last Punt   247

Aftermath   264

PART ONE

1970–71

1

A Knock on the Door

TEN-FIFTEEN ON the morning of 15 October 1970. I was dozing in bed in the house at 71 Castelnau.

"*Raindrops keep falling on my head…*"

What a maddening song. Sue must have left the radio on.

"*But that doesn't mean my eyes will soon be turning red. Crying's not for me, cos I ain't gonna stop the rain by complaining.*"

Must be Tony Blackburn's morning show on Radio One. Couldn't he play something else?

"*Because I'm free. Nothing's troub-er-ling me.*"

It was almost a relief when two long buzzes from the electric doorbell disturbed my reverie. But I couldn't hear anybody going to open the door. Where was Sue? Had she taken our son to an early appointment at the dental hospital? Someone else would have to answer it.

"Keith!" I yelled.

My pal, Keith Wilkinson. He had crashed for the night in the bedroom across the hall. But he'd be groggy and confused, even if he was awake. We had been up late, eating rabbit stew and listening to Deep Purple on my new NAD amplifier and Wharfedale speakers from Tottenham Court Road. And had smoked a lot of dope.

I waited, but there was no sound from Keith. Suppressing a groan, I rolled onto my back and looked around the room for the Patagonian poncho I wore only as a dressing gown; I didn't do hippy fashions as a rule. The poncho was on our lopsided ottoman; the kids had broken one of its legs. I sat on it carefully, rubbed my eyes and enshrouded myself.

The bedroom Sue and I shared was a big one off the ground floor, opposite the living room, in our house in Castelnau, the road just south of Hammersmith Bridge in west London. Two beams of light, as from a lighthouse, penetrated the heavy, needle-worked felt of the cashmere curtains that Sue had made. At least it looked nice outside. The bell rang again, rather insistently it seemed to me, so I went to the window that looked out over the driveway. The huge chestnuts, maples and weeping beeches down the street were rusting, the magnolias naked. The acacia remained brilliant.

No Citroen there, so Sue was gone. Just Keith's Vespa scooter, the Bentley Flying Spur – and a Mini Cooper. Whose was that? A man in a sheepskin driver's coat stood in the drive. How ironic. I knew sheepskins well and his was no Morland – my family had been making them for decades – but some cheap import from Pakistan. The man looked in his early thirties, already losing his hair and a veteran of acne. Emerging from the portico was a younger, taller man with long, shaggy hair. He was looking up towards the roof, as though checking something. Then he disappeared again. I heard him lift the letterbox; he must have been peering in.

Two more blasts on the doorbell. I had a nasty feeling about this.

Out in the hall, two grandfather clocks ticked away. One had come from my parents' farm at Tendring, in Essex; the other was its match from Lots Road auction house. They suited that hall: granny-takes-a-trip chic. Tina, our *au pair*, had painted the filigreed dial spaces in psychedelic colours to give a touch of eccentricity; otherwise the décor was pretty conventional. That was how I liked to seem to outsiders: boringly normal. Both clock dials said it was now 10.20. I unchained and opened the door to the daylight and my visitors.

They had "fuzz" written all over them. The one who seemed to be in charge wore what looked like a cashmere coat, had long hair and a stylish self-confidence. The other, in the sheepskin, looked as though he'd been dragged through a hedge backwards but didn't mind you knowing it. I imagined he could fend for himself in a boxing ring.

"Francis Morland?" asked the shorter, scruffier one.

"You are Francis Morland," concluded the other confidently. "We already know you. Can we come in?"

They stepped in before I could answer and looked around. They were phonily impressed.

"Nice place you got here," said the smaller one. "Must have cost you a bit?"

"Yes, we like it," I said. "We got it ten years ago. Got it cheap."

"Had the cash did you? Always an advantage. Hey, hey, hey! Look at that garden. You could play a good game of rugby on that!"

This was the younger, taller one.

They stepped out onto the small veranda overlooking the garden.

"What are those red and pink things, Francis?"

"They're my sculptures. It's what I do." We all gazed down at my sculptures.

"Sculpture? That? More like chopsticks and spaghetti."

They both chuckled at this, but I didn't rise to it.

"Can you sell that stuff, Francis? Serious?"

"Those three are sold to Jeremy Fry." I indicated three fibreglass cylinders, pink, orange and red. "A thousand pounds," I said, stiffly.

"Get on, Francis."

For a while, we contemplated these big pieces that I'd had to store in the garden after leaving my studio in Kilburn. I had expected to show and sell them all at the Whitechapel Gallery, where I had been promised an exhibition. But I didn't tell them that.

"So, Francis. And the Roller out the front? Making a good living are we?"

"It's a Bentley. I get by. Who's asking?"

I guess that was cheeky. But I knew by now.

I was busted.

Still, I had only twenty-five kilos in the country, and it wasn't in Castelnau. I had to keep calm. I knew Keith must have some too, and just hoped to God he didn't have it somewhere on the Vespa, or with him in the spare room.

"I'm Norman Pilcher," said the tough, scruffy one. "This is Pritchard. Drug Squad, Scotland Yard. Who else is in the house?"

So it was the infamous Detective Sergeant Norman "Nobby" Pilcher, scourge of spliff-smoking rock stars and darling of the Sunday scandal sheets. He had busted the Rolling Stones and the Beatles. Now he was onto me. Hmmm.

I explained about Keith Wilkinson. He had split up with Jean, his wife, and was staying with us for now. You could say he was my best friend. Well, he was my partner, for all his faults. Keith was the sharp, hyperactive type. The son of a Northumbrian butcher, he now had a scooter shop in the Wandsworth Bridge Road. Bit of a mod in his time. Good looking, dressed expensively and snappily: flowered shirts and suits from Lord John. Girls loved him. For my taste he smoked and drank too much, but he was my partner. And he liked to oversleep; well, he was still asleep right next to us. I also explained that we let the top floor to a lodger, though there was probably no-one in.

They produced a set of handcuffs and I let them cuff me in case I impeded their search. It turned out to be a long morning. First there was a sniffer spaniel with a handler. Then they called up more troops in plain clothes and some officers in uniform from Barnes. There was a lot of whistling at my apparent affluence: the American skis, the new kitchen, the NAD. They searched and they searched.

Then it was Keith's turn. It seemed Keith did have some gear with him: a kilo. In the bed, would you believe, the idiot. So he too was nicked. To this day he claims it was a plant. I have my doubts. On me or elsewhere in my house, they found virtually nothing.

Then events turned bad. In off the street walked Mike O'Shea, right into the arms of the law.

"Welcome to the party, Sunshine," said one of the detectives. "Where's your car?"

"I walked here."

"Oh yeah? Pull the other, it's got bells on it. Nobby, send one out. We're looking for an Austin Princess. Shouldn't be too hard to find."

They found the car and in it were another ten kilos. Poor Mike. He was my friend Damien Enright's gopher, twice dropped by the jumpy Damien from this particular scam but reinstated and now tarnished with involvement in an international drug conspiracy. Actually in the end he was only done for the ten kilos, which was a reasonable result for him.

For me, it went from bad to worse. The telephone rang.

"You going to answer it, Francis?"

"Oh. Well, yes." To speak to anybody would be a bonus, surely, especially if it was Sue or Tina. They'd get the hint and stay away.

"Pick up down there, will you," Pilcher shouted to his men searching the basement, where there was another phone on the same line. "We'll be listening, Francis."

I picked up. It was Khaled. My Lebanese supplier. *Fuck.*

"Hi, Khaled. How are you?"

"I'm okay. Hope you are. All cool there with you?"

I didn't answer for a while, hoping he would suss what was going on. Then I said, "Where are you?"

"In Rome. I haven't got long. Tell me, did Pat get back okay?"

I hesitated again.

"Yeah, yeah. He enjoyed his break. He, er, he brought Sue that olive oil."

"Good, good. Hey, listen, I've got to go." The line went dead.

"Who's Pat, Francis?" asked one of the Drug Squad.

"He's a friend of Sue."

"Nice try, Francis. That's Pat Newsome you and Khaled were talking about. Useful runner, eh?"

I looked aghast. This was terrible. Did they know everything?

"Wise up, Francis. We box clever. We're not guessing. We've got your number. You'd better spill everything."

I was allowed to leave a message with Tina for Sue, before we were driven to Cannon Row Police Station.

I didn't trust the Drug Squad one inch. They had a reputation. *Friendz* magazine was always on about these "pigs" and their antics: planting drugs, faking evidence. At Cannon Row, I started to get the picture. They had busted Bob Palacios, our yachtsman, somewhere in Barnes with 150 kilos of our most recent shipment. He had been bringing it into London for us to sell. That was a blow, but even worse they had his catamaran, the *Letitia*, at Cowes on the Isle of Wight, and his newly acquired Rolls-Royce.

They hinted at doing deals, playing Keith Wilkinson off against Bob Palacios and vice versa. I wasn't too worried about Keith. He never stopped talking and thought he was cleverer than he was, but he was loyal. Yet somehow they already knew about Khaled, Fulton Dunbar and Pat Newsome. Someone had been singing like the proverbial in the mine.

As for me, I'm dyslexic and distrust anyone writing things down. It all added up to me remaining pretty silent, for a while. That didn't stop them trying, and eventually resignation set in. Meanwhile my mother and adopted sisters, who had been alerted, ran about the place instructing solicitors and discussing QCs. I remained taciturn about everything except a few snippets that I knew made no difference but which would allow me to listen to their questions and conversations to piece together what had happened.

Whatever it was, it sounded like most of our little group had been busted. There was Keith Wilkinson, my partner; Khaled Mouneimne, our supplier; Bob Palacios, the boat skipper; Fulton Dunbar, the international courier; Pat Newsome, the money-mover; Mick O'Shea, the runner. And me, I suppose the overall organiser of what the Press would soon call "a huge international drugs smuggling ring".

Although I never aspired to be Mr Big.

POOR BOB Palacios was quite out of his depth. He was twenty-seven years old, a nice, clean American boy who had made some money crop-dusting. He had a rich daddy in San Francisco and one way or another he'd bought a catamaran to sail about in the Med and hang out in the Balearic marinas with not enough to do. We shouldn't have got him into this, but his offer was too tempting. I had been running dope for three or four years and was getting tired of the great hauls across Europe by car to get to my contact, Mohammed, in Ketama, in the Rif mountains of Morocco, then coming back with just ten or twenty kilos. Bob's offer to bring 200 kilos in one go right into London, while I had my feet up in Castelnau, was irresistible. Hell, he didn't even like smoking the stuff.

It was to be the new me. I would be in charge of logistics. I had the contacts in Morocco and Lebanon. I hung out with yachtsmen. Once the load was delivered to the UK, I was going to hand it over to Pat Newsome and my good friend Damien Enright. They could get their hands dirty hanging around hippy gaffs doing the onward distribution. Carving it up and dealing with small-time hipsters was not my scene. I could sit back and count the money.

All credit to Bob, he had done it. He and his unsuspecting sister had sailed the cat into Cowes with the full load. Then he had picked up a mooring and rowed his dinghy ashore with twenty kilos in a suitcase, coming to London on the Southampton stopper – for some reason he thought express trains attracted attention – into Waterloo. There he put the case in a locker. Damien sent his fellow Irishman Mick O'Shea to meet Bob near his hotel in Earls Court and get the key to the left luggage at Waterloo. Bob then holed up with his girlfriend and sister at the hotel and awaited instructions. I had them all to supper to meet Damien, and we told Bob to rejoin his boat.

The next day, Mick O'Shea set off down the Great West Road to collect the bulk of the remaining gear from Cowes, but was stopped by the diplomatic protection police. They were expecting royalty in from the airport but were also apparently looking out for Mick in the Princess as a favour to the Drug Squad. He had nothing in his car, but only because he was on his way out rather than back. That made Damien go all windy and he called Mick off. So now I was back to looking after Bob, who was also nervy about what had happened to Mick and came back up to London.

I gave Bob his cash to reassure him, because he was completely trustworthy. He was also completely lost in England. He'd barely been out of San Francisco all his life and here he was in London gazing about in wonder and awe. That meant we had to go to the Harrods depository to get him his £4,000, a huge sum then. I showed him some sights and took him to the Cumberland Carvery at Marble Arch. It was a phenomenon at the time: as much roast as you could eat for thirty bob, in an English gents' club atmosphere. The lad loved it. I would only learn later that we had been tailed there, and a man-and-woman team from the Drug Squad were sitting at a nearby table, watching our every move. They had been onto us for months, even tapping our phones, and were preparing to close the net.

Anyway, it all went to Bob's head. I told him he was going to have to bring the load to London himself. He needed a car to do that. So what does he do? He goes from Marble Arch to Berkeley Square, walks into the Rolls-Royce concession and chooses a maroon Rolls coupé, pays cash there and then and drives it off to Hampshire and then over to Cowes. He was tailed surreptitiously by the cops, but then he was hardly inconspicuous. Call it boyish naivety. I should have stopped him and told him to slow down.

Bob collected most of the remaining blocks of Moroccan resin, loading them from the catamaran in boxes onto a dinghy, rowing them ashore and putting them in the boot of the Rolls. He knew how to get to my place by now, so he was told to drive to Lonsdale Road, round the corner. There he would be met by Mick O'Shea, who had recovered his nerve and who would lead him to a lock-up I rented in Barnes. The cops seemed to know all of this, and not all of it could have come from Bob: they were waiting there to meet him and arrested him outside a phone box in south-west London with the cannabis in his car.

But miles worse than any of this, for me, was that I had been there on the beach at Club Med when he had brought his catamaran in – and that, Bob obviously did know about. If he blabbed, he could land me right in it.

Club Med was his idea, which I thought was bonkers. I took no part in the loading. I heard the *fellaheen* who had brought the resin down on the donkeys couldn't resist ogling a lot of French teenagers in bikinis and apparently walked down the jetty and threw the boxes into the anchor lockers without anyone batting an eyelid.

Still, at that stage, I had no idea that Bob was going to spill the beans.

The case against me was sounding circumstantial, so I bided my time at Cannon Row and sat there with an upmarket family solicitor, shocked to his core that a Morland could be dabbling in drug dealing. On this scale! But the right to remain silent is engraved on every lawyer's heart and he gravely assented to my careful wielding of this shield.

At this stage the pitch was this: I was a sculptor and car restorer. I knew nothing about drugs. If anyone was saying I did, I would wait until my trial to refute them. I was not going to give any hostages to fortune by speaking now or make any trouble for my co-accused, whatever wickedness they may have been up to.

But the time gained by my silence was no help, as it turned out. Initially four of us – Keith Wilkinson, Bob Palacios, Mick O'Shea and I – were charged with conspiracy to contravene the Dangerous Drugs Act of 1965. The police opposed bail and we were remanded in custody for a week. Sue, who had been arrested too, was granted bail by the magistrates at Bow Street on her own recognisance of £500, plus one surety of £1,000. When she was asked if she could find the surety, what the newspapers described as a "long-haired man" stood up in the public gallery and shouted that he would stand for it: it was my friend Jay Mirdel.

They found my lock-up, but too late. Little Jim, a gopher head we used for running about, had cleared it for me. I had told my solicitor to ring him and tell him where to find the "money" I owed him – Jim knew what this rather unsubtle code meant. I still thought I had a chance. Then Damien and Tina and the Newsomes hit the mattresses. Tina had rushed down to Tunbridge Wells, where Damien and his second wife were living, to find the place deserted, the front door swinging open. He had sensibly fled to Ireland. Tina, with her latest boyfriend, Roger, and a mate, took the hint and hurried off to Ibiza.

For me, things started to go downhill when Bob Palacios's dad flew over. Bob's dad was an operator. Not for him expensive solicitors and academic speculations about what might happen at trial. He got straight onto Vic Kelaher, the head of the Drug Squad, and went on a charm offensive. He was outraged that our laws had been violated. He was furious with his son. Boy, he would get it in the neck when he got him back to America. Meanwhile how could he put things right?

"Get the boy to make a statement nailing Francis Morland," said Kelaher.

"Consider it done," said Palacios senior. He got daily visiting rights to his boy in Brixton Prison, and before Keith and I could get to him we were transferred to Wormwood Scrubs. Bob was released on bail. Next, he was promised a brown envelope when he came to be sentenced, for "invaluable assistance to the prosecution" – when he had almost single-handedly sailed 200 kilos of cannabis from the coastal town of M'diq to Cowes. How had he got that? He had nailed that arrogant, posh bastard Morland, that's how. In due course, young Bob would get off with a fine of £4,000, in effect what I had paid him and what he had spent on the Rolls.

The cops were not as smart as they thought, however. Their actions had opened a chink for me. If the police could be so relaxed about Palacios getting bail, why couldn't Morland have bail too? Innocent until proved guilty was the presumption and that meant, on the face of it, that all accused were equally eligible for bail until they or a jury said they were guilty, providing they wouldn't escape or commit other crimes.

A bail application then was a short affair, usually conducted between 10 and 10.30 A.M. before the real day's work – hours of men in seedy wigs badgering police officers by about their paperwork during the investigation, with a lot of looking over the tops of their glasses at sleepy jurors – of the Old Bailey began. There is little time to go into details at these short hearings and the defendants are not present. I had a fashionable silk of the times, Michael Sherrard QC, who made two applications for me, paid for by my uncle but then repaid by me.

The pitch was this: I was the scion of a well known and utterly respectable family of devout Quakers. I was a reputed sculptor who had exhibited in Paris and New York. I was a husband with children who had lived in his own house for the past ten years. Ten thousand pounds could be found as security, and so on and so on. Morland maintained his complete innocence of any role in this importation. It was tosh, of course. I had thrown in the towel by this time and made an exhaustive confession. But that was par for the course in those days. The Old Bailey rang loud to the sound of outraged counsel saying that confessions were faked.

Sherrard had a flair for the theatrical courtroom flourish – it was said of him that he had "the nerve to bring a full murder trial to a dead, silent stop for a whole physical minute, just to prove a point of possible human fallibility" – and he didn't hold back. As far as bail was concerned, the scoundrel youth from America with no roots or ties in this country, and who was going to plead guilty, was to be a free man on the basis of his father's promises alone. How could that be just? Apparently no-one from the Drug Squad was there that day in December to contest him – they'd had their office party the previous evening – and the judge bought it. My mother and my uncle put up £5,000 each and Peter Dobbs, my father's best friend, paid £10,000 into court, and after five weeks in HMP Brixton I was granted bail. I was still meant to be confined to quarters as part of the conditions, but at least I was free. I moved fast. I collected on the twenty-five kilos I'd had from the Waterloo left luggage, and gave £10,000 to Peter Dobbs's wife to give to my uncle if "anything happened". My mother would have to shoulder the loss, poor thing.

It all had been an appalling shock to her. Her late husband, my dad, had been a leading TB consultant and oldest in the male line heir to Morland industries, at that time an internationally known and respected firm. She herself had been a director of the Institute of Contemporary Arts and a significant figure in the London Modernist movement. She had led a colourful life, and had leading figures in the art world as personal friends: Ben Nicholson, Herbert Read, Henry Moore, Mark Gertler and so on. She just never could take on board that her only blood child and son was a criminal.

As for me, I went to a friend of a friend in Chiswick, who introduced me to a Greek called Vasiliou. Vasiliou had an antique documents business off the high street, selling old maps and other oddities. No doubt a lot of them were forged because his other business was buying and selling stolen passports, and amending them to suit those who for one reason or another did not wish to stick with their true identities. It was snowing heavily on my second visit but by the time I emerged I was Charles Hamilton Brice, and was to remain so for a while. A year-and-a-half later I was still giving this name on automatic, although who the real Charles Hamilton Brice was I never knew.

What next? You'd think I'd want to discuss the fix I was in with my friends. But I didn't.

I had two groups of friends. The first you might call my "respectable" circle, some of them members of the British establishment, like Jeremy Fry and Tony Armstrong. They also included friends from the art world such as my mentor, Eduardo Paolozzi, Nigel Henderson, Phillip King, Tony Caro, the jazz singer George Melly, and others who are now knights of the realm. But what could I discuss with them? The pros and cons of becoming an eternal outlaw? Committing to a life of crime?

Certainly they were trustworthy. The class loyalty of the small, privileged London elite at the apex of the "modernist", sophisticated, educated world I had matured in would never overlap with Vic Kelaher's Drug Squad, downing their pints at rugby matches, leching over the girls in the typing pool and rotating onto on the Vice Squad. But none of them had ever been in my predicament, even if the occasional cottager had felt obliged to relocate to Paris. I knew what their advice would be: get an expensive silk, take your punishment and change your ways. I wasn't going to take it. I had other plans, already in train.

My other group of friends was my "associates": Keith, Damien Enright, Mike O'Shea, Pat Newsome, John McDonald, Charlie Radcliffe and others that you will eventually meet. The trouble with them was that, on the law of averages, they would also in their time fall into the hands of Nobby Pilcher or his colleague George Pritchard. Some of the bigger fish might have had a running licence from Vic Kelaher, head of the Drug Squad, who got from them a little stream of information about those lower in the feeding chain to keep them sweet. There was some honour among thieves but it often ran out. Even a remand in custody without charge was very disruptive in this tense world, where the loss of a load meant debts froze where they lay, leading to anger and hatreds. I don't want to exaggerate; the wholesale importation of cannabis was still in the hands of relative amateurs who had stumbled into the business during the Sixties more because of opportunity than criminal breeding. Yachtsmen were a vital link in this world. It was still a small world, but getting bigger and attracting attention. Kelaher had enjoyed walking Mick Jagger handcuffed into Chichester Magistrates Court. Release, a cool

Portobello collective run by Caroline Coon to help busted potheads, and Oppenheims, the with-it solicitors who worked with them, were fashionable gossip in those days.

So I wasn't discussing it with them either. I'd always been guarded. I didn't talk a lot anyway. I liked doing things on my own. I never shared much unless I was working or talking about work. And this was a turning point in my life. I was thirty-five and about to make a crucial decision. My life was mine; others would have to fend for themselves. But Sue had to be told, and I did prepare a little for that. She loves her food, so I booked a table for two at the Hungry Horse. I'm afraid I planned to deceive her. I made out I had to make a tactical move.

We packed the children, Joyce and Lee, off to bed. I wore the dove-grey suit that had been my father's until he died and which I had worn at my wedding. Sue wore a kaftan; maybe she was putting on a bit of weight. The Bentley was going the next day, so why not? We drove it, the gangster and his moll. I smoked a light joint on the way.

Sue was a respectable housewife. She never asked to share in my work life or enquired into it unless there was a crisis. She ran the house, collected the rent from our tenants, bought the food, paid the bills, took the children to school and cooked. She'd be in the kitchen and I'd be next door scheming with Keith and Damien, but we didn't stop talking if she came in. If it wasn't a subject that interested her – music or films or food or children or schools – she'd pick up the latest copy of *Queen*, put on a record, light a cigarette and hum to herself. She was a very easy person to be with. She never smoked joints and she cooked beautifully for all of us. She never queried my comings and goings even though she guessed at my flings with students.

I knew I was lucky.

We ordered, the waiters fussed. We sat with our glasses of wine and began to get serious. I put one hand over one of hers on the white tablecloth between us. I had tucked a napkin into my shirt top, French-style, which always amused her.

"Bob's made a statement. Apparently I fixed his boat for him in Formentera and then started making demands of him. Like, 'You owe it to me. You just need to take a package to London,' and so on. He says I lost my temper and called him a guttersnipe and rat. And threatened to burn his boat under him. I had lots of criminal friends who loved to plant some dope on a boat. Says I told him it was too late, I'd already stored dope on his boat."

"But that's rubbish. You've never harmed a mouse."

"Who knows that?" I mused thoughtfully. "People say what they like in court, Sue. Suppose you went to court and said I regularly beat you? In private. Very hard to disprove. No smoke without fire. To a jury, that can be 'not guilty because Palacios might have acted under duress from a powerful older criminal'. But for me? Well, I'd be sunk."

"I'll come and say it's a laughable idea," said Sue, loyally. And it was laughable. I wasn't violent although I didn't mind breaking a rabbit's neck or throttling a goose if it was for the pot or oven.

"You're sweet. I know you would. But what wife wouldn't. Same with family."

"What about Princess Margaret?" She could be very naïve, Sue. The idea that the Queen's younger sister would pitch up at the Old Bailey to give a character reference for someone she only knew from house parties and ski chalets was ridiculous. Naïve Sue was, in those days. She'd wise up fast in the coming years.

"Are you kidding?" I dismissed the idea peremptorily. "Richard says a cutthroat trial is a bloodbath, a pleasure for the prosecution as the defendants fall over themselves to blame each other. And that's where my trial is heading." Richard was my silk.

"Oh, no. You're going to go down? All that money on lawyers and you're going down. How long?"

I pretended to be thoughtful, carefully filleting my red mullet. It was all very white, the Hungry Horse, in a minimalist but groovy way. I didn't really like it, but I knew Sue did. She liked its staginess and the cool people who ate there. I looked around to make sure no-one was listening.

"For a long time. Unless I can cut loose from the others."

"But how can you do that?"

"By disappearing for a while."

I seemed to develop the thought as I filleted the fish and stripped some rosemary over the potatoes.

"You see, it wouldn't be so bad if I were on trial alone. If Keith and Mick and Palacios were out of the way. Dealt with separately."

There could have been some truth in this. Bob was going to plead guilty and it was unlikely the jury would hear from him, which would be good for me. But the truth was that by the time Pilcher had finished with me, I had made a full confession. Sue didn't know this. I was done for anyway, despite the theoretical possibility of contesting the confession. But for present purposes it sounded tactical and crafty and Sue fell for that kind of thing.

"I'm clearing off for a while. Just until they've been tried, until it's all blown over. Bob will be back in America, Keith doing a short term. Then I'll come back to face the music on my own."

On the way home in the Bentley, Sue cried a bit, then wiped her eyes and lit a cigarette. She was a practical girl and well able to keep the show on the road. I think she trusted me and knew she and the children would be looked after.

Next I went to see Pilcher at a magistrates court to pick up my personal belongings, the ones I would be allowed have back.

"I suppose you'll be on your toes?" he asked cheerfully.

"What does that mean?" I retained my dignity.

"Plenty of dough in the family kitty, eh? Well, shouldn't be giving you any ideas, should I? You'll be back. Guaranteed."

"I'm not going anywhere. I'm a father and husband, remember."

Still, he seemed to be almost implying I should disappear. It made me uneasy.

TWO DAYS later, I set off with Tim, a lad Keith had found for me, in a very poor-condition Ford Escort to Newhaven. From there we crossed the Channel to Dieppe, then drove across France and over the border into Franco's Spain at Perpignan. The Pyrenees looked splendid, freshly laundered in snow. I would have loved to have had some skiing, but had only £3,000 left and needed to get back to work. Still, we were back in the sun, albeit a wintry one, and a long way from the sleet falling on Hammersmith Bridge.

I left Tim and the car in Barcelona and told him to drive on to Marbella. Then I took the ferry to Palma, on the island of Majorca. I had with me a heavy load. It included a sextant and *Hiscock on Cruising*, which I had bought at Captain Watts's chandlery in Bond Street. I had a five-gallon can of caulking grout and at least twenty yards of rope of one kind or another. I had pulleys, swivels, shackles, even an air conditioning unit. If I'd had more money there would have been a ship-to-shore radio and maybe radar, but my Palacios load had gone down and taken the profits with it, I'd had to pay lawyers and sureties off, and I had to provide for Sue and our children, Joyce and Lee. I was nearly broke, despite selling the Rolls and a few other bits and pieces.

The next morning I staggered off the ferry and straight on down to the marina. I was looking for the *Beaver*.

2

Crossing the Atlantic

THE *BEAVER* WAS a forty-seven-foot, pitch-pine ketch with a middle wheelhouse and an old eighty-horsepower diesel engine. Built for the High Commissioner to Montreal in 1928, it had three cabins, a comfortable saloon and even a full-sized bath. I had bought it for £5,000 in Gibraltar, where it had been the houseboat of a gay retired naval officer and his Moroccan houseboy. The interior was all mahogany and brass. It had no electric circuit but relied on paraffin lighting and Primus technology for cooking. It had not been to sea for a long time and was not fit for useful work.

I had bought it with two partners in 1969. One was Harvey Bramham, who I hoped to find with the boat now. Harvey was another young hippy who had fallen for the Ibiza scene, one of those hedonistic, lotus-eating remittance men who hung out in the Old Town stoned on dope and New Age thinking. They loved their Ouspensky and Taoism, and talked about acid as if it was a holy sacrament. Not for me.

Harvey had been on Bob Palacios's catamaran when he introduced us, but he didn't have a rich dad and needed to turn his hand to making a bit of bread. Actually I'd first met Harvey in the boatyard when I had been scouting out the *Beaver* with Ken Nagle; Ken was sharing in this "investment". He was a New Yorker and I had sent three electric organs to his business there from London, each stuffed with cannabis. The mark-up for Moroccan resin in New York at that time was huge, even though they had a ready supply of Mexican grass. Ken was keen to move this business along and Harvey, who had done even less sailing than I had, was up for it.

Harvey had been a roadie for a lot of big bands in the UK, including the Pretty Things and Fairport Convention. One morning in 1969 he had been driving members of Fairport back to London from a gig in Birmingham when his Transit van overturned on the M1 motorway. The drummer, Martin Lamble, was killed, as was Jeannie Franklyn, the girlfriend of guitarist Richard Thompson. Harvey was thrown ninety feet and broke both his legs. He faced a court case for dangerous driving and served a short prison sentence. The accident had upset him and his employers badly, which is why he lit off to the Med and wanted to be away from the music scene. He had rustled up the money somehow and, like me, now urgently wanted a return on his investment.

By rights the *Beaver* should have been in Gibraltar with Harvey living on her; the deck planks were unpitched and parted and she should never have gone to sea in that state. But Harvey had panicked when two police launches had moored on either side, and suddenly took her out at dead of night, bound for Majorca. At least he'd paid the marina fees. As he was alone, he couldn't handle the sails and had motored the whole way. Anyway, I was glad not to have to show my face in Gibraltar.

I found the *Beaver* but no-one on board, so I dumped the gear and took a room at the Majestic in Palma. There were two reasons for this. Hotels are places where, unlike marinas, you are not expected to explain your presence. A more important reason was communications. In those days there were no mobile phones or email and even fax machines were a rarity. All communication was by fixed telephone or letter. Doing what I did required constant communication with others and that meant either a home telephone, which required the permission of the subscriber, or a public telephone box, at best in a café, at worst an open booth in a busy station with people waiting. In many countries you couldn't receive phone calls from public phone boxes, only make them. Even if you could receive them, you had to book the return call with the operator and wait about. Communications before the advent of mobile phones were the slowest, most time-consuming and most maddening obstacles in my chosen trade. Mobiles had only just started to appear when my career ended. God, they would have made life easier. Not that I am forgetting their downside: they leave an easily retrieved record.

The best solution was a hotel. It's the reason people like me booked into them even if they had somewhere to put their head down. I rang Ken and Keith and Damien, the latter hiding in Cork. Damien told me Tina had lain low with him, but was now in Ibiza. I traced Harvey, who was also in Ibiza, house-sitting a yacht. Eventually he got a message at the *capitainerie* and rang me at the hotel. He was astonished to be speaking to me. News of our bust in the UK had reached the Balearics alright. A sharp rise in the price of pot there was flatteringly attributed to my absence from the scene.

"So what are we going to do next?" asked Harvey.

"I certainly can't hang around here too long. From what you tell me I'm the talk of Ibiza."

Actually one was perfectly safe from extradition in Franco's Spain, but it was a police state with a few concessions to the tourist industry. They'd certainly keep an eye on a cannabis smuggler if they got to hear about him.

"Morocco?" I suggested.

"Yeah? You still want to do the big one?"

"All the more so. I now have to."

"And from there?"

"You know where."

He did know where we would go from there because he knew about the 3,000 per cent mark-up that Ken and I had been so triumphant about. But it still deserved a moment of reverence.

"The US of fucking A," he observed quietly. "In the *Beaver*. Who've we got?"

"Maybe Jim. But it may just be you and me."

Tina, our *au pair*, who at my arrest had run for it with her latest boyfriend, Roger Law, was with Harvey, so we were now quite a party. Actually Tina was a one-girl party, full of bubble, everybody's *au pair* at one time or another, with a fatal willingness to sleep with anyone who would party with her, often the father of the children she looked after. Tina eventually married Charlie Radcliffe, a member of our group until he got fed up with me. He was a striking personality, politically motivated in the style of the times, a very alternative, situationist-anarchist who was always storming student meetings and clashing with the police. He helped set up *Friendz* with Alan Marcuson, making it the rioting students' house magazine, with a credo that getting out of your head was revolutionary. I guess I was not really his type.

It was a few days before they all joined me, but there was plenty to do in the meantime. The trouble was I didn't want to be seen too much in the marina. Sooner or later, I was thinking, someone would turn up who knew me, so I holed up for a while in the hotel, reading the book on navigation I'd bought at the chandlers in Bond Street, studying my charts and practising on the hotel terrace with my sextant in the dead hours between lunch and supper. I did manage to start the old diesel one night, clearing the traps and running up the mainsail briefly, but I didn't dare to sit on the deck in the sun freeing up the shackles and splicing and trimming lines, even though such labour is true happiness for me. That would have to wait until Harvey joined me and the air had cleared.

Finally Harvey arrived with his guitar and with Tina and Roger in tow. My confidence was rising. There had been no mention of my disappearance either in the media or on the grapevine in England. The story was that I was staying at our small farmhouse in Malta, awaiting my trial. So I gave up my hotel room and came out into the open.

We spent a month in Palma. We pitched the decks, greased the pulleys, repaired the canvas sails and ran them up. There were no winches except on the anchor chain; it was all double pulleys redoubled on the uphauls to get the sails up, and just one lorry battery. Our lack of ship-to-shore radio and navigation aids, other than my handbook on cruising with its dead reckoning instructions, made Harvey nervous and I finally agreed to buy a wireless direction finder, although we had to buy a new but not very powerful one. This was a method whereby the navigator rotated a handheld monitor 360 degrees to see if he could pick up a wireless signal transmitting in Morse code. If you got one and it came from a mast in the system, you could then look up its identity and direction according to how loud it was when pointing in that direction, but it told you almost nothing about its distance other than that it was in range. Out on the oceans it was useless, as most of the masts were coastal. From then on we would have to rely on my skills with the sextant. We had no radar either and that meant a constant watch was necessary, in four-hour sessions. The speed log was a trailed spinner. We carried 100 gallons of fuel, which meant we only had 100 hours of motoring. All other propulsion was by wind power on the main and mizzen masts.

We did have one shock. Harvey was stopped by the *carabinieri* at the marina entrance one evening and asked if a pop group called "Francis Morland" was on the boat. He fiercely denied it but it was time to make a move.

On a blustery day in late February we set off, to Marbella, where the construction of the current glitzy, yacht-based utopia had only just begun and the marina was virtually unsupervised. At six in the morning, we started up the diesel and left it running while we went and declared our departure, bound for the Costa del Sol for the purposes of tourism.

Two days later, we arrived and tied up, having completed my first overnight sail ever, all the lights correct, shipshape and Bristol fashion, the flags properly dressed, not a frown on any official's brow. As yet, however, I had still never sailed out of sight of land.

We were joined by Jim, who was going to sail with us, and Tim, who was to shadow us in the Escort for our next step. His first move was to drive, via the car ferry to Ceuta, to Al Hoceima, a grubby but sound fishing port which was as close to Ketama as you could get by sea. The price for his services was two kilos of the product.

Our plans took a blow one evening when Jim got drunk and started playing air guitar in the wheelhouse, in accompaniment to Pink Floyd. I told him to go down and start the engine. This had to be hand-cranked under the saloon table. He came down with his bare foot onto a bottle from which he'd been drinking and it smashed under his weight. He was a heavy fellow and the resulting wound had to be treated at hospital. The doctor told Tina he wouldn't be able to walk for at least a month, so he was discharged from the ship's crew. Harvey and I were alone again.

Jim was no loss, as far as I was concerned. He came with the reputation of being a sailing instructor, although it turned out he'd done little more on that front than manage a boating lake. Harvey had a misplaced faith in Jim's competence, quoting him whenever he disagreed with me. Jim had apparently said that you never fully sheet-in the mainsail however close-hauled you are, which is nonsense.

ONE MORNING, we slipped our moorings and motored out to sea, following the coast down to near Gibraltar and over to Morocco. We closed with Al Hoceima two days later, where we refuelled. This worried the nervy Harvey. We had used half our fuel on one-fiftieth of our journey. The other worry was that the battery would not support our navigation lights for more than a few nights, let alone the weeks we expected to be at sea. We'd have to run the engine every morning to recharge.

Another thing that made us nervous was that we were the only yacht in the harbour. All the other vessels were fishing boats, unbelievably rusted and shabby. It was a busy harbour and at night a fleet of up to thirty shrimpers would set out and drift along the coast off the very beaches on which we had planned to make the pickup. They were a lovely sight, twinkling at night, but would be the bane of my life in all my future travels on this coastline, until I caught up with ship-to-shore radios.

Would we be noticed? Was there any reason to be there other than the reason we were there? We decided we needed to behave like tourists. We drank endless tea at the harbour cafes and ooh-ed and aah-ed at the glorious vegetable and fruit displays in the market behind the front. A flock of little boys followed us wherever we went, asking endless questions in pidgin French, and we developed the story that we had broken down and needed to make repairs before we continued to Tangier, which everyone in Hoceima described as heaven.

It was true that I was dismantling the alternator and getting it rewound in the hope it would charge the battery quicker, and little by little we were victualling the boat for the long haul ahead. We stored ten-kilo bags of onions, dozens of tins of tomatoes to go with forty packets of spaghetti and chorizo sausages, a whole sack of pulses, another of polenta, and a sack of flour, with which we intended to make fresh bread daily in our small gas oven. Plums too were abundant and I spent many happy hours on deck boiling them to make jam to go on my future bread. There were four chickens, and tins of sardines and anchovies.

The harbour master, who we called Mr Haj because he had a red beard, was a delightful man who made us welcome and allowed us to tie up on the main quay for as long as we liked. He may have had an idea of our mission, and he had a constant smirk on his face and disconcerting, smiling eyes. But he liked explaining Islam to us and his attitude to women, from which we tried to dissuade him. He gently mocked our corrupt western ways. He was fascinated by the idea that respectable girls wore bikinis.

Whether or not he guessed our plans, I'll never know. Although cannabis was not strictly legal, Moroccans assumed that one of the reasons European tourists were so keen on visiting their main cities was to smoke dope, and young men on the quay were always offering to get us some. In the end we thought it might look more normal to get a bit, so we did.

Finally Tim arrived at a crawl in the Escort, limping and listing to one side. He had suffered various problems. The suspension leaf springs had snapped, which distorted the chassis, making it unfit for what we were planning on very rough roads. This was a worry. We were on the edge of spectacularly beautiful but mountainous country, thickly forested near the coast and getting wilder as one went inland. Only the coast road and one east–west inland road were metalled; roads to the excellent sand beaches near Hoceima, beyond the Pointe des Pêcheurs, were very poor. None of us was in a position to hire a car, so eventually we resolved to load the boat off the quay, Bob Palacios-style, when the moment came and run for it before anyone clocked us. Even so, I had to go to work with a polyester and fibreglass resin solution to the suspension problem. It looked horrible, like a hairy white rugby ball replacing the suspension bars. But I thought it might work, and it survived a severe road test when we deliberately cantered the car down a potholed road from a height above Al Hoceima.

It was time for me to go to Mohammed, a man I had known for six years and whose farm between Targuist and Taounate I knew well. I was always very welcome there and my little presents of radios and pressure cookers were always fallen on with joy by the womenfolk.

The roads into Ketama province are precipitous and endlessly winding, the landscape dotted with flyblown villages, sometimes fortified, always with a mosque and often a Christian church too. Round the village there were a few orchards and grazing for goats. Down at the valley bottoms lay bigger farms with cattle and crops. But the crop for which Ketama is most famous is *cannabis sativa*.

It is an ugly, straggly, weed-like plant that can grow taller than a tall man. It was originally grown for hemp, to be made into textiles and more recently rope. Since the advent of Indian and American cotton and man-made fibres, its practical functions have been displaced by its psychotropic ones. The female flowering ends, if gathered and processed in a number of possible ways, produce the most famous recreational drug after alcohol: dope.

Moroccan history is the story of tough desert tribes falling on the pampered coastal agriculturists and enslaving them in sometimes very cruel regimes. Hassan I of the Alawites, who rule over Morocco to this day, oversaw a typical civil war in which Ketama province was loyal to him in a way that earned them a reward. They were to be permitted to continue to cultivate and use cannabis without interference from the authorities even after it was banned in the rest of Morocco. It was their culture, a lifestyle deemed worthy of preservation.

Realistically, cannabis was the main crop of the place and grew everywhere. It was pretty much the only cash crop there and when one got to the top of a pass, one looked out over an endless vista of its distinctive green, broken with the occasional patches of beans and pulses. Western tourists find it spectacularly beautiful. The natives all want to get out, down to the towns on the coast, and there is only one way to make the break: get big in the cannabis trade. Do that and it's a villa above Tangier, with respectful and awed visitors from the clan left behind in the Rif mountains.

Officially the drug was not tolerated outside Ketama, so although one could without interference drive up to Mohammed's farm and buy large quantities of his produce, it could not be taken legally out of the province. Since the roads were few, this was quite easy to enforce, and a large amount presented a problem. The much smaller quantities that I had been buying from Mohammed in previous years were another matter. They could be stowed under a fender and no one was likely to bother you. Indeed my lifelong love of Citroens, particularly the DS, was founded on the ease with which its panels came off and its self-raising suspension that disguised the size of a heavy load. In Amsterdam, I had freed the only bolt holding the rear wing and carried the dope in broad daylight into the café where I was delivering. But now we were talking more than a ton. And that was another matter.

How did I know Mohammed?

It had started in the fly-blown government hotel in Ketama town, a sad straggle of crumbling bungalows and dismal shops connected by sagging electric wires. The concierge had got me my first single kilos. Later he introduced me to people further up the chain. That's how I came to be urging the feeble Escort up to Mohammed's, although the approach to his farm involved fording a steep-banked stream at that time of year. He had a lovely place, lined with cypresses and eucalyptus and the usual oleander and bougainvillea. Long white walls surrounded a group of single-storey buildings set loosely round a big paved courtyard. Long arcades looked over this yard and the rooms behind were either open or divided by hangings. There was a well in the middle of the yard with a tank next to it, and there were always women washing clothes and hanging them out along the arcades.

The rooms were very simply furnished but also comfortable, clean and stylish. Lots of hangings, kilim rugs and great cushions furnished the main rooms, or at least the ones I saw. The effect was slightly spoilt by some access they had up there to endless blocks of foam, which made up the beds and sofas. All the wiring hung loose and dangled over any decorative effects in the stone work. Whole areas were for women only and I was politely excluded from them during my stays. Any water had to come from the well. I once offered to bring Mohammed a water pump, because the place had electricity from the village generator. He had declined with a frown and a dip of his head, which meant the idea was distasteful and better dropped.

"What would I do with that? The women can raise the water."

Whenever I stayed, I was waited on hand and foot. I had only to raise a hand to have mint tea brought to me. In the evenings we sat in a circle round a ceramic oven heated by coals and from which marvellous breads emerged, to be eaten with those elaborate olive stews for which the place is famous. At breakfast, earthenware dishes were coated in olive oil, heated in the oven and then had eggs broken into them, which sizzled while we communally dipped in the fresh bread. It was my favourite meal.

Nearby were large barns. I would spend my waiting time there watching the work. Lines of peasants, all men, day-recruited and kept separate from the household, stripped the pollen from the cannabis crop, crushed them through sieves, and then pounded them in plastic bags with olivewood mallets to a resin. From that, they were turned into kilo bars, wrapped in hessian and stored. Every twenty minutes, the men stopped to escape the heat and drink water.

At that time, in the late Sixties, you could sell wholesale in the UK for six times the purchase price; in the USA, for thirty times the price. The cost to me, delivered to the coast, was about $30 a kilo. Mohammed had been told by postcard that I was up for 1,000 kilos – in those days a huge amount – and Mohammed was ready for that. He had been paid half the money six months earlier and Harvey had now managed to find the other half. Mohammed had a lot of donkeys on the farm and could hire more elsewhere. Each donkey could struggle along with 100 kilos on its back. Once this little baggage train was loaded, it would take the donkeys three or four days to get to the wooded areas behind the beach, which was as near as the drovers were willing to take them. The Palacios load had gone into a hire car and been driven up to the Club Med, with a couple of the donkey drovers to then carry it down the jetty.

In the end we had decided that a beach loading of this quantity was too difficult. Equally, no way could this little mule train process through the streets of Hoceima without drawing attention. There was going to have to be a transfer to the struggling Escort for the final leg onto our quay, or Mohammed would have to agree to drive it down.

I had never accompanied these donkey excursions, but an associate of mine, Philip de Bere, once did. He went with five donkeys, each with its drover, and they travelled only at night. This was more to avoid the heat of the day than for security, but it meant they travelled by torchlight, up endless boulder-strewn gullies and pathways between farms and through forests. He tripped over at least once an hour and arrived exhausted and bruised all over. They ran out of water and everyone was in a bad temper, which is not a good state for the tense finale of signalling to the boat, hooking up, loading dinghies and floundering out to the boat, which was on the edge of grounding and hence making the skipper cross and flustered too.

For an extra payment to bribe police controls, Mohammed did agree in this case to drive the load to Hoceima. The donkey men had to be tipped too for missing out on the delivery. As it transpired, when they arrived near Hoceima, in the middle of the night, an envoy was sent to me saying the drivers were panicky, as usual, and unwilling to drive to the quay. We would have to go and meet them five kilometres out and do the final leg ourselves.

The logistics of the illicit drug trade are always fraught. No excursion of mine ever went off without flaw and this one was no exception. We couldn't put more than half a ton into the Escort at a time, which meant two runs. All hands were needed to load the boat quickly, so half the load had to be left with the Fiat driver, plus Mohammed and another man in two more cars. Everyone was edgy and anxious to be off.

On our way through the empty streets of Hoceima, the suspension did a lurch but held, although a sinister grinding emanated from the back axle. We staggered to the boat, quarrelling bitterly about Tim's failure to get it properly fixed in Tangier as I had asked him to do. We slung the cannabis bricks through the deck hatch straight into the forward cabin. I checked under the suspension. Could we keep going? My absurd makeshift sculpture was beginning to crack but what could we do but carry on? By the time we got back, our little caravan had gone. Happily they had left the balance of the dope in a ditch. This took us half an hour to find and load.

We crept back through the now-stirring streets of Hoceima at five miles an hour. Worse, there were people on the quay as the shrimpers returned, so we sacked up the remaining 500 kilos, staggered along with the heavy sacks and dropped them, in front of the shrimpers, with loud thumps onto the deck.

I was casting off the mooring ropes before the last of the load was stowed. Tim left with the Escort, hoping to get it fixed before returning to Europe with his two kilos, and to my intense relief the *Beaver* rounded the further breakwater of the harbour as the sun emerged in all its glory across the bay. Behind me, at the light on the harbour quay, I could see Mr Haj waving to us. We hauled up the sails, killed the engine and peace returned to our souls.

We would not touch land again for six weeks.

OH, THE PEACE of the sea. I love it. It suits my unsociable soul. I look at the land and think of jostling humanity struggling for a bit of space to call its own, quarrelling, compromising, the sweat of work, and all the things that go wrong. I was free of all that, with not a boat to be seen and needing only the wind to keep moving. Some may say that makes me a selfish person; many of my family indeed do say that. Perhaps it is true. In some ways I had been an only child, largely left by my mother during the War and after, at the farm in Tendring, having to fend for myself and find my own amusements: shooting rabbits, fishing, playing at Swallows and Amazons at Landermere on the sailing skiff my dad had bought me. I am as I am.

Although we felt as though we were moving as we went through the Straits of Gibraltar, we weren't. I started the engine, which brought Harvey up. He hated using the engine unless it was an emergency.

"Why are you motoring?"

"Because we're not getting anywhere."

"What do you mean? Look at our wake. Remember, speed doesn't matter."

I stopped the engine and told him to line up a stay with a hilltop in Ceuta. He watched for a while.

"You're right. We are going backwards."

Two hours later, we turned south and left the tidal stream that pours through the Straits. Silence returned. As dusk fell, the land dropped away. For the first time in my life I was sailing an ocean in a twenty-ton ketch, with a twenty-five-year-old who, like me, had never been out of sight of land before.

Two days later, we made our first landfall: the Canary Islands. It was gratifying that my charts seem to accord with the real world. Harvey was keen to stop; I wasn't. Reporting to the Spanish authorities, filling in forms at the marina, declaring our destination and so on was a risk there was no good reason to take. I insisted we sail on, and I prevailed. It was not the only time I quarrelled with Harvey. We bickered a lot about my rota for watches, which became all the more important when the alternator expired with a loud report, so that we no longer had lights.

We left Santa Cruz de la Palma to starboard and by that evening it had sunk below the horizon. We sailed on south.

"How much longer are we heading south for?" asked Harvey, at the start of one of his watches.

"Until the butter melts, is the old adage. Then we turn right." We did actually leave a curl of Moroccan butter on a plate on the watch. On we pitched, at a steady four or five knots, the wind astern, still in heavy sweaters and donkey jackets when on deck.

Below, I made my first attempt at alleviating our endless diet of spaghetti, tinned tomatoes, or powdered bolognaise, onions and chorizo. Although my dough looked good, and kneaded, it wouldn't prove or rise properly in the oven. It may have been the sea air; it may be that the oven burnt too high. It remained doughy, dense and flat.

At midday every day I braced myself against the wheelhouse and hung myself from a line, holding the sextant, to steady my attitude against the movement of the boat. I noted the exact time that the sun reached the zenith – its highest point – and its height in the sky. The former told me our longitude compared to the 0° line that runs down from Greenwich, otherwise known as the Prime Meridian of the World; the latter told me how far south we were. At this stage I was more concerned with the latter, and everyday the sun got higher in the sky. Another guide we made use of was seeing what radio programmes of neighbouring nations we could pick up on long wave. For a long time they were Mauritanian, then nothing.

On the whole the weather just got better, but four days past the Canaries the Northerly got up and we careened along, pitching sharply. At about two in the morning, during Harvey's watch, there was a sudden, appalling crash and at first I thought we'd hit something. I'd caught Harvey dozing before on watch and I went up expecting the worst. The boat had come to a halt and we were wallowing.

Up on deck I found some kind of beam swinging violently, suspended on lines. It was crashing against the stays and spars, threatening to tear them from their housings. The genoa was partly collapsed and slapping around in our faces. We needed to get that down. Releasing the uphaul only brought it part way down, so we set about detaching and wrapping it in the bows, which at last we managed.

Now I could see what had happened, and it wasn't Harvey's fault. The top mast, a twenty-foot extension of the main mast bound to it with bolts and metal straps, had broken free and fallen towards the deck. Fortunately various stays and lines had stopped it actually hitting the deck, where it could have done considerable damage. We needed to secure it and stop it swinging. I got lines and Harvey held the torch while I secured the top mast to the main mast and restored calm. The swinging, slapping and twanging stopped and we sat waiting for first light. It was a terrifying few hours. We might be totally crippled. We might have to fire off rockets to get help. We might lose the boat – and all our treasure.

To Harvey I remained impassive, a picture of *sang froid*.

Daylight revealed that all was not lost. I needed to go up the mast to cut free the section that had broken loose, disentangle the lines and stays, re-secure the stays to the new mast top, and rearrange the pulleys and shackles so that the smaller jib could be rigged to our new mast, twenty feet shorter. The taller genoa, which depended on this extension, was to find another mission in life.

Just as sailors in Nelson's time couldn't swim, I had a weakness that made me an inappropriate sailor, and that was seasickness. Generally it wears off, but climbing fifty feet into the sky, perching up there while the boat rolled ten degrees one way then ten degrees the other, was utterly nauseating and I had to come down every fifteen minutes to recover. As a result we lost most of that day, before finally we could re-rig the mainsail, turn the boat back towards the wind and resume our drive, heeled but not rolling on south.

Over the next few days, the wind dropped and dropped. We shed our sweaters. One morning Harvey was topless as he rigged the record player on deck, but still the butter had not melted.

"That's modern butter for you," observed Harvey. "Full of preservatives."

"I agree. It's time to turn west."

It was textbook, really. We drifted rather aimlessly for a day and then we found them: the famous trade winds that blew the commerce of the early British Empire from Africa to the New World. A marvellous eight-to-ten-knot wind blew steadily from behind for the rest of our journey. We secured the tiller to and gaffed out the booms and foresail. Then the tiller, the bearing and the set of the sails had to be balanced so that they corrected each other to the right bearing. A marvellous peace settled over the boat. So quiet is a following wind that you have to put out the speed log to realise you are moving at all. Now we could go about the business of keeping the boat shipshape, on deck in our bathing trunks.

Two dolphins joined us, not just to check us out but to keep us company for a couple of days, skipping and careening around us sometimes when playful, sometimes just cruising behind, sometimes disappearing for an hour or so. We offered them chorizo sausage but they didn't like that. Then we played them music to see what they liked best. They seemed to prefer my limited classics to Harvey's Love album. It definitely made them more playful. We tried trailing a line and baited hook to catch them some fish, but our steady five knots was too fast for this to succeed. A couple of flying fish landed on our deck one morning but by then the dolphins had gone. So we sautéed them for ourselves and they were good, tasting like mackerel.

Another time, a basking shark set up camp beneath us, with two pilot fish to keep it company. We trailed a sock of mine filled with sardines and anchovies, to no effect. So I got diving with the harpoon, which drove off the shark, leaving the pilot fish to confuse the *Beaver* with their mother shark. Even so, I couldn't get near them.

Every Sunday lunch we had a chicken, but they were gone after a month and the endless mushiness of powdered mash and polenta and sardine mixes made us start to fantasise about the joys of crunchy food on land. I read a lot, mainly Asimov but also some Russian classics like *Fathers and Sons* and *The Idiot*. I did think about the family I had left behind. The sad truth is I did not miss them in an immediate sense. I felt a sense of duty towards them, in that I had to provide for them, but in all honesty I did not miss the queue on Hammersmith Bridge on the school run. Instead I had formed a vague project to move the clan to our small farmhouse in Malta and bring them up as a boating Mediterranean family. At other times I resolved that this was a one-off operation to set me up for life without further smuggling. I would resume my original career as a sculptor. Only time would tell. For the moment, I had plenty of time to spare.

Twice more we attempted to make bread, even trying to get our lumps of dough to rise in the midday sun, but nothing availed. We put this unappetizing mix into reserve in case we sprang a leak that needed caulking. Soon we alternated our sack of pulses with spaghetti to vary the diet and ate the jam naked to keep scurvy at bay.

For a day or two, we kept company with a sleek, seventy-foot Camper and Nicholson boat and flagged it in the usual way, but I was glad not to have them able to raise us by radio and was careful to rumple the side panel that carried the name of our ship. On another day, a heavy tanker ploughed past us and knocked us around with its wake. I dug out our flags for a coordinates request but they can't have seen them. Anyway, we were in the Tropics and that was all I really needed to know.

Another time, we seemed to be off course. I tried to correct, but couldn't. The tiller was dead, stiff, and I didn't want to break it, so once again we turned back into the wind and, with sails aflutter, I plunged into the ocean. The rudder stock was gummed up with crab barnacles. I spent an enjoyable hour with the snorkel and a knife. I love to be in the sea with the sun burning me through a film of water, even if twenty tons of wood is bouncing above me. At least my prison pallor was gone.

So the weeks went by. Despite having this great cargo of cannabis on board, we only smoked it once and agreed the hangover spoilt the perfect peace that we enjoyed during this perfect crossing. As we approached the West Indies, my confidence was growing.

Then we saw a turtle. The chorizo was finished and a turtle stew would have been just the ticket, followed by a gallon of soup. So we started up the engine, and what a business that was. It had no starter motor and had to be hand cranked. The compression on a diesel is terrific and has to be released by a lever to enable the cranking to take place. Once you have got the flywheel spinning, you release the lever and the momentum of the flywheel gets you about four cycles of the engine. Along with this, you have to prime the inlets with the right amount of fuel and not flood it.

We had been starting the engine every two days for an hour to charge our battery and keep the mast-top light on at night, and it was warm. So it started and we circled the turtle. We had a spring-loaded harpoon gun on the boat, and while I was at the helm, Harvey leapt around trying to get a good aim on the turtle. Eventually he fell in the sea. To his credit he stayed in and swam about trying to catch the turtle, still carrying the harpoon gun.

Finally he gave up and made his way round the boat to climb back on board. He was completely unable to. And it had taken us three-quarters of an hour to turn the boat around. It dawned us for the first time that if one or both fell in during some crisis, the moving boat would become the *Marie Celeste*. From then on we trailed a rope from the stern until I fashioned a rope ladder in Christiansted, in the Virgin Islands. As it got hotter, it was a standby so that we could trail behind the boat, cooling off.

We were also getting low on water. That was always going to be a problem. Our hope of some rain was ill-founded. We took to boiling bottles of white wine to evaporate the alcohol, producing a filthy-tasting drink.

Harvey took to climbing the main and sitting astride the upper spar to read a book.

"Why do you do that? It looks fucking uncomfortable."

"No, it's good. I might clock another turtle."

"Fat chance. You're looking out for land, aren't you?"

Harvey was getting stir crazy. I'm ten years older than him, liked reading and Mozart and binding rope ends, stitching the jib that kept parting and sanding bits of flaking varnish. He was young and fit. He wanted land, meat, chips, beer, girls. And why not? We had been five weeks and two days at sea.

In the end it was me who first saw land. I was on the dawn watch and suddenly there it unmistakably was. At first it looked like a rock in the ocean, but during the day, as it gradually raised itself, it became quite a large island. We mobilised the radio direction finder and worked it all day. It was Antigua, one of the outermost of the Windward Islands. A near perfect landfall.

I congratulate myself that this was down to my faultless sextant reading and dead reckoning, but with the wisdom of years I now realise that half of it was pure luck. The ease with which a heavy yacht might be written off by a margin of a few miles because of a tiny navigation error was to be brought home to me later in life – that would also be in the Caribbean, behind the Windwards, where shallows and reefs are as numerous as islands above the water. Until these things happen, the innocent can be fearless. I had been blithely unconscious of the great care I should have taken for this landfall. Suppose Antigua had appeared in the evening? By the following morning we'd have been perilously close.

We had started to pick up long-wave radio again, and went silent at one particular news item. President Nixon had declared a "war on drugs". We looked at each other aghast. He was going to set up something called the Drug Enforcement Agency. Did he know we were coming?

In other respects, God and good fortune were on my side. That night, as we took bearings on mountain tops and lighthouses with our hand-held compass, our charts pinned down on the navigation desk became covered in triangulated "cocked hats", drawn with pencil, to give our positions. But we had no tide tables, and the considerable tidal flows between the Windward Islands remained guessed-at mysteries. As I say, God was on our side.

Still, I had the good sense to leave Antigua to port (our south) and pass between St Kitts and Montserrat to less tidal seas behind, and only then turn north towards our destination, still a day and a night's sailing away.

Harvey was beside himself with excitement, begging me to take us into Charleston for a night on the tiles. But I was adamant. We were stopping nowhere until we'd buried our booty. Harvey was so wound up by now that he kept permanent watch in the bows virtually for the whole of the next twenty-four hours, whilst I took the helm. This was a good thing because I could quickly start the engine if necessary, whilst having set a safe course.

The British Virgin Islands are a cluster of scrub-clad mini mountains set on boundless coral reefs and sand bars. Their fringes are white sand beaches with palms reaching out diagonally across them and, when we got close enough, the endless charm of beachside bars, restaurants and jaunty, wood-clad hotels. This sybaritic utopia is so well known I won't attempt to describe it.

The first island we approached was called Virgin Gorda. It is one of the bigger ones but was then only thinly populated. Nevertheless Harvey, gazing longingly through the binoculars, let forth a huge whoop. At the end of a wooden jetty, he had spied an English telephone box. And on the beach were girls in swimming suits. We skirted various bays, each more beautiful than the last: Dog Bay, Handsome Bay, Taylors Bay, all empty but for the occasional villa roof in the dense green background. Finally I was persuaded to drop the sails and test the anchor off Crooks Bay as a practice for our final target, Fallen Jerusalem.

Harvey, his excitement rising at the prospect of female company, launched into a fantasy commentary as we slipped past silent bays. Weeks at sea can do that to a man. In his vivid imagination he was slipping into the sea, swimming smoothly to the beach. Girls turned to watch over their sunglasses this weather-tanned figure emerge from the waves in his cut-off denims and make for the bar, where they were cooking pizzas in wood ovens and serving pina coladas in tall, slim glasses. An eighteen-year-old Australian heiress joined him. Where was he from? He nodded casually at the boat, towards which she now cast a languorous gaze. We had just arrived from Europe. She invited him back to her villa to wash and sleep …

We paused to allow me to test the anchor chain run-out and winch while he burbled on dreamily. Then it was three in the afternoon and time to move on. We took turns winding the winch and hauled up the anchor, then engaged forward and nosed our way round the corner, bringing Fallen Jerusalem into sight.

It's a small island which had no water or inhabitants at that time. No doubt the yachting community sometimes picnicked there but this afternoon it was deserted. We motored between it and Gorda, rounded the leeward side into a bay out of sight of Gorda and dropped anchor the second time. It was time to go to work.

Although the bay was wide, access to small runs of sand was very limited due to the huge boulders that shielded the island and gave it its name. The Avon inflatable had to be pumped up and the Seagull two-stroke engine mounted and fuelled with our small jerrycan of petrol. It was reluctant to start and it seemed like an hour in the sun was spent fiddling with its carburettor and hauling on the starting rope. Eventually it spluttered and then roared, sending up a cloud of blue smoke, only to stop equally suddenly. Finally it purred and we were ready.

Here was the routine. I took Harvey and a spade from Hoceima ashore. His job was to go to just above the high water line and dig into an embankment formed by the roots of a kind of mango tree, at a point providing maximum cover from the rain. This gallery, the size of a grave, was lined with the now useless genoa, and the burial could proceed. My job was to go to and from the *Beaver*, climbing aboard and loading 100 kilos a time and bring it up the beach to Harvey, who was to bury it tidily. I'd then walk up to a small headland to check if there were any boats in sight. One small yacht did pause in the mouth of the bay, obviously wondering whether to stop. We pretended to be boisterous tourists, splashing in the sea and spoiling the peace. They moved on.

One of our difficulties was one that every blue-sea sailor knows: a long period at sea, rolling and pitching, has an effect on the inner ear and sets the gyroscope in there counter-rolling and pitching. This can continue for six or seven hours after stepping on land, causing one to feel that the land is rocking, making one feel dizzy and unsafe. But we worked away, cooling off now and then in the sea, and puttered to and fro until all but forty kilos were buried and covered with our redundant genoa. Then we recited to each other the number of palms lining the bay and where our particular tree, the weeping mango, lay in the configuration. The final forty kilos remained on board for our immediate float. We had barely £100 in cash between us. Finally we motored out of the bay, for all the world as though we were tourists drunk with too much sun and moving back to civilisation in Devil's Bay.

Imagine the burden of worry that had lifted from my shoulders. Although Harvey was to have some close scrapes with the law, up until now he had basked in a hippy complacency that cannabis smuggling was an evangelising adventure which only a few "pigs" cared about, and they were too stupid to fear. For my part, I had been fully busted, faced many years in prison, and was now on the run with enough dope on board to see me locked up into old age. Unloading it on Fallen Jerusalem was a delicious relief.

We went ashore in Devil's Bay back on Virgin Gorda, a one-hour crossing, and climbed a potted road. Beat this: we rounded a corner and there was a pub. Yes, a pub, called the Wild Dog, empty and waiting for us. I rubbed my eyes in disbelief. The publican, a heavy-bellied RAF retiree, sized us up wordlessly, took our orders for steak and kidney pudding and yam mash, and pulled our pints of Shepherd Neame for all the world as though we were two walkers arriving off Exmoor at a village in North Devon. He also took our English money without turning a hair. This surreal scene was completed by two screeching peacocks on the lawn.

The alcohol went to my head and it was Harvey who for once was hushing me as we rehearsed late into the night all we had been through. Finally we got the barman to fill our twenty-litre jerrycan with water and left. It was past midnight when we flopped into the Avon and blundered around adrift as we struggled to start the Seagull. A breeze carried us back to the *Beaver*.

We had made it. We had crossed the Atlantic with a ton of cannabis and landed it in the New World.

3

New York

OUR PLAN WAS based on a chap called Ken Wainman, who we had known in the Balearics. Ken was an American whose parents had kept a holiday home on St Croix, the most southerly of the American Virgins, so he knew the place well. According to him, Christiansted, one of its main settlements, was a laid-back port full of lotus eaters like himself. It was also a well developed, fully functioning piece of America and, even more importantly, it had an international airport with regular flights to Miami and New York. According to Ken, once you landed on St Croix you were officially in the United States, so if you then caught a plane to Miami or New York you were effectively just taking an internal flight, without having to run the gauntlet of customs and immigration. That sounded good.

So at six o'clock in the morning, we hauled anchor, ran up the sails and headed south for St Croix, where we hoped to complete our business.

We sailed all day, and it was late afternoon before we spotted the familiar volcanic humps that characterise the Virgin Islands. Like all these islands, St Croix was also surrounded by treacherous coral reefs, behind which lurked fabled lagoons of azure water on white sand. Generally these lagoons had breaks in them through which a river or the small tides there could flow. You needed local knowledge to negotiate these, although if you were going into a significant port, as we were, the approaches were carefully buoyed.

It was dark and moonlit when we picked up the first red port marker buoy and took a line, leaving the sequence to our left. Twice I felt the boat judder as it skidded, happily only on sand. We widened our distance from the red buoys, although they were getting harder and harder to pick out in the gathering gloom. Then came another skid. Then a wreck – yes, a wreck – only a hundred yards to our starboard.

"It's a fucking trap," shouted Harvey. "They make their living as wreckers."

I swerved back towards the buoys and shouted to Harvey to trail our weighted line which passed as a depth finder. Weirdly it seemed to get deeper the nearer we got to the buoys. Even stranger, the sandbank that we had to avoid to port seemed a long way off in the moonlight, whilst the island that we needed to skirt to our starboard seemed almost under our bows, looming out of the darkness. I threw caution to the winds and went over to the other side of the fading line of buoys.

At last the shape of Gallows Bay opened up, fringed with lights, and then the lighthouse that marked the entrance to Christiansted harbour. I shut my eyes and drove straight for it. Harvey says that when I am scared I am good at not showing it. It's true; I go silent. I was deathly silent for that last half mile. But I may have been flustered because once we had passed under the end of the curved harbour wall, I told Harvey to drop anchor. Sadly it was too close to a rich man's schooner and we fouled his anchor rope. So we paid our anchor out and edged up to the jetty and tied up. I was a semi-professional diver so the anchor could await the next morning. We were on dry land proper now: banks, boatyards, telephones, cafes and air conditioning.

There was even a Howard Johnson, legendary at that time for its burger and fries. This was where we rewarded ourselves and where Harvey got to talking to a local called Eddy. He explained our terrifying approach to the harbour.

"Heck. You guys don't know a thing. Reckon I had heard that over there they do their buoys the wrong way round. No, no, no," he chuckled. "The right way round is red buoys to starboard on your way in, to port on your way out."

"Actually it's we English who say what's right in these matters," I contributed, contentiously. "Port means left. Leave to your left when approaching port. Not leaving port. Anyone can leave a port."

He loved it. "With that accent you could kill a mule!"

Pretty soon Eddy was our best friend and took us out for a drink. Later he showed us the Stone Balloon bar, which was to become our headquarters, although I didn't encourage Eddy to go in with us. He was great, Eddy, a sort of would-be Hemingway, bearded, paunchy and mad for heavy duty fishing on his derelict-looking Grand Banks motorboat. He was longing to take us out with him the next day and eventually I did go out with him and had a tremendous day. Although his drinking worried me.

The next day, refreshed and confident, I went diving to recover the anchor. Then we reported to Customs and Immigration. Our story was that we had been cruising the other Virgins with the owner, a New Yorker, and he had gone home. We were here to fix up the boat, re-victual and so on. We expected to be based in town for at least a month, when the owner was due to rejoin us. Then we booked a slot in the boatyard for the following day and got permission to remain on the jetty until then.

Then it was time to report to the Stone Balloon, a louche coffee bar, favourite with the young and, apparently, with draft dodgers avoiding the Vietnam War, long haired and well into "the scene", for whom we would become willing suppliers. The walls were draped with posters of Che Guevara, Marsha Hunt and Huey Long, worn copies of *Rolling Stone* magazine lay scattered about and the Grateful Dead played on the jukebox. The barman was an elegant black guy, a retired police officer from New York. I loved it.

Harvey told the barman we were looking for Ken Wainman and soon we were round at a crash-pad of a flat a block away. Ken would be back from Miami that night, a Joan Baez lookalike told us. We told her we'd be in the Stone Balloon. Meanwhile we looked around.

Christiansted was typically American. Big, red-roofed bungalows ran in straight lines, ending in boulevards lined with palms. Most of them had swimming pools and fizzing garden sprinklers, Chevy Impalas being cleaned by their owners and those ubiquitous mailboxes on stands. On the hills round about, the rich had their mini estates and picture postcard views. Between there and the airport was a black shanty town. Downtown was the port, which was to be our home for the next month. Here there were some grander and less American buildings from the 19th century, in fine French chateau style. The colours were more vibrant and bright, typically yellow. This looked like a nice place to settle.

Ken seemed a bit shifty when we met. He was with someone called William Heerwagen. Heerwagen was apparently a trustafarian heir to the Uncle Ben's Rice fortune, but he had fallen out with his parents because of his alternative lifestyle. That lifestyle was clearly drug orientated. He'd got through a lot of LSD in his time and claimed to be softening its aftermath with controlled quantities of heroin. But he had money, and Ken had got him to buy a Land Rover which we drove around the island.

Ken was amazed to hear what we had come with.

"A ton? You're kidding me." He didn't seem that pleased. "How are we going to move a ton here?"

"Here," I spelt out, "is the biggest market in the world."

"What? A hundred hippies?"

"No. I mean the United States of America."

"Oh, the US. Who is going to take it there?"

"Well, you are, aren't you? You said you could get girls to fly it over there twenty ki at a time."

"You seen what a bottle of whiskey costs here? They're giving it away. Why do you think that is?"

I had noticed this phenomenon: lines of shops selling watches and cameras at giveaway prices.

"Because they are duty free?"

"Exactly."

"Meaning?"

"Arriving in the US from here is the same as from everywhere else. Worse in fact. Because of its duty free status, they are especially careful about smuggling."

"Why the fuck didn't you tell us that?"

Ken tried to pretend that this was something new in some way. But the truth was he'd been guessing. And dreaming. So it was back to the drawing board.

Over the next few weeks we sold a kilo on the island so that we had some money to fix the boat and live. Forty kilos we buried inland with Ken and William. This was hard work, finding a safe, suitable place in a wood inland. Coming back we got lost and asked directions of a man who appeared to be loading a pickup. He turned towards us. His face was bleeding like a pig.

"It's those fucking blacks. I'm getting the fuck out of here." Even the Virgins reproduced America's racial warfare of the time.

This forty kilos was later moved in Heerwagen's Land Rover to Miami, where they were busted. At the time we were at sea, believing that Ken had arranged for us to be met at Providence, Rhode Island. That was where we planned to move the bulk of our cargo. We were to be met by his sister, who had a place there. I suspect that either he or the barman at the Stone Balloon tipped off the DEA, or ICE as it was then, in Miami, about our plan. I reckon the cops called up their old employee, prompted by their fortuitous bust of Ken and William, for which the hapless Heerwagen took most of the blame because the Land Rover was his.

All that lay ahead. Meanwhile the *Beaver* was patched up and became quite a draw for the local hip crowd. There was a cute American psychedelic painter who light-heartedly shacked up with me and there were a lot of seafood and barbecue suppers on deck. However, I had to call the whole thing closed after a while when the dope smoking and music got out of hand.

Harvey was resolved to fly to New England, where the Woodstock Festival was coming up. He needed to warm up some contacts there for our eventual delivery. He said he needed to arrange bank accounts in Switzerland and that he would take charge of the money side of things. That was a huge burden off my mind, because it was not my plan to sail home with $1 million in cash stashed in my hold, to a Europe now no doubt on the lookout for me. There was many a slip between cup and lip.

So I needed a crew and that meant talking with the hip crowd who hung round the boat to find reliable lads, lads who would pick up at New Jerusalem, sail up the coast of America and deliver to Rhode Island. Once I had them, I needed to move fast.

Having been there well over six weeks, it was July by the time we left. I was getting nervous about the approaching hurricane season. With me were Red and Brad, both in their early twenties with barely delayed military call-ups to avoid. To my surprise, Red turned out a good sailor and Brad a good cook. They also liked the boat to be shipshape. They were to get five kilos apiece for their work, on delivery. In fact they were not there for delivery and they were pissed off when I gave them just half of that. But I don't blame them for what happened in the end.

On a hot and windless day, we motored slowly up to Fallen Jerusalem and anchored. Brad ran about the beach catching coconut crabs which we barbecued on the sand. We had put out a very long, marked warp fore and aft so as to be able to pull the dinghy to and fro. It would also deter other boats coming in too through our narrow entrance. Only one sailed by, no doubt just enjoying the serenity of the scene, so we set about sunbathing.

I also challenged the boys to find the stash as a kind of game. While they were off searching around the corner, I actually dug it up, separated forty kilos, and reburied it nearby. Now I was the only person who knew where it was. My ace in the hole. Intrepid treasure hunters may like to seek it out, for I never went back to get it, although what nature has done to it I dare not guess.

Then we were off. The journey took three weeks and was beset by a lack of wind for days at a time. We followed the coast of America, perhaps 300 miles out, and there were times when heavy mist fell and we seemed to be moving through a muffled cloud of steam. As well as creating a fuel shortage through motoring too much, this caused a problem with navigation. My well-honed navigation skills with the sextant were rendered useless and for days at a time we didn't have a clue where the sun or we were.

Then one day, looming out of the mist in a pool of ghostly light, was a huge trawler, or maybe a mothership. It had the familiar red-dot Japanese flag flying from its stern, and it was stationary and silent. They could tell us where we were.

As we approached this spectre, to our astonishment, it moved off. Now it was we who were giving chase. This was a change from feeling the chased one. After moving only about a mile, she stopped and this time allowed us to come alongside. For a while nothing happened. Then over the side was lowered a wicker basket with paper and pencil.

We wrote: "Where are we?"

Up went the basket. Down it came again. Inside, holding down the reply, was a small bottle of fiery liquid and a number of porcelain bowls. We filled them and drank a toast to the invisible crew, put the bowls back in the basket and up it went again. On the paper were our coordinates. We were about level with Charleston, South Carolina, and had drifted much further inland than we had expected. But our fuel was low and we were going to have to make an unscheduled stop.

We chose Cape May at the mouth of the Delaware to make landfall. It was a poor choice. As we started up the one-mile channel that links the lagoon to the Atlantic, a US Customs cutter loomed up behind us at speed, then started to overtake us. A man in uniform photographed us. Brad was being sick overboard and I barely stopped him from diving into the sea and swimming for shore. One of the officers waved at us and they disappeared into the lagoon. As it happened, we had chosen the main Customs training and operational base on the Eastern Coast.

Fortunately the lion often fails to notice the fly that has landed on its lip. We found a refuelling barge, took on water and fuel without having to land and report, and did not waste any time on seeing the sights. We got out of there.

The three of us talked a lot on the way up. Brad, who knew Ken well, was clearly windy about his scheme to meet us on Rhode Island. He didn't trust him. I wasn't sure I did. Brad was also unwilling to go to Rhode Island because he feared our reception there. I was for cutting to the chase, where the market was: New York. The watchful predator scans the horizon and often misses what is under its nose. That was my thinking.

"You want to sail up the Hudson and dock in New York?" exclaimed the astonished Red at my proposal. "No way! More pigs there than a Chicago abattoir."

Brad was of the same view. They had the typical amateur understanding of smuggling: find a small cove, land the cargo at night, rent a car, etcetera. This is a huge mistake made by smugglers and dealers who believe that farms and empty country with no cop station for miles and miles ought to be safer than the main street of a great city. They're wrong. Life is empty and uneventful in the country. Each person's business is everybody's. Everything gets noticed and tongues wag in the bar of the local town. You're safer operating out of an arches lockup on the Bethnal Green Road than any remote croft in Scotland.

Unloading by dinghy and making a series of drives in a hire car into New York would take days and days. Endless ripples would run.

"I want to hit the dock and hail a yellow cab," I said.

"And how many times you gonna do that?"

"A dozen. There's plenty of cabs there."

"You crazy? The place is stiff with cops."

And so we went on. But they were adamant. They would go up the Hudson with me, but then they were off. They were having nothing to do with the unloading.

I did agree that I needed to reconnoitre the 79th Street marina, on the Upper West Side, and book a slot. And it would be wise to make some phone calls to see the lie of the land.

And that is how we came to make our first stop in Sandy Bay, opposite Manhattan. This has a low lying, slightly dreary New Jersey foreshore used mainly by working boats, as the hinterland is industrial. I certainly didn't want to stay long. It was not an obvious place for a stylish yacht to spend its time. I dinghied ashore, walked for what seemed miles before I could find a cab, then went into New York City and booked into the Chelsea Hotel on 23rd Street. It was time to make some phone calls.

Harvey was at Woodstock but said he'd fly straight down to New York. He thought he had a buyer there for most of the load. Ken was incommunicado. There was a rumour he'd been busted in Miami, and his sister wouldn't return calls. Harvey agreed that a fast delivery to New York was our best chance. I was back on the boat that night.

At seven the next morning, we saluted the Statue of Liberty as I, "Charles Hamilton Brice", skipper of the *Beaver* with his mutinous crew, sailed past and up the Hudson to arrive with over a ton of cannabis resin in the heart of New York City, at the 79th Street Basin.

AUGUST IS a killer in New York. The humidity was terrific, the heat dense and oppressive. Walking a block put you in a muck sweat. Brad and Red were willing to moor but thereafter I was on my own.

The boat basin is a largish marina next to Riverside Park, while 79th Street, which terminates there at a roundabout, is an important cross-island thoroughfare. Looking up river, the Washington Bridge loomed in the summer haze. You could say it was bang in the middle of Manhattan, although in those days the area north of Riverside Park was regarded by white people as a dangerous reserve for drug-deranged blacks called Harlem. The embankment opposite the basin is raised high and built into it is a large restaurant extending out onto a deep terrace. This was packed on our arrival, so we didn't lack for an audience, which made my crew all the jumpier. They left me, bags slung over their shoulders and American passports in hand, and disappeared into the basin office.

For my part I set about folding and rolling sails, making good the lines and sheets, and adjusting the fenders, watchful for I knew not what. Eventually a basin official with a classic New York girth rolled up.

"Where you come from, buddy?"

"American Virgins, St Croix," I said.

"That's a way. You stop anywhere?"

"Cape May and Sandy Bay."

"You British, or something?"

"I am."

"Staying?"

"For a while. I need to replace my crew."

"Those boys just gone in your crew?"

"They were."

"Hey, they're just lads. And this here is the flesh market of the world. You alone now?"

"Whole place is mine. Call me Hamilton." I stretched out my hand to shake his and he gripped in warmly.

"Right, Hamilton. Welcome to New York. You got anything you shouldn't have?"

"Like what?"

"Food, animals, plants, things like that?"

"Nothing like that. Bit of cheap booze maybe."

He chuckled.

"Hammy, fill in this form and bring your passport by. And have a nice stay."

It seemed I was in and, as is my wont, I slowly went back to the business in hand.

Later I walked to the roundabout behind the café. Cabs were no problem, although hauling the product up the slope was going to be hot work. I returned to the Chelsea Hotel some way downtown and extended my stay there to a week.

I had previously exhibited in New York and stayed at this very hotel. It was a cool place, proud of its slightly flophouse atmosphere even though it had all the mod cons. Being long-haired and bearded, as I now was, I went with the flow. The only danger was if someone recognised me, but I doubted that. Sadly, I hadn't made that much of a splash.

Best of all, the Chelsea had telephones in all the rooms, and air conditioning. A remarkable feature of New York at this time was the ubiquitous spread of air conditioning. Every building was festooned with add-on white-boxed machines purring without pause. The most wretched diner would greet you with a blast of cold air and litre glasses of ice and water. If you had a cab waiting out the front of the hotel, you could get through most of the day feeling the heat only in sudden wafts as you ran between cab and building and vice versa.

I got to work straight away, hammering the telephone. Harvey told me to introduce myself to a William Linus, who worked in a printworks-cum-publishing office called something like Alternative Publishing, somewhere around 50th. So I took a cab there and buzzed the entry phone.

It was a handsome, brick-built industrial warehouse block tucked between the familiar skyscrapers. Each floor was open plan with stays and pulleys in 1920s ironwork still attached to the supporting columns. Between the floors were caged iron staircases and in the corners on each floor were simple cabins open to the floor, where people worked at desks and came and went. Over the open areas were hundreds of boxes, some baled, some packed, there were rolls of newsprint and somewhere I could hear the hydraulic churn of a heavy press. The business was a stack of alternative publication businesses, a different one on each floor. Linus was on the third. Posters, flyers, local newspapers, pamphlets, books and other junk bestrewed his space.

William, or Bill, was an entrepreneur, tall, slim, dressed in denim and a pioneer of the ponytail. He invited me into his office, a chaotic swirl of signed photos of authors and sexy silhouettes of afro-headed nudes, and sat me down. He'd been expecting me. I introduced myself by putting a kilo block on the desk in front of him. He was cool about that.

"Mind if I roll up?"

"Sure. You'll like it."

He rolled a joint there and then on the desk, lit up and drew deep. Other employees came and went without batting an eyelid. To some of them he offered a toke, and they savoured it like oenophiles with a good Bordeaux. To my dismay, Bill seemed to be getting sleepy.

"That's a heavy high," he sighed eventually. "What do you want for it?"

"Harvey didn't tell you?"

"He said you'd be greedy."

"Yeah, he's a pal. Eight hundred dollars per kilo, if you take the lot. A thousand dollars if you take only half and climbing if I have to sweat round this greenhouse to find other buyers."

"And the whole lot is?"

"A ton."

To my surprise he did not do the usual intake of breath and whistling stuff. He got right up.

"I'll need to talk to some guys." And he was gone.

Half an hour later, during which time I read a booklet called *How to Bust the Bust*, a half-finished handbook on being arrested with drugs, he came back. He handed over an envelope with pictures of Madison inside. I counted them. Eight hundred dollars. I looked up.

"So the lot?"

"We'll try and take it all. If we can't move the whole lot in ten days we'll look at the price again. Meanwhile, cash on delivery?"

"Harvey'll be dealing with the money. All I want is a receipt."

"You're a cool dude," said Bill. "Your British gentleman's word, huh?"

With $800 in my pocket I could get to work. The first thing I needed to do was get all the dope off the boat, and for that I needed somewhere to stow it. I rented a one-bed service flat for $300 a fortnight, renewable, on 53rd Street, nice and close to Alternative Publishing. The plan was to move the dope in 100-kilo goes to the flat until the boat was clean and empty. Then I could concentrate on distribution.

I had two Revelation suitcases, my dad's, which had completed the trip from England with me. Both the hinges and the catches were on a ratchet so you could double the size of the case and force it down tight against the ratchet. I could get anything up to sixty kilos in with a coating disguise of clothes without it looking too absurdly heavy.

And so my routine began: loading the cases on the boat, getting the basin trolley, rolling it up the ramps to the roundabout, calling a cab, loading the cab, taking the trolley back, back to the cab and off to 53rd Street. Pay off the cab, haul the cases up three storeys to the flat, unpack and stow it and back down with the empty Revelations, into a cab and back to the boat. For some of this I eventually rented a car out at the airport, which I could leave in a car park stack next to the basin.

One time when I was in a heavy sweat pushing the trolley up the ramp to the roundabout, two cops in full uniform joined me, one on either side. I thought they were seizing the trolley but they weren't. They were helping me. I was so dumbstruck I went into a kind of Terry-Thomas impersonation.

"Jolly decent of you chaps. You'd never get a British bobby helping out like that."

They were thrown by this.

"Always glad to help, sir. Have a nice day."

At some point I would go to the Chelsea and phone from my room. Harvey had arrived from Woodstock and was still windy about Ken and his girlfriend being off the radar. He wanted me to get the stuff shifted by making daily deliveries of fifty kilos to Alternative Publishing, starting now.

My average day would start with breakfast with Harvey at a diner next to the Chelsea, and thence to the boat. Harvey wouldn't come near it. He had sunk more and more into the alternative scene and was picking up the rising paranoia of acid abuse, Nixon and Vietnam. To me it was water off a duck's back. I was happy for him to look after the money and leave all this handling work to me. I'm no good with figures and paperwork. I was happier putting baggy wrinklies round the mooring lines to stop them fraying.

I would then do maybe one, maybe two, excursions with the Revelation cases: boat, cab, flat, cab, boat. At some time during the day, I'd go round to Alternative Publishing with fifty kilos in a Revelation case, again by cab. Often I'd hang out there for a while and maybe eat takeaway pastrami-and-ryes with the staff. One evening a group of us went to an Ionescu play at one of the many theatres round my hotel. Another time we went to Max's Kansas City restaurant, one of those eternal stars in the constellation for steak-eating Americans.

Meanwhile there was work to do on the boat, so I was also busy painting the wheelhouse and resealing the hatches. I had told the guy at the Basin office that I might be selling the boat. That was indeed the plan, so it was not that surprising that one late afternoon a couple of men who looked like father and son appeared on the pontoon, admiring the *Beaver*'s lines.

"Hi there. You Hamilton Brice?"

I stopped my work and went over to their side.

"Cute-looking boat. Kinda old, no?" I told them about the boat and its history.

"My dad's winding down," said the younger one. "He was thinking of like a retirement thing. A boat he could live in for some of the year with Mom, like the winter months, down Florida and Bahamas. You know what I mean? He wants a good-size yawl."

And so on. They had a quick look around and purported to consider where a grandchild could sleep and things like that. Then they left.

No sailor would mistake the *Beaver* for a yawl, mizzen on the stern. I didn't like it. But what could I do? Keep moving the dope.

Harvey was more wary. He had accumulated a big stash of dough, around $200,000, and we agreed he would fly back to Europe with it. He clearly thought I was doomed.

"Why not wait until we've sold the lot?" I asked.

"In case we don't sell the lot."

"You think it's going to come on top?"

"It's what I fear," he said.

"And you're going to leave me to face the music?"

"Better you face the music with some money in the bank." He was right. There was no point us both being wiped out.

After he had gone, it reached a stage where there were about forty kilos on the boat and 400 kilos in the flat; the rest had been delivered and paid for. My deliveries were becoming fewer and clearly I was stretching the capacity of our buyer. Time seemed to slow down, yet there was an unpleasant expectancy in the air. How could this all be so easy?

It came on top one lunchtime. I was eating peaches out of a tin with a fork on the pontoon when they appeared at one end, a young man and a girl in plain clothes and three other men in boiler suits with the ICE (Institution of Customs Enforcement) slogan across their chests.

"Hamilton Brice?"

"That's me."

"We have reason to believe you have a large quantity of cannabis resin on board this boat and I have here a warrant to search. You want to tell us about it or are you going to make us do it the hard way?"

We walked back together to the boat. Do it the hard way, I thought. "I'll help you as much as I can," is what I said.

Well I was a goner as far as the dope on the boat was concerned. But the reference to "on this boat" implied they didn't know about the flat. I've said this before and others believe it too about me: I don't panic, and I give myself time to think. I'm not a brilliant thinker, in fact most of what has happened to me makes me seem an idiot. I try to do too much on my own, and though I didn't know it then, ahead of me lay numerous imprisonments for ill-planned operations. But what helps a little is that I lack imagination. I don't in the moment of crisis see the disastrous times that loom ahead, and so I never go to pieces.

"You'll find it in the forecabin. About forty kilos. When you've got that we'll talk some more."

They found it alright. They searched me and bagged my belongings, then they sat me down in the saloon. While the girl made some tea – "That's what you Brits like, right?" – they grilled me.

It was time for my damage limitation story. I told them a black guy in a bar in Christiansted had asked me to deliver this forty ki to a guy in New York. That was my revenge for what I believed had happened with the ex-cop barman there. They had found Harvey's number but he was safely back in the UK. So OK, I said, it might have been this guy Harvey. I was to take this dope to the Chelsea Hotel and eventually he was going to come in a cab and pick it up. In fact he was due this afternoon. I had been about to take a cab there. This was sort of true. The last forty kilos was packed into one of the Revelations, although it wasn't going to the Chelsea.

In the event this was a clever piece of improvisation, because what they wanted to do next was stake out the Chelsea with me and ambush whoever came to collect. I was cuffed and marched up the ramp to their cars, one marked, two unmarked. On the way up we met the Basin office guy. I shrugged my shoulders to him as though I didn't know what this was all about.

"Nothing to do with me, pal," he said, his palms opened out, Al Pacino style.

Our little convoy proceeded through the midtown traffic to the Chelsea. The fact I had a room there seemed to confirm my story, although if they'd known I had been there nearly two weeks it might have raised questions. They forgot to ask and didn't want to alert the staff there to an impending bust. The young man and the girl walked me into the hotel, I got the key and we went up to my room. I had passed the attitude test and I was no longer cuffed. We stowed the case and they searched the joint. Then we went downstairs and waited in the foyer.

An hour went by.

A yellow cab drew up, and a young couple got out and were paying the driver. I rose to my feet.

"It's them," I whispered urgently. "I'll go and get them in. Wait there!" Amazingly, they did. I walked fast out into 23rd Street and hustled the arrivals away from the driver's door.

"Don't worry. I'll pay. I need this cab. Just go!" To the cabbie, I said, "Just go, go, go! I'm being chased. Go! There's a hundred bucks in it if you can get me away from here."

It was a complete lie; I didn't have a penny. But he went; unbelievably, he went. As fast as he could. Which, unfortunately in the traffic, was very slowly indeed.

I should have run.

There followed a farcical twenty minutes in which we were blocked in slow-moving traffic, only able to turn right and right again. I was spluttering an incoherent account of being caught up in error in some gang shootout and all the time we were working our way round the block back to where we started. Then a hue and cry went up, police sirens everywhere, blue lights flashing and NYPD cars cutting through the late- afternoon logjam. Back on the corner of 23rd, I could see and hear prowl cars on their way to the hotel. A similar racket of police activity was going on behind.

I left the cab as quickly as I had got into it, chucking my wristwatch to the cabbie as payment, and sprinted across the road. I had seen a barber and I hadn't shaved or had a haircut for a while. Maybe if it was all shaved off, I would get away.

No sooner was I inside the barber's parlour than I could see a cop walking towards us. I ducked back out and ran down towards First Avenue. Coming the other way were two fit and determined-looking plainclothesmen. I surrendered.

They led me to their vehicle and bundled me in. No sooner had they done that than two traffic cops came up and tried to stop them. It was the narcotics Feds that now had me, in the form of the Bureau of Narcotics and Dangerous Drugs (BNDD), and they were setting off. An unholy turf war broke out as to whose prisoner I was. After a lot of crackling radio and heavy swearing, calm was restored and it was conceded that I was the property of ICE, and the narcotics department handed over their prize. Not that it made any difference.

The BNDD had raided Alternative Publications that very afternoon and had been planning to pick me up at the Chelsea, where they knew I had been staying. They'd recovered fifty kilos from Alternative and arrested four or five people there. An even more calamitous sequel was that a sharp-eyed exhibits officer puzzled over the boat keys. One looked familiar to him. It was of unusual manufacture and mainly issued by one particular New York locksmith. After some cunning tracing work, they identified the flat on 53rd, and 400 kilos more were recovered.

I was a goner.

All that remained was identifying me. Unless I wished to hide from my family that I was to spend the next four years in a federal penitentiary, that too was a foregone conclusion.

Exactly a year after my first arrest at 71 Castelnau, I was collected from one of the twenty-man cages that filled a federal warehouse in the Bronx, was taken to the US District Court South, and pleaded guilty in front of Justice Croake. That winter I was sentenced to eight years in prison.

My luck had run out. How had it come to this?

PART TWO

1934–71

4

The Morlands

I WAS BORN out of a TB clinic in Norfolk in 1934.

Yet the first years that I can recall were spent not in East Anglia but at Inyswytrin, a large, handsome, 15th century manor house with a walled vegetable garden and a beautiful view, halfway up the Tor at Glastonbury. Why I was in Somerset I am not quite sure; possibly because war was approaching, together with the fact that Glastonbury had long been the family fiefdom.

My father, Andrew, was the oldest son of John Colby Morland, who lived at Inyswytrin (the name means "Isle of Glass" and is what the Celts called Glastonbury Tor), and the grandson of John Morland, founder of the family dynasty. Old John had been a Quaker, and by the middle of the 19th century Quakers were a network of virtuous, like-minded nonconformists, stricter and more self-disciplined even than Methodists. They believed in the endless betterment of mankind through work and worship. They also disliked hierarchic authority, nowhere more so than in their meeting houses. Whereas the Protestant upheaval in Northern Europe had downgraded the special status of priests from chosen messengers of God to mere leaders of their congregations, Quakers dispensed with them altogether. Instead they had "elders", who played a similarly influential role over their flocks. When they met, in their bleak, undecorated meeting houses on a Sunday, they waited for God to inspire them directly, making them "quake" or hold forth in some kind of ecstasy, hence the name.

Many of them became very successful. The Fry and the Cadbury families were among the richest in England. Barclays, Lloyds and Friends Provident all have Quaker origins. Those that made money disposed of it modestly, donating handsomely to charities and the Liberal Party. Within the family they promoted the ablest, as they saw it, rather than the oldest. They didn't drink, or smoke, or spend long hours at the dinner table late into the night. So supper at Inyswytrin was over by seven, and there was no radio to while away the remaining hours. Grace was said before and after meals, the food was virtuous and dull and we all fell silent if my grandfather appeared.

The house was on the edge of town and had plenty of land, indeed a farm. An elegant, copper-roofed canopy ran around two sides of the house, overlooking lawns and gardens which ended in a sharp drop to a gully from the Tor. It looked south across a finger of the levels to a line of hills opposite. Down the steep road was Glastonbury. Glastonbury was long famous for its Saxon Tor and the Thorn tree planted by Joseph of Arimathea and Arthur.

It was also a company town, and that company was Morland and Co. Its founder, my aforementioned great-grandfather John, had married into another Quaker family, the Clarks, in 1865. The Clarks had established themselves in a bleak town called Street on the edge of the Somerset levels. Street was downriver from Glastonbury on the River Brue, which originally must have flowed into the sea nearby. Later the Somerset levels were drained by Huguenots fleeing

Henry IV and Louis XIV of France, and the freed-up land confirmed the area's status as one of the principal sheep and wool trade centres of England. It also had historic claims to nonconformism. George Jeffreys, the notorious "Hanging Judge", was at his bloodiest here against the local support for Monmouth, whose rebellion against James II's attempts to restore Roman Catholicism at the end of the Stuart dynasty was brutally suppressed.

Leather tanning is a smelly, dirty business, involving heavy-duty chemicals and drying agents, preservatives, relaxants, oils and so on. It requires a lot of water and is not popular in bigger towns, even downstream. The Clarks of Street got big in the tanning business, buying up the local sheepskins, treating them and turning them into saleable products. They covered the whole range. Now they make only shoes and are a household name.

When John Morland married Mary Clark, he went to Street with her. The Clark family must have been pleased with him, for in 1875 they hived off to John all their business in which the wool was kept on the skin, whilst Clarks concentrated on naked leather. Morland and Company prospered enormously, particularly during wars when sheepskin coats and jackets were in huge demand from the armed forces. At the time I was born, Morlands had a factory on the edge of Glastonbury that sprawled over eighty acres; its chimneys could be seen almost from Taunton. It employed over 1,000 people there and in smaller plants elsewhere and bought most of the sheepskin production of Patagonia, which is why I said that Glastonbury was a company town.

We were a big clan and at any one time at least four or five of the family worked at the factory at Northover. Up the Coombe, in Wick Hollow, were four other Morland households, in houses designed by a cousin. My father and his brothers and sisters were brought up at Inyswytrin and educated at the Quaker Eton, Sidcot School, near the Mendips. They had the smell of tanning in their blood from an early age. The immediate neighbour, in a large thatched house, was my Aunt Elizabeth, married to Harry Scott Stokes, the sometime mayor of Glastonbury and managing director of John Morland. Humphrey, another uncle, was working his way up the management scale. My friendship with John, the son of yet another uncle, was another reason for me to spend time at Inyswytrin.

But my father had a wandering, cosmopolitan instinct, which I would inherit, and Wick Hollow was suffocating. Medicine was considered a virtuous profession by Quakers and was the one my father chose. He came to it as a result of a familiar Quaker experience in war, a Friends Ambulance Unit. This now venerable institution satisfied the problem of conscientious objection to war: Quakers were pacifists. It was they who set up this prototype, centrally run ambulance unit at the beginning of the First World War.

My dad was driving such an ambulance near the front at Cambrai, in northern France, when he was the collateral victim of a gas attack. His lungs were damaged, and it was this that led him to specialise in his training on lung disease, particularly tuberculosis. Becoming a renowned expert, he later combined his love of walking and skiing in the Alps with an interest in a TB clinic in Davos, and had consultancies at other clinics there, on top of a burgeoning practice in London. He spent seven years on the staff of Mundesley Sanatorium in Norfolk, which is why I was born there, and was to treat George Orwell and the painter Mark Gertler among others, until finally succumbing to the occupational hazard himself in 1957. TB was a curse of the times and its spread and cure were not well understood. Until antibiotics came, it was a disease that was managed with regimes of rest and dry air.

So not for Dad the dreary routines of Inyswytrin that his father had instituted. He bought a house in Harley Street to promote his practice and to all intents and purposes, until the War came, that was our home. I remember the living quarters upstairs, but only slightly. Apparently a monkey cage was constructed outside the nursery window, in which I could be suspended in mid-air and have lots of fresh air.

I don't believe my mother, Dorothy, could have liked Inyswytrin either and I don't remember her being there much. She had met my father somewhere in the Swiss Alps because she too had succumbed to tuberculosis and lost a lung, and had gone to recuperate in the mountain air. She was a glamorous figure trying to become an actress, tall, slim and elegant, more Parisian in style than the Somerset Morland women, who were prone to mild frumpiness.

Although she was to adopt two girls almost as an afterthought – my sisters Gil and Susannah – Dorothy was not interested in children the way modern mothers are. It was one's duty then to have a family, but endless cuddling and finger painting with them was not called for. Among adults she had a highly social instinct and never stopped acquiring friends from all quarters of life. We must have been well off, but the bohemian chaos of the interiors of our various homes, although chic in their way, would never have given this away. Dorothy was also left-wing by instinct and campaigned for the Labour Party in the aftermath of the War. Dad was one of the few consultants in private practice to support the setting up of the National Health Service and the only one in Harley Street to put up a "Vote Labour" poster.

When the Second World War began I had one sister, Gil. She was some kind of an orphan who was invited to Inyswytrin to play with me one summer. My mother was so pleased at how well we got on that she adopted her. My next sister was acquired in an equally casual way. Susannah was the daughter of someone known to my father who was at his wits' end as to what to do with her now that war had started. He had lost his wife and it seems my mother had put it about that she was taking me and Gil to Canada. Susannah's father asked if she could join us. So she did. Only we didn't go to Canada, we went to a house near a village called Bovingdon, in Hertfordshire, on the edge of the Chilterns, and Susannah became my second sister.

The house was an Elizabethan manor called 2 Rent Street Barns, for some reason. It had a kind of archway entrance through which you passed into a yard that was a cross between a farmyard and an elegant court. At the back of the house were orchards and a paddock and a duck pond and a poultry house and so on. My parents took this house with a family called Dobbs: mother and father, both doctors, and two children. Dad was an expert skier and Mr Dobbs was his partner in the British ski team, as well as his best friend. During the week there would be Phyllis Dobbs, my mother, us four children and a succession of household helps, and occasionally a cook. At weekends the fathers would appear and sometimes bring delicacies from London such as chocolate, which their patients had given them.

In those days the country round about *was* country, by which I mean fields with cows and crops on them, woods and streams. There were no cars on the road and the village started about half a mile down the lane. We children were allowed to go where we liked, including the village. These days, well-preserved mums plough their new four-wheel drives through glossy suburbs of executive houses, riding schools, golf courses, garden centres and children's activity areas. Everything is manicured and cute. Not then.

Against this background, we children led a life of benign neglect. There was no restriction on tree climbing or on trespassing on other farms, clambering on their tractors, in their milk parlours and their sawmills. We could bicycle where we wanted. We baited a particularly aggressive gander we kept at Rent Barns with shield and sword, for he was the scourge of our visitors. He went mad in the end and attacked my mother so badly that she had to be hospitalised, but she insisted on keeping him because he was a good breeder.

At age seven, I started school. This was about four miles away in Kings Langley. Although doctors had access to petrol and we had a car, this was not wasted on me. I rode to school on my bicycle every morning with Simon Dobbs, and back in the evenings. The school was an eccentric place run by two pacifist sisters; another sister of theirs was the novelist Ivy Compton-Burnett. They believed that the way to stop war was not to mention it. This was some achievement during an event as huge as the Second World War, but it contributed to the fact that I barely noticed the conflict. It was only at the end that I had a sighting of a doodlebug that had wandered off course in the Watford direction. Nor do I remember my father mentioning the Blitz, which he must have witnessed.

One of my fellow pupils was a very intense, clever boy – unlike me – called Jonathan Miller. It was no surprise when he became a lion of British intellectual life. Another was Nicholas Garland, later a famous cartoonist. I did not prosper at school, and it became clear that I was dyslexic and unlikely to go to university or be an intellectual of the kind my parents favoured. It was a damning prognosis in those days but it spared me from going to Sidcot, the Quaker school in the Mendip Hills, and boarding away from home, the idea of which would have dismayed me greatly.

At weekends we often entertained guests, no doubt ferried around on my father's petrol exemption. I remember Herbert Read, the anarchist poet and literary critic, coming to visit, as well as Tom Garland, a communist agitator and father of my schoolmate Nicholas. He was to become my mother's lover. Tom specialised in industrial medicine, which meant that union leaders and industrial workers were exposed to him and his radical ideas, even during the war.

It must have been during this period that my mother became interested in, and a collector of, modern art. I dare say it was pretty cheap at the time. Tom Garland's wife, Peggy, lived in Kings Langley and had a sculpture studio there. She was school of Barbara Hepworth. I remember visiting and wandering into her studio and smelling the bubbling beeswax and feeling the smoothness of the alabaster she had been polishing. It made a lasting impression.

There was an American base at Bovingdon and our little clan befriended their officers, who regularly came to lunch in full uniform. My dad embarrassed us by handing out Morlands flying jackets, which I doubt they'd have been allowed to fly in. They would bring as house presents swing and jazz records that my mother had no way of getting even if she'd known of them. We all loved this music and I played it on the gramophone as much as my mother allowed.

Once, when a lot of visitors were coming for the weekend and my mother was preparing for them, she casually instructed me and

Simon that we would need a goose killed. We had no idea how that should be done. We took down the washing line and tied a running loop on it, then chased the geese around trying to lasso one; I rode cowboy-style on my bike while Simon ran after me holding the free end. That didn't work, so finally we herded the geese into their shed where our selected victim had no room to move. Finally we got a loop over the neck of the one we hated and then tightened.

So we had one by the neck. But what next? We dragged him over to the orchard and threw the loose end over a branch and hauled him up. We were under the impression that any animal hanged by its neck would eventually die. But he didn't, he kept right on flapping and honking. So we got a cricket bat and set about his head until it was a bloody mess and the goose finally gave up the ghost.

We presented this grisly corpse to my mother.

"I didn't tell you to kill the gander," she said. "Anyway," she added dreamily, "he'll have more meat on him. Now you can pluck him."

One summer we went by train to St Mawes in Cornwall. The journey took all day. I was very disappointed that no bombing was going on in London – we had to go to Paddington for our connection – and that there were no aircraft in the sky. Down at St Mawes, my father commandeered a sailing dinghy and we had a marvellous week skidding round the bay and occasionally capsizing. He also taught me to play tennis. On another occasion I remember visiting the abstract painter Ben Nicholson in St Ives and playing French cricket with him in the sand. The architect Leslie Martin, a friend of my parents and designer of the Royal Festival Hall, was supporting Nicholson and buying all his paintings.

As I have said, it was a life of benign neglect. And although we were a skinny bunch of children I don't remember ever being hungry or missing meals. So I was sad when the War ended and the Dobbses went their own way. But no one could have complained about where we Morlands went to live next.

Our new home was a magnificent Georgian mansion seemingly in the middle of Hampstead Heath: number 1 East Heath Road (which now belongs to the television personality Esther Rantzen) was in a row of equally lovely houses and fine gardens sticking out like a finger of Hampstead village into the Heath. My father rented the house from a Quaker flower painter who made a fortune selling his kitsch paintings to hang on the walls of doctors' waiting rooms.

This would be my home from the age of eleven more or less until I married and got the house in Castelnau fifteen years later. These formative years were to be rich in encounters and discovery, in large part because of my background. It had been a privileged childhood, and that is more evident with the benefit of hindsight. Children take their families and their homes for granted. They assume that everyone else's life is a mild variation on their own. I was no different.

Every year we went to Switzerland to ski, either at Klosters or Davos. It was a young sport which had become popular with the rich, particularly the English rich, during the 1920s. A £50 limit imposed on currency taken abroad after the War did not inhibit us, as my grandfather had an interest in a hotel in Verbier. It was normally for summer hikers but he acquired it to keep it open in winter, when the factory in Glastonbury was slack. The resort was free of ski lifts. You climbed all morning, picnicked, then skied back down through immaculate powder. At least that's how I remember it.

There was also a clinic in Davos, in the valley of Klosters and St Moritz, the home of downhill skiing. We had free access to the clinic because my father consulted and sent patients there. Later, because of the spread of antibiotics, the cure for TB, it became in stages a guesthouse and finally a hotel. In the meantime it allowed us to live comfortably whilst skiing, although I can't remember who didn't live well in our circle. My father was a good friend of Arthur Lunn, who was a driving force in the growth of skiing in the Swiss Alps and became a tycoon in the travel business. He also oversaw competitions, clubs and parties at the hotels in which he had an interest, and was integral in the formation of the Ski Club of Great Britain. I took to skiing like a duck to water, and later, in my twenties, brought a little glory for my country.

As for school, it was ordained that I would not thrive at Sidcot because of my dyslexia and so I was sent to a Burgess Hill day school, over the hill in Hampstead. I could get to it walking through the village. Hampstead was not the home of the super-rich as it is today, but more a colony of left-wing intellectuals from the Jewish diaspora and the English Left. I walked past the Everyman cinema on my way to school and occasionally was taken to virtuous showings of subtitled French films and Soviet propaganda. I remember one where a factory that stamped out metal panels came to a halt with a great flash of lightning. A handsome worker pulled heavy power cables out of some kind of fuse box and, amid a mass of sparking and flashing, held the cables together with his bare hands. This allowed the factory to complete its night shift, when electricians would arrive. Meanwhile our hero had died from his exertions. Uplifting though this was, I would much rather have been down the hill watching an Alan Ladd blockbuster at the Playhouse.

My next school was a bit more academic, King Alfred's, over the hill in Golders Green. I could bicycle there over the Heath, which has many paths. These impressed me particularly because all paths had disappeared from the country in the war, ploughed up for the war effort. To have the Heath, with all these paths, as your back garden was very heaven. Another of the eccentricities of the Heath was the Saturday night nude bathing in the ponds, which attracted a lot of ribaldry.

My cousin John lived nearby and, although a bit older than me, was a close friend. Nevertheless I was deemed to be corrupting with my wild ways. Once we took an airgun and shot at the ducks on Hampstead pond, where the women swam. I winged one, which swam in increasingly small circles among the bathers and a great hue and cry went up. We were caught, cuffed and marched home, where my mother dressed me down, principally for getting good John into trouble. John blamed me for all sorts of misdemeanours, including firing an airgun in a cinema and a 12-bore in his bedroom.

On Monday nights there was a regular salon at our house. George Melly, a good friend of my mother's, sang bawdy songs and much wine was drunk. John Williams, Jonathan Miller and other younger artistic people came and went without need of invitation. There was very little in the way of musical entertainment in London if you were into swing and jazz, so these salons continued well into the 1950s.

But my greatest source of happiness was Pilcox. Pilcox was a long, low manor house on a farm near Tendring, in Essex. My parents bought it as some kind of hedge against death duties which were the great spectre to the post-war generation of well-off people. Another consideration was the possibility that I might take to farming when I grew up. There was a farm manager, related to us, who shared the house, living at one end. It was 250 acres of mixed arable, dairy and beef and never made any money. But there was Peter the pony, a quarry to shoot rabbits in, a collection of .410 shotguns, a pair of ferrets from which I bred, and Philip, the son of one of the workers, who was well up for any fun.

We went there every weekend, high day and holy day, and my parents extended their very sociable lives to house parties. There were fewer doctors and more artists as my mother became increasingly absorbed with modern artists, whose small house presents were often mini sculptures and quick paintings. I remember Peter Gregory, Leslie Martin and Henry Moore staying there, already well known in those circles, although there were many others.

We had a tennis court and regularly made up tennis parties with neighbours on the circuit. Among these were the Stevens family, who owned a magical hamlet called Landermere on the edge of the sea marshes at Hamford Water, which beset the low-lying Essex coast about three miles away. One of my greatest pleasures was to put Peter between the shafts of the trap and ride cross-country with Philip, bypassing Thorpe-le-Soken, to the Stevenses' place next to the bay.

It was here that we kept our sailing boat, bought for me by my father after the success of our sailing holidays in St Mawes. This twenty-two-foot, clinker-built sloop was quite heavy and had a little cover in the bows. My father found it in the barn of a nearby farm and I was with him when we went to look at it. The farmer told us he had never used it but that there was a story behind it. The boat had turned up one blustery night in 1941, when a shivering young man wearing a feather quilt encased within oilskins appeared at the door. He spoke very little English but it was clear he was starving and in bad need of a bit of care. He was given supper and put to bed. Only the next day did his story became clear. He had escaped from

Nazi-occupied Norway three days earlier, had crossed the North Sea and had run aground on one of the islands in Hamford Water. He said that if the farmer would buy him a ticket to London, he could keep the boat. The farmer took him to Clacton, having contacted the Norwegian government-in-exile to come and meet him, and put him on a train to Liverpool Street. Then he claimed his prize. I insisted my dad buy the boat and move it to Landermere.

At high tide, water fills the entire bay, leaving half a dozen islands above water, some occupied only by rabbits. At low tide, just three or four channels carve their way through the mudflats and reed beds, feeding all the way into the Essex countryside, where the stone-lined levies admit the streams from the gently rolling lowland countryside beyond, and keep the sea at bay. There were cockles, crabs, mullet and, on the islands – before myxomatosis – rabbits to be shot as well as shelduck. Elsewhere oystercatchers, redshanks and avocets busied themselves to the mournful cry of the terns.

The worst that could happen to a boy would be to become stranded by the falling tide in the marshes and have to wade and scramble to shore. Otherwise anchor could be dropped anywhere, and the islands visited along wooden causeways. Here a boy's imagination could run wild. Skipper Island, the main one, features in Arthur Ransome's early boat adventures.

Once, Philip and I terrified the weekend cruisers moored on their reach near Skipper Island, by emerging from the mist, adrift on the running tide, whooping and hollering as we thrashed our rabbits against the side of the boat, splattered with blood, as a way of eviscerating them, whilst the ferrets took cover up the mast. They bought our catch for five bob, more in terror than for lack of supper, I suspect.

One dirt track that leads to this area ends in a line of tiny, two-storey fishermen's cottages opposite a one-time Georgian inn known as the Kings Head. This for a long time has been owned privately with the rest of the hamlet. Outside this house runs a channel which abuts a mud- and wood-stayed quay, usable when the tide is in by boats with shallow draughts such as mine. The Stevenses, who lived there in arty bohemian squalor, had a telephone which I could use to ring home after a day on the water, and eventually as they became more friendly, I could leave Peter grazing in their orchard. When the Stevenses died, they left the estate to their daughter Judith. Making up a fourth for a tennis party at Tendring was Nigel Henderson, husband of Judith and a photographer and artist. When I was a bit older, he became a regular companion of mine for sailing in the bay.

Nigel Henderson was an important mentor to me. During the war, he had been an observational cameraman and pilot in the RAF and coastal command. Photography and graphics became his profession. He had a studio at Landermere and I would often help him with layouts and collages, which quickened my interest particularly in the plastic arts. He taught at the Central School of Art and was abreast of all that was happening in the Modernist movement. He was a close friend of Eduardo Paolozzi. My mother adored Eduardo and invited him to live in our house in Hampstead. The whole basement became his studio. He had a smelter in the back garden with a reversed vacuum cleaner to pump it. Later she would encourage the two of them with exhibitions at the Institute of Contemporary Arts, of which she was director for eighteen years, it having been established by a rich Quaker, Roland Penrose, together with Herbert Read, Peter Gregory and Simon Watson just after the war.

It was because of these two that I became more determined about my career as a sculptor. Another sculptor friend of Nigel's was William Turnbull, who had a beautiful Chinese girlfriend and later too became very successful. Richard Hamilton was another of this fabled group who taught at Saint Martin's School of Art (later Central St Martins), and were hugely influential.

When the Stevenses died, Nigel and Judith left the East End, a risqué place to live in those days, to live full time at Landermere. Later they brought Eduardo with them and set up a business there called Hammer Prints, which prospered. Eduardo and his wife occupied two of the cottages, and one of the outbuildings of Nigel's house was the studio – until Eduardo disappeared to London, leaving his wife stuck in the Essex marshes.

But by then I had grown up. I would have to make my own way.

5

Skier

EVER SINCE I had seen the beeswax bubbling in Peggy Garland's studio and felt the polished alabaster of one of her pieces and smelt the shellac and the gelatin, I had wanted to become a sculptor. Nor was my mother opposed to that, given that sculpture and painting were now her principal interest. Most days she spent at the ICA, which had recently been set up in Dover Street to promote and exhibit "modernist" art and to encourage its exponents. Life seemed to flow very easily in those days. They held a raffle at Dover Street where I did the draw. Lots of middle-aged men in rollneck sweaters and beards smoked heavily amidst an exhibition of sculpture while I read out the winner – of a Cézanne painting!

In those halcyon days, anyone could go to university or art school with minimal effort and there were grants galore to pay for it. Nigel Henderson worked one day a week at Saint Martin's and told me I needed only to turn up to do a leisurely "pre-dip", or pre-diploma, on which students were likely to have had only a minimal preparation for art. So that's where I went in 1951, aged seventeen, to start my adult life. I also passed my driving test and had free use of my mother's Austin A40. It was a nice life, driving down to Southampton Row and going about in my Black Watch tartan trousers and Nigel's

Bomber Command Morland flying jacket, with two-and-six, or half a crown, a day to feed myself. I was never the typical student who wore duffle coats and scarves, according to a casting director who rejected me as an extra for a film about the beatniks.

The college canteen had a genuine Italian espresso machine where we mingled, carrying our earnest satchels, to work out what to do about the opposite sex. Central was a mixed school, and art student girls were generally cool about nudity and loved advanced theatre, sincerity and living together – even "free love". Sex had a remote, ungrounded aspect to it for most girls. Those who were interested mainly revealed themselves by reading D.H. Lawrence – not that Lady Chatterley had reached us yet – smoking cigarettes, and on Friday evening having parties in their digs, where revolting Algerian wine was drunk and the racier girls necked with their tutors. I myself broke ice with a Jewish girl from Golders Green following the Art School Christmas party, a huge event in those days.

Central enjoyed a lot of kudos because of its William Morris, Arts and Crafts lineage. It suited me. It was very hands-on and provided facilities to cast and fire clay, bend and weld metal, cut and chisel wood, and polish and grind glass. As I was only doing a pre-dip, there was a limit to how dirty I could get my hands, and unlike the girls who were settling into a three-year stint, I and most of my fellows faced a gloomy spectre from which there was no easy escape: National Service.

My plan was to do it in the RAF. Nigel said photography was the coming thing. It was he who made the most creative use of the two darkrooms at Central for developing film, still a complex and technical process which I greatly enjoyed. So my plan was to announce that I wanted to do photo reconnaissance in the newly announced Gloster Meteor jets reconnaissance section. Every schoolboy knew about Sir Frank Whittle and the Meteor, the first jet-engined aircraft ever to take to the air. To use them just to take photographs seemed the ultimate in cool and suited my vague Quaker pacifism.

That's what I told a bristling, red-faced major, sitting between two equally angry-looking sergeants, when I came before the board at the old Knightsbridge barracks.

"I'm at art school doing photography," I explained. "I've handled cameras and know a bit about developing. So I think it would be a useful training for me."

"Who do you think you are addressing?" barked one of the sergeants.

"Well, him," I suggested shyly.

"And who is 'him'?" he barked even more loudly. "Some friend of yours?"

"No. The officer there," I said, nodding at the major, who glared at me with a disbelieving expression.

"An officer is not known to you as 'him'," thundered the sergeant. "He is only known to an ignorant student like you as 'sir'!"

"Yes, sir. So sorry, sir. As I was saying, I want to learn all I can about photography."

"You do, do you? You think the armed services exist to help you with your career?" said the major, menacingly.

"Your letter did say the soldier could learn some useful trades."

"Sir!" barked the sergeant.

"Sir!" I barked back. I was getting the hang of this.

"We will train you. When we've finished with you, you will be trained to run a mile carrying a fifty-pound ammunition box. Report to the King's Own Rifles barracks in Winchester, 8 a.m., Monday morning. And get a haircut. Understood?"

"Sir!" I yelled back.

And so it was that one cold April morning I took the train, using my warrant from Waterloo, in a carriage full of Cadet Corps Etonians, my hair cut, my BEA cabin bag over my shoulders. They were much more cheerful than I was. After training they were to go and do WASBE, the acronym for War Office Selection Board, to become officers. "Another six weeks of fagging," one of them described it as. After that it was a gravy train.

The Malayan Emergency and the Korean War were at their height when I went into training and my mother was terrified that I might be sent to either. In fact we were sent to Paderborn in Northern Germany, the tedium of which had no equal in my life before or since. At Winchester there were the usual square-bashing and spud-peeling punishments. A little more fun for young men was rifle and machine gun handling. One of the exercises was marksmanship at a local quarry. I proved to be good at this and got a sniper's certificate and a prize. My work would have been cut out for Korea, I was told. In reality we were never destined for the Far East. Our job was to hold back the Russian hordes on the North German plain.

I had been called up to quite a smart regiment, largely officered by Etonians, with an armoured vehicle called the Bren Gun Carrier as its main weapon. But morale was at rock bottom; how the Malayan insurgency was put down I'll never know. The carrier was a pointless machine manned by an utterly exposed mobile machine gunner;

it was actually a mere Bren gun plus a driver with a signalman to support him, also exposed chest up. They weren't even much fun to drive.

My platoon sergeant on field training on Luneburg Heath, when we used these carriers, loaded his with cases of bottled beer. When at the end of the day we had still failed to find the tank group we were meant to be supporting, and had disconsolately put up our tents, he would fall asleep in his sleeping bag out on the open plain while we tried to keep warm around petrol stoves on which we tried to cook our beans. When an officer turned up to get our reports, we would gesture at the sergeant and the officer would roll his eyes in despair and drive off with a tired, "Carry on, men." We would bed down in our tents and the next morning this sergeant would make out it was our fault that we were lost.

Most of the recruits were East End lads who couldn't bear to take these crucial years of their lives off, away from home, just to sit in Nissen huts earning twenty-two shillings a week. But their torment was not over. Thereafter a National Service man had to be on standby for another five years. I once saw how this worked. Most of them reported to the training depot in Winchester for their two weeks' training. There they refused to have a haircut. The punishment for this was confinement to barracks until such time as the refusal ended. They were dedicated Teddy boys and preferred to spend the two weeks locked up in the guardhouse than lose their carefully crafted hairstyles.

Fun consisted in getting a group together to be bussed to a neighbouring barracks, where there was a Nissen hut showing *The Dam Busters* or *In Which We Serve*. Once, when I had leave coming up, my mother and father turned up in a Jaguar, which hugely impressed my fellow squaddies. They took me off to Hamburg, where my mother was having an ICA gathering of her modernist artists. We drove through large areas of the city that were still rubble, and at points trams diverted slowly along wooden runners where clearances on the metal rails had not yet been completed, before getting back to the track proper.

Otherwise the tedium was hardly bearable. Two years of this! And I was eighteen, and in my prime. What escape could there be? That was what I told Dorothy and Andrew.

Escape came in the form of skiing. The following November, I reported to Winterborne, the army ski centre two hours away in the Harz mountains. The army has long had a ski training arm. Theoretically this was is in case we had to go to the rescue of Finland. In reality it was because the officer part of the army is hard put to think of what to do with himself or with his men in times of peace. I have often seen the army yachts, *Zulu* and *Drumbeat*, beautiful boats kept on the Solent. It's a good way for well-off young men to learn team spirit, apparently. Others might say it is an expensive sport supplied for nothing. I'm not complaining. It saved me.

It was clear at Winterborne that I needed no coaching. Nor did they demur when I applied to enter the army championships, which were held annually at Bad Gastein, near Salzburg, Austria. You made your own way there, chose a hotel and booked in; the army might eventually settle the bill. Qualification was determined by how you did in the downhill. Skis were still wooden and the boot held by a bear trap into which the toe of the boot was jammed by a sprung cable going round the heel of the boot. We were a long way from plastic and carbon-fibre skis rigidly attached at heel and toe, and it called for much more skill in turning.

At the downhill we were released every thirty seconds, and our descents were timed. When I was released I found that I was lapping two skiers who were ahead of me in the seeding, either because they had fallen or were locked into a series of slow-motion snow ploughs. At the end of the events, I was sixth. I had made my name with the army.

From now I had endless opportunities to extend my leave each year to ski, and I took full advantage. The army had just begun to take on other organisations in a sort of surrogate international competition. This would take the form of a series of events in different places and at different times, rather like the golf or tennis circuit. We'd turn up at Mürren, in Switzerland, and be accommodated free by the hotel, which benefited from the excitement that the big competitions generated. Mürren had the Inferno, which has been called the world's most spectacular ski race. When you got as far as the lifts would take you, you still faced another three hours of climbing. There you would find the Italian army Alpino team, or the Canadian Mounties, the French chasseurs, the Swiss rescue service, and so on.

Before the big day, you would go up four or five times to practise and get to know the descent. It took about twenty-five minutes normally, through fresh powder, over roads and railways, through vineyards, woods and gullies, including a mile of flat *langlaufing*. It was exhausting. Each day we would return to the Palace Hotel, where Field Marshal Montgomery had a suite and by reason of his rank would preside over us. We had to join him at his table for supper at six o'clock, where he twinkled away, taking each of us to our place by the arm, or with an arm over a shoulder, holding forth all the while. He neither ate nor drank; his greatest pleasure was to hold us rapt while he told us of incidents in the desert, or Europe during the war, in which he had fallen into a tank trap, or a rain tank, with a handsome youth and been forced to rescue him despite having so much else on his mind. We, who represented golden youth, then showed gratitude on their behalf. In return he would speak to our commanding officers and get us long extensions on our ski leave.

The trouble with these suppers was that we had eaten by the time the other guests came down to start their cocktails to warm them up for supper at 8.30 or 9 P.M., with the band starting up at ten. It was difficult to gear ourselves up for this fun and my amorous development was again held up. At least we were fit. I was twenty-third in the race, coming down in eighteen minutes, easily beating the record set in 1939 of twenty-two minutes, albeit there were twenty-eight others who also achieved this distinction.

The next season was the same. I did well in the Lowlanders race at Val d'Isère, and then moved on to the Parsenn Derby in Klosters. This meant I could stay at the old clinic my father patronised in Davos, and while I was there I had my first introduction to affairs of the heart. Breakfast was a self-help affair and I usually had ham and eggs. Next to me one morning was a tall, blonde woman, about thirty-five years old, with a slightly puffy but cute face, very carefully made up. She was tremendously confident and without compunction started talking, in very broken English. Somehow she knew I was competing in the Parsenn, which was still a week away.

"Not eating eggs for fitness," she counselled. "Winner eat yoghurt. Not eating meat."

"English champions eats eggs and bacon," I countered.

"English not winning ski."

This, incidentally, was true. Despite the fact that it was the English who invented downhill skiing, they were not even allowed to compete in the first league when it came to international competition.

"You could help me win?" I asked.

"Of course. You sitting, me serving."

Well, I put myself in her hands and for the next fortnight I ate all my meals with her and she chose what I ate. And that night, after supper – no wine allowed – she expertly led me up to my room and put me to bed. So began a very charming young man's fling.

This lady before the War had been a Czech film starlet known as "Manloever". At some stage Goebbels had taken her as his mistress and this got her into trouble after Germany's surrender. As a result she had been held in custody for a while by the British. When she re-emerged she had tuberculosis, and my father had sponsored her at this clinic. The British taxpayer seemed to be footing the bill for her to live there in some comfort, at what was later to turn into a luxurious hotel. If ever I asked her about the war years and what happened to her, she always referred to "naughty things", as in, "You don't need to know these naughty things, why you want to know naughty things?" Anyway I never learnt more than what my father told me.

Soon after this, and before the big race, I broke my leg badly and was flown back to England. This then led to me being invalided out of the army, to my enormous joy and relief. At last, at twenty years old, I could have that entitlement of the young: two more years of student life.

Back to London. Back to Hampstead. Back to working with Eduardo in the basement. Back to weekends at Landermere. Back to Bloomsbury, albeit now to the Slade School of Fine Art, part of University College in Gower Street.

At around this time, Eduardo Paolozzi had a show at the Hanover Gallery. It included a bronze that came from a cast I had made, albeit in his studio. I was annoyed by this, and told him I would have expected an attribution. He laughed this off and was in a position to do so, as he was becoming recognised. So I asked him for one of the six bronzes that the cast generated. He refused this too. This led to coldness between us, since he was generous about things like that with friends and associates of his who did well in life, such as George Melly. I, on the other hand, was a newcomer in the art world. Later I had a kind of petty revenge on him that I am too ashamed to describe.

But this was not the end of my skiing. We were two years off the Winter Olympics, which were to take place in 1956. England's performance in 1952 had been abysmal, relying on ageing pre-war heroes such as John Botages, and it was clear that the Ski Club of England was looking for new blood. The Ski Club was a marvellous institution with a big house in Eaton Square with a smoking room, reading room, log fires, leather armchairs and the typical terrible food in the dining room: endless shepherd's pie and macaroni cheese. I've already said that it was rich English who invented the sport and there was no better evidence of support available than this sumptuous club, Arnold Lunn and his hotels, the Downhill club in Wengen and so on.

To me, an attempt at qualifying for the English team in 1956 was not a self-denying ordinance as it would be in most other sports. It was an opportunity to ski for two seasons absolutely free. Such was the power of the Ski Club in the main resorts that English skiers entering the qualifying races, many of which were organised by the Club, stayed in the hotels free, their lift passes were free and often so was the bar bill. To qualify for the England team you needed to do well in a particular series of races, two of which I have mentioned, the Parssen Derby, the Inferno, the Wiesband in St Moritz and the British Ski Championships.

Having qualified, which I did, you then competed in the Duke of Kent, the Lowlander Slalom, the Kandahar and the Gonegrat. And if you did well in these you didn't have much to congratulate yourselves about. You were only in the Championship League. The Premier Division were competing at the Lauberhorn, the Hahnenkamm in Kitzbühel, which none of us would dare descend, and at Cortina in Italy.

I remember Toni Sailer, the Austrian champion, who won all the downhills at the Cortina Olympics. I bought some skis from him and he said he'd learnt his English working in a café on the M1 motorway. It was a revelation to me that such a humble young man could rise to such heights in the pampered world of skiing.

The English team was a busted flush. It very much depended on one family, the Mackingtoshes. Father Mackingtosh was a skiing friend of my father, and his children, Charlotte and Douglas, had kept the flag flying for Britain but the team badly needed an injection of youth, and to be anything less than useless it also needed two months' training, which was expensive with no government help. Which was why I had a chance. Also I was an insider. It had long been a family affair. Dad and the Dobbs brothers were the best in

1928, but no longer. Skiing for a nation was a six-week project. Each day or two could mean a different race in a different place. We were based in St Moritz, where we had our two weeks of training. Then the first race. If I came no lower than second or third, I was in.

Then there was the inter-university race going on at the same time. The Oxford-Cambridge presumptive team got the free accommodation at the palace, whereas I, from London, and the champion, Nigel Gardner, weren't put up there, even though we were better than their team. This was against Swiss Universities, who always won. There was a regular second cup for a British Universities team in my dad's time which he had won on one occasion and Lunn, the towering figure of British winter sport, in his excitement threw his leg caliper through the window of his hotel. Luckily it was his hotel. (His son still enters the Inferno and will retire when he comes last.)

I qualified for the British team, albeit they only competed on the B circuit. I also represented England for three years running, from 1954 to '56. I did not make the Olympic team, although this was more because I had gone to work for Morlands by then, than for lack of ability. However skiing in the run-up to the Olympics, with people like Jean-Claude Killy and Sailer dominating, was at last leaving its rich-boy, amateur status behind for the English. My best had been coming second to a Dane in the Lowland at Val d'Isère. And I think one year the English team came third in their group.

I WAS AT the Slade until 1956. Bunking off was par for the course, so from January to March, I was a ski bum. Our captain was Peter Waddell, a delightful man whose parents lived above the Ski Club. Another skier was Rupert de Larrinaga, from a shipbuilding family.

He had an enormous American brake and we drove from resort to resort, all six of us, with all our equipment in it. Rupert was mad about equipment, which he believed was the secret to winning and the lack of which was holding him back. He was forever trying out new technologies. One was having his skis coated in a newly discovered material, PTF. This was done at an Oxford research lab, which declared he would gain thirty per cent in velocity on a ten-degree slope. Any steeper, it turned out, and there was no gain. The next year he tried new piston grips to hold the heel. This too failed to make him a champion skier or persuade us others to allow him to be anything other than a reserve. However, like many an accidental English genius he had identified the two big changes that were in the offing for skis: plastic surfaces and gripped heels.

Another of our number, actually our best, was Noel Harrison, the son of Rex Harrison the movie star. Not only was he an excellent skier but he also played guitar very well, and did so when we were in Klosters, where his mother had a boutique. Back in England he played in a club called Esmeralda's Barn, which was reputed to belong to the Krays, two sinister young gangsters who were just beginning to be talked about. Christine Keeler used to dance there with the smart young men, but privileged people getting down and dirty for a thrill was not to my taste. Rex Harrison must have made it by then because I remember him driving us all to a restaurant out of town in his yellow Rolls-Royce and singing songs from *My Fair Lady* to amuse us. Also letting their hair down with us were Robin Brock-Hollinshead, who made the Olympic team, and the British Army champion Sutton-Pratt.

We motored from resort to resort, staying in each three or four days at a time. Hotels like the Palace in Mürren and Badrutt's Palace in

St Moritz were free to us, though we would have to dress for supper in black tie. There was a lot of Bullingdon Club, Sloaney yobbery. There was the Cresta Run gang, devoted to dangerous tobogganing, for which a lot of armour was worn. Its practitioners were well-off bankers, constantly drunk, especially during races. There were plenty of cups to be won by the "pot hunters" on the C circuit and these yob skiers could knock off cups aplenty if they wanted them, doing little more than weaving back down an anchor lift run.

I've mentioned the Downhill Only club, a true Bullingdon of the slopes. They had a team in the British Ski championships in Klosters in 1950, before I had even joined the army. I was with my family in Davos but went over, having entered the race. The day before the race James Palmer Tomkinson, who with John Boyagis was a hero of the old regime, dashed his brains out during a practice run. The shocked race organisers made last-minute changes to the gates and everyone was wrongfooted, including myself. Boyagis missed a gate and was penalised five seconds, though still did enough to win by a hair over Noel Harrison, who would have been justified in complaining that Boyagis had not been disqualified as the rules required. Later the FIS suspended this as a recognised event. This was my first encounter with my future team-mates. Their arrogance was legendary and they regularly overrode the rules of competitive skiing on the grounds that they owned it. In Wengen one year they were banned from all competitions because of their rude behaviour. But being young is fun; I tell it like this now with the benefit of sober hindsight.

When Julie Andrews was singing and the Duke of Kent was on drums at the Cheza Gruchina, in Klosters, and you were staying in a rich friend's chalet with Princess Margaret, what wasn't there to enjoy? Margaret was a friend of Jeremy Fry and was a regular guest at his various establishments.

The fun continued back in England. Art school in the Fifties was a pleasant affair. You were allowed to get on with what you wanted. I spent more time as Eduardo's assistant in Hampstead than I did in Gower Street. However, fibreglass and resin were coming in, and the Slade gave me very good insights into their potential, which determined later developments in my career. I made big advances in achieving proportion in clay sculpture. I also took a welding course.

Two or three nights a week, I went to one of a small handful of jazz venues. You might say that jazz was rather an esoteric interest to have, but there was no other. If you liked jazz and jiving there were only two great places: the 100 Club and the Flamingo. I would head there with friends from Central or the Slade. Somewhere, I suppose, rock music was sowing its seeds, but I wasn't aware of it. George Melly, a former regular at my mother's Tuesday evening *soirées*, had become a good friend and we would try to turn out every time if he was to sing.

It was at the 100 Club that I met Sue. I bumped into her on the fire escape, where people went to cool off. I'd seen her dancing and she was a dedicated follower of dance fashion. She was a champ, the type happy to dance with another girl if they made a better partner. People clapped sometimes when she really got going, so I had a crack on the floor with her. She found me useless, but we got to talking and to looking out for each other at the next session. She was quite a big-boned girl, boyish, with bobbed short hair, pretty, fun and with a no-nonsense, pragmatic approach to life that appealed to me. She was a partly trained nurse, with humble parents originally from the

North but now living in Taunton, not far from Glastonbury. She still had flat vowels in her speech but was not remotely daunted by meeting my rather haughty mother, who adopted a snobbish attitude towards her. Sue was working in Bell and Croyden, the pharmacists in Wigmore Street, and mentioned that she sold condoms. My mother didn't like this. Nevertheless we became nearly inseparable.

Then came a time when my mother announced that Sue was to go with Peggy Garland's daughter to Paris to be an *au pair*. This was to be a trial separation, as my mother didn't think Sue was right for her only son. It would widen her horizons, was her way of putting it. Peggy's daughter went to a grand Parisian family to look after a single child in Neuilly, with servants to help, while Sue was banished to a dreary suburb to look after three children with a working mother. Sue loves children, eventually becoming a paediatric nurse and a marvellous mother, but this was too much for her at eighteen and she made her apologies and went off to Juan-les-Pins with a mate, hitchhiking.

Another cloud over the passing of youth was that my father had become sick. He, better than anyone, knew the likely consequence of TB getting to one's kidneys and he had wound up his practice at an early age, knowing he would not last long. For a lot of my second year at the Slade he was upstairs, ill in bed, looked after by our marvellous Jamaican live-in servant, Derwin. My father, from a different perspective, was worrying about the future of his only son after his death. He must have summoned a conference of the family, because in the summer of 1956 I was ordered to join the family firm, albeit on terms that I found acceptable.

I was to be trained to become Morlands' head foreign expert in skin quality and purchase, and so my youth ended and the world of work intruded.

6

Business and Pleasure

IN THE LATE summer of 1956, Sue and I set off in brilliant sunshine in my Citroen Light 16 to a village near Glastonbury, where I had found a second-hand, twenty-two-foot caravan for sale for £250. The décor was shabby and outdated and it had hardly been used. We had it towed to Inyswytrin and parked it at the end of the garden under a row of palm trees. There we were allowed to connect it to my uncle's electricity supply and a hosepipe laid to a nearby tap provided water. Outside I built a covered wooden deck where I had my table and chairs. Soon Sue was spotted sunbathing on it by a cousin walking her dog on the other side of the valley and Morland tongues wagged disapprovingly. We spent a happy week in lovely weather, painting the caravan, cooking pasta on the two-ringed gas cooker and basking in deckchairs on the lawn.

My arrival was not a flash in the pan. It was all change in the family firm. Harry Scott Stokes, my uncle, had retired from managing Morlands, although he continued as mayor of Glastonbury for a further term while I was there. My uncle Humphrey was his replacement and the changes he instituted at Inyswytrin, which he had acquired on coming to power, were typical of his stewardship generally, which was pedestrian and unimaginative.

He decided to sell the Tudor house to a developer, who converted it into flats and sold them. As a result, a fine manor was converted on the cheap into a dull, three-storey block of flats, for very little financial gain but enough to allow Humphrey to build a new house – designed by his cousin, Jack Hepworth, the factory architect based in Bristol, whose style was 1950s municipal. At least it was stone, unlike the one Jack had recently built for my cousin John further up the Tor, with its mainly framed glass-and-concrete frontage, widely accepted as hideous. This sort of thing was easy for the Morlands, as Humphrey was chair of the relevant planning committee. I'm sure this is true up and down England in company towns.

Cousin John, my childhood friend who had lived nearby on Hampstead Heath, was by now in charge of production and was, while I was still there, a young director. He was only two years older than me but was married, to Jan, and had two children, of whom Sue was fond. I was often up at their newly built house, Shehallion, for meals and baths, and sometimes John and I went fishing. John was also a very good draughtsman. When my uncle was foolish enough to quarrel with him, he left the firm and set up a poster company in Glastonbury producing his beautiful, intricate, Dadd-like illustrations.

It was to John that the firm owed the Morland driving coat, which was to be one of its mainstays until the end of the Sixties, when car heating improved and open sports cars fell out of fashion. Meanwhile foolish Humphrey had closed the flying jacket line on the spurious grounds that people wanted to forget the war. Henry Scott Stokes and I wrote him a letter urging him to reopen this line but got the usual smug response.

At the sight of my caravan at Inyswytrin, the Morlands used to joke that I had my "tank on their lawn", but the truth was my heart was never in the family business. Humphrey's sister, Gladys, lived up the Morland lane and once took me to task for taking the factory girls on a swimming party on the river. I assured her I did not foresee spending the rest of my life at Morlands, to her surprise.

This was the plan: I was to do two years at the Northover factory working in every department until I thoroughly understood the business. For this I was to be paid £9 per week. Thereafter I was to continue on this wage but return to live in London. There I would be at the beck and call of the company as their controller of quality and purchaser of skins in South America in their slaughter season, our spring. It was expected that I would spend two months of my time in Argentina and Chile, visiting the slaughterhouses and the *frigorificos*, which baled and sold the skins. This was regarded by Humphrey as part of a strategic approach to pricing on a world market in skins. He was not wrong about that. Later the next Morland, Pat, made an understandable but fatal decision on forward buying in the 1970s. He bought forward five years, without a hedge, on the Australian sheepskin market, which committed the firm to a price that turned out to be double what the competition was paying when overproduction of meat swept the world in that period. This was to prove the first nail in the coffin of Morlands.

Pat Morland had some other foolish ideas that contributed to the demise of the firm. One was a decision to buy up sheep farms in the UK. No Morland had ever been on a farm, let alone worked one. It was a huge capital expense that provided about one per cent of the skins needed for the business. Another mistake he made was to open a chain of Morlands-only shops. The range we made was much too limited to justify a whole shop on the high street and they thoroughly annoyed our other outlets, who stopped stocking our lines.

As a young man, however, I had been made a nice offer: a small but steady income, comfortable travel all over South America, and an entrée into a business where I would get preferential treatment if my real hope of being a sculptor foundered. So I set to it with a will. It started with me reporting to Humphrey for a lecture in his office in what is now the Red House, the brick-built part of the factory where administration took place, and which abutted the road out of Glastonbury towards Street.

"Very glad you're joining us. Andrew was a bit above us all, I know. Look what it's done for him," said Humphrey, referring to my father's illness. "We're all family here, really, even if not called Morland. We pull together and if it's all hands to the pump we don't expect a lot of overtime chits or union consultations."

He continued in this vein for a while until I butted in.

"So you won't want me to clock in every day?"

Clocking in and out was compulsory at Morlands and the terms of employment were not generous at all by Quaker standards, with no profit-sharing schemes or lavish pension arrangements.

"Hah, that! Your grandfather brought that in. Yes, there were a few raised eyebrows. But do you know what? Your workman likes it. It means he's not always looking over his shoulder at his neighbour, feeling resentful because he was off home early the previous evening, and only to get to the darts competition in the pub. If you get my meaning." Uncle Humphrey prided himself on his insights into working class mentality. "No, no. We don't go for privilege here. You're just one of the chaps. Unless you come to the boardroom."

The boardroom was a classic in mahogany and walnut burr. In my grandfather's time it had a kitchen with lunch cooked for the directors every day. To Humphrey's credit he had stopped this and moved the managers and directors, apart from himself, into the canteen, albeit on a separate table.

John took me round the factory. There was the raw skin department and the dry skin department, which graded the skins; the rugs department; and the biggest department, longhair quality control, where cousin John was. The skins were soaked, washed, and scraped by machine, rolled over a blade for height, dry cleaned in benzene, chrome-tanned, and softened in cages full of rotating pebbles. I loved those. Then there were various cutting departments and so on, until one came to the stitching and finishing and packing areas, from which emerged slippers, boots, travel rugs, domestic rugs and, slightly absurdly, pram canopies, a niche hangover from the Thirties.

Humphrey was very proud of the fact that sales were computerised while I was there. Morlands was one of the pioneers of computerised invoice printouts and I was told this had saved the wages of twelve people. The machine was a desk made of white Bakelite with tiny, circular-valve TV screens and green-on-black lettering. The angled slab facing the desk worker had a large grid of red lights and a number of switches and paddles. Punched cards were fed into a letterbox on the side, followed by the satisfying sound of a deck of cards being riffled. It was dazzling, I must say, although it was the printer that went with it that really caught my attention. The speed with which its golf ball could spit out whole sentences as well as straight lines and primitive circles had me thinking, and I was so impressed I showed Nigel Henderson its details.

Elsewhere, the factory was little changed from the Thirties. Large barns with roofs all raking in the same direction were held up by bare A-frames above our heads. Beneath, in the middle, were huge, heavy, wooden tables, while along the walls were belt-driven cutting machines, all in open-plan caverns with bleak neon lighting above. It was actually very poorly organised according to Jack Townhill, who developed the computer cards I spoke of and who had a roving commission to rationalise the factory. The task proved to be beyond him.

A lot of the workforce were quite old, especially the skilled ones, who were proving hard to replace. I got on best with them; they seemed to accept me with good humour. Although I was a Morland among them, they did not worry that I might be spying on the workforce for the bosses. There was one we tormented because he was always evangelising and invoking the devil. On one occasion we told him we had seen an escaped lunatic creeping across the levels towards the factory. As our evangelist had very poor eyesight, we easily convinced him. We put together an assembly of red-dyed sheep skins and young Harry Stokes, exercising a Morland entitlement of summer work at the time, helped me get up a ladder to appear at the window. The old boy swallowed it hook, line and sinker and fainted from the shock. It took a while for the department to recover.

A lot of trainee life was very dull but the Christmas party was a boys' fantasy. The girls of the rug department got completely liquored up, they imprisoned and smothered John in a rug box, and chased me like a monkey up into the rafters, where they poked at me with staves until I dropped into a stack of rugs, where they fell on me.

Still, I was quite interested in the processes, and particularly the grading; the amount of chemicals, bleaches, oils and beating that needed to be applied to a skin depended on it. A healthy, well-fed English sheep, skinned by an experienced hand and cold-stored at the right time of year, required much less processing than one slaughtered in the southern hemisphere and left baking in the sun. Even wool length was another factor, as were wool count, fibre thickness and colour. The best skins went into John's new line in driving coats. I was going to need to understand these things when I stepped into my part as Morland rep with the producers of South America.

Sometimes Sue came down at weekends and stayed with me in the caravan. My mother had been right; her tour of the Cote d'Azur had turned her into quite a foodie and she cooked up a storm of pasta, garlic and charcuterie she brought down from Soho. At other times I went up to London, to Hampstead, where Sue had been appointed *maitre d'hotel* to run the house, oversee the care of my father and release my mother to her life at the ICA. A strange feature of my parents' relationship was that my father knew that Dorothy and Tom Garland had for a long time been in love with each other but held off in the interests of their families. My father now gave his leave for my mother to go to Tom if she wished, and she did. After my father's death in 1957, they started living together and would remain so for the next fifteen years.

Down west, George Melly introduced me to someone who was to become a lifelong friend. This was Jeremy Fry, who lived near Bath and was one of the stars of his generation in high-tech engineering. His family, also Quakers, had a firm called Frenchay Products, which made various kind of couplings for the pumping industry. Jeremy took one of their products, actuated valves – valves that opened on electrical actuation according to a programme – and made them big time. The firm he started to do this was called Rotork. He became a rich man in his own right as a result.

He was related to the famous Quaker Frys and found time for a huge number of interests including sculpture, painting and metalwork. He was to become a significant patron of my works, commissioning a threesome fibreglass set for Rotork which I am still trying to track down. He still found time to entertain at weekends at his beautiful house near Bath, the 250-year-old Widcombe Manor. We were looked after royally there by him and his wife, Camilla. There were always many guests. Tony Armstrong-Jones was a regular and in due course his wife, Princess Margaret. She and Melly played the piano and sang songs in the evening, and come winter we all skied together from a villa he took outside Davos.

Jeremy had what he called a boat house – a comfortable home, to you and me – on Restronguet Point, in Cornwall. There he kept a beautiful sailing boat, the *Flicker*. It was only twenty-eight feet long and came from a class of Baltic design much favoured by the Hitlerjugend organisation, which had melded recreation with preparation for war training for Hitler's navy. They are now known as Volk boats because at the end of the War the whole lot were taken as reparations. They were hugely loved by the English for their design. They were very low in the water, with stylish, low-lying coachwork and in those days were often made of varnished clinker or carvel wood. If you used the head (the loo), your own head would emerge above the deck level. Four people could just about camp on them.

Jeremy lent us *Flicker* and Sue and I and the children sailed to the Scillies and pottered around among the islands one idyllic summer. At one point we found a group of young men living off the beach in a mix of bathing huts and groundsheet canopies. They were diving on a sunken Liberty boat with a huge bronze propeller which they wanted to get at to sell. This was right up my street. It was quite a project. Using oxyacetylene cutting equipment underwater was too skilled a craft for them, so they had explosives with them and we set about blowing the shaft apart to separate the propeller. While the children built sandcastles above, I was below setting off explosions. Sue hated it. Nor did she like my habit of slipping overboard from the *Flicker*, leaving her alone to man the boat while I scooted about below looking for the wonders of the seabed.

As a hobby, Jeremy bought an abandoned village, Le Grand Banc, on a mountain top near Apt, in the Luberon of Provence, and turned it into an exotic settlement for his clan, employees and servants. Much of his marvellous collection is there, including Lewises, Nolans and Warhols. Some of my sculptures are still there, but not the threesome. The reason Grand Banc had been abandoned was apparently this: two of its inhabitants claimed the coveted title of *boulanger* in the village, so there were two bread-shops competing for this very small trade. This could not help but divide the village, like the Yorks and the Lancasters in the Wars of the Roses. Eventually a decent life could not be comfortably led there and it was deserted en masse during the Fifties.

The nearest shop was in a village called Oppedette, at the bottom of the hill. It clung to a crag and had magnificent views. Oppedette too was mainly abandoned, so it may well be that these events occurred against the background of post-war development that led to draining the countryside of its peasantry. This trend was soon to be balanced by a returning tide of citizens who had prospered in Avignon, Marseilles, Lyons and elsewhere, turning these peasant dwellings into exquisite *maisons secondaires*. You should see Oppedette today: every dry stone wall is impeccable and crowned with lobelia and oleander beds.

On and off until Jeremy died, I looked in on Grand Banc when I was in the area, or went there for holidays with my family. This was quite often: I made copious use of the French canal system and often passed through Avignon. There was always work for idle hands, especially carpentry. Little by little, Grand Banc became what it is today. The cobbling of the streets is immaculate. This house is a guest quarter, that one the owner's sitting room, another his bedroom suite; here the winter kitchen, there the summer one behind a big terrace with a dining table for sixteen, looking towards the Alps. A whole street will accommodate the support staff, with a huge swimming pool, bread oven and so on.

On one such visit, a cousin of his was staying. Linda was about twenty, blonde, beautiful in an English way and rather sulky and spoilt in the manner of the rich. Once she came with me to do a big shop in Apt and told me what she was so miffed about. Back in Bristol she had had a boyfriend, her first. Her mother, with whom she quarrelled in the typical mother–daughter style, had seduced her boyfriend off her and that was the reason she was feeling hard done by. By my standards she was touchingly transparent and, like Forrest Gump, said what she thought, including the most embarrassing things at meals. Her project in life was to marry a rich man and she was marking time until that inevitable moment. This made her vulnerable to a married man. Like me.

For a while she captured my heart. Later I engineered it so that we would be in Malta at the same time. I did this by persuading Jeremy Fry that Malta was the gem of the Mediterranean and that he should come and buy a castle for sale there. Jeremy, Linda and her mother all came out and we were able to see a lot of each other. Jeremy did, in fact, buy the castle but later lost interest and sold it.

A diving companion of mine was one of a pair of brothers, the Blacks, who had a place there. They were very rich for some reason. So when we all went out for supper at a restaurant one night, Linda spotted a bird of the same feather. To my slight relief by then, and Sue's, Linda knew where her true interests lay. As far as I know they are still married to this day.

As for Jeremy, his marriage too was under strain. A sculptor we knew called Lynn Chadwick was very successful and had the means to do up a Gothic-fantasy Victorian castle in Gloucestershire. Jeremy took a hand in this. The dining room table appeared to be the wing of an aeroplane and was heated. The shower rooms were what are now called wet rooms, with under-floor heating and were the size of many people's drawing rooms, to the intense pleasure of my children, who used them as skid pans.

Unfortunately Jeremy fell in love with Frances, Lynn's second wife, and a very unhappy love affair ensued, which tore them and their families apart. Frances committed suicide. Jeremy spent more and more of his time in France, between a flat he had in Cannes and Grand Banc. Next he came out as gay and led the frantic life of a newly gay man. Finally he calmed down and settled with an opera producer called Didier.

But I have digressed considerably.

My stay in Glastonbury was coming to an end. Growing up never pauses for pleasant interludes. I needed to make my way. Between 1958 and 1962, I made annual visits to Buenos Aires and set forth from there to all points south in the interests of sheepskin for the mother company. My visits occurred during the slaughter season in February and March. And by slaughter, I mean slaughter.

I made my first visit by ship, Castle Line from Southampton. I travelled first class and wore black tie for supper every evening. This enabled me to make friends with a charming Anglo-Argentinian family who had been seeing their son off to school in England. They had a comfortable villa in Buenos Aires and a play *estancia* out in the foothills of the Andes, where an English climate and apple orchards could be enjoyed. Their wealth, needless to say, was related to the refrigerated shipping of meat.

In 1958, Buenos Aires was the meat capital of the world. Uruguay and Argentina produced half the good quality beef of the whole globe. Huge companies such as Armour and Swift, from Chicago, and Vesteys, from England, dominated this industry. Vesteys had their plants, abattoirs and processors in Montevideo, over the River Plate from Buenos Aires. Armour and Swift were based in a specially built workers' paradise, La Plata, about twenty miles south of Buenos Aires. Although a company town, it was heavily unionised and the unions had their trough filled by Juan Peron, to whom they delivered their privileged blue collar vote. During the killing season herds would be brought in, thousands of head at a time, to the great slaughter plants of La Plata. For miles around you could smell cattle, cattle and more cattle.

I had only been off the ship one day when I was taken to see what this was all about. I was picked up from the luxurious grandeur of the Plaza Hotel (£2 a night) by a couple of American managers from Armour in a huge gangster's car and taken to La Plata. This was a new, circular, purpose-built town with a huge plaza in the middle and boulevards radiating outwards and intersecting with circular roads all the way to the perimeter. Everywhere there were statues to previous dictators, but pride of place in the centre was reserved for Peron. To him, I was told, they owed good hospitals, cheap canteens, cathedrals, museums, endless steaks, pensions and schools. He'd been able to afford La Plata because of the war, which had jacked meat prices up all over the world. It was a state/company town on a huge scale.

Just out of town on a canal port were lined the great cathedrals of meat. We went to one of them. Soon after arrival, in great stockholding yards, twenty or thirty of the cattle at a time would be herded up a ramp to the top of a three-storey plant and from there fed into narrow concrete walkways with low walls, like long railway cars, standing proud of the main side walls, allowing a *peon* to stand astride each of these passages. He had a metal sledgehammer surfaced in wood and as he passed over the bullock between his splayed legs, he'd bring this down on its forehead and it would fall stunned to the ground. He then moved to the next.

The ground was a metal grid, which, with each thirty or so stunned animals covering it, swung down and released its cargo onto the floor below. There they were awaited by vast, sumo-wrestler-sized men, who swiftly shackled the hind legs of the bullocks, pushed a button on a hanging cable, and they were raised to hang just above grid-covered drains that ran the length of the hall. Then their throats were cut with a single flourish of a machete, which otherwise hung from the men's waists. The blood poured into the drain and flowed into vast vats on the floor below.

Next, with huge accuracy and skill, an incision was made down both buttocks of each bullock before these colossi re-sheathed their knives. Now they seized the hide of the beasts and their huge size came into play. In one clean piece of theatre, these one-ton bullocks where stripped naked with a single searing howl of flesh. Then there was some trimming round head and legs and finally a single skin was thrown into a funnel, dropping to the floor below.

Finally the chained-up carcasses started a macabre journey across the floor into a neighbouring chamber, where the line rose to waist height, and there other men with chainsaws sliced the animals in half from tail to head, and the excised guts fell onto a moving belt beneath, to disappear into a further hole. Nothing was wasted. And so the great slaughter continued without break, day and night, for months every year.

This was my introduction to the business. The Armour manager who had picked me up at the Plaza told me it was his favourite job, showing new boys the real world they were joining. And for extras, during the performance I attended, something went wrong. One of the bulls was less than stunned when it fell to the floor below, got up before it could be chained and started to career around the skinning chamber, bucking and kicking and swinging its horns. Howls of derision rose from all sides. A sledgehammer was dropped down to the sumo wrestler whose animal it was and he set off, weaving and ducking through the swinging carcasses, trying to head off the maddened animal. Finally he caught up with him in one of the aisles and burst through a curtain of hung beasts in time to deliver a coup de grâce. Then he gave a little bow and, with a flourish, returned the sledgehammer to the cowboy above. I was not shocked; I had enjoyed the spectacle as much as anyone, though apparently some *novicados* were sick after attending these opening performances.

There was no reason for me to be taken on this expedition to La Plata. I suspect it was done more to entertain Armour managers than to teach me anything I needed to know. There were no sheep at this plant, and sheep were anyway only a small part of the Armour operation in Buenos Aires, but they did control some of the stations in the south.

In Buenos Aires, I went to various traders' warehouses, got them to open up bales of their skins and inspected them. I'd then report back on the condition of the skins and make field reports about drought conditions, likely quantities and so on. On the basis of this, Morlands would make an offer and generally take half the product. So I was a VIP as far as the traders were concerned, quite apart from my name. I was endlessly entertained, which in Argentina means *assados*, *assados* and more *assados*: barbecues to you and me.

Signor Nealson was a favourite of mine because he could take me out into the spectacular ocean of Pampas that surrounds Buenos Aires and had friends who would let me ride their ponies over these vast grasslands with their stands of alfalfa and cane, filled with butterflies, and their lakes with flocks of teal, flamingos, ostriches and birds of every variety. Every ten miles or so would be an *estancia* settlement heralded by a rampart of Lombardy poplars turned in to make an avenue leading to the arcaded bungalow. Within this there were peach, quince and cherry orchards, in fruit at my time of year, and the occasional huge willow. Mulberry bushes lined the pathways round the house. Round about there were barns and smaller houses, and endless, chirruping children came out to see rider visitors and brought them peaches.

Less enjoyable was the rest of my job. Most of the sheep in Argentina are in the south, in Patagonia. In some ways it was a dispiriting tour. It started with a flight in a Dakota to Puerto Madryn, which you could call the northern border of Patagonia, a huge territory of bleak, grey, treeless, flat semi-desert cut through at intervals by rivers coming down from the eastern slopes of the Andes. These valleys were lush and made delicious breaks in the otherwise endless landscape. The weather too became much less clement than around the capital, with huge storms sweeping up from the Southern Ocean to be trapped by the Andes towering high over this strange, almost uninhabited land. And it could get very cold in winter.

The *rios*, or rivers, were a vivid contrast. They were lined with willows and glinted like liquid mercury through cherry orchards, rush marshes and broom and berry shrubs clustered up the sides of the valleys, which could be deep and shaded. There were partridges or similar to be shot and vultures and the occasional condor wheeling above. Near the mouths of these *rios* were the ports which supported the European, largely British, settlers. Elsewhere the only native animals I noticed were the guanaco, a small camel, ostriches and huge flocks of upland goose. This was land made fit only for sheep. The same was true of the flora, a prolific covering without any variety.

In February and March the *estancias*, some big and prosperous as they were in the north, others bleak, impoverished hill farms, drove their flocks towards the ports. The ports were at the mouths of the rivers and consisted of little more than a jetty to accommodate one or two ships, and the *frigorificos*, as they were generically known: the abattoir and the refrigerated warehouse that went with it. Beyond that there would be little more than a bank, a supermarket and a post office, and housing for those that ran the town. I didn't envy them.

My arrival was an important event and the manager would meet me at the airport in person and drive me to his home. There I was fed and made a fuss of. There would also be a ritual litany of complaint about the weather and the erosion of the soil that was gradually degrading the land between the rivers, resulting in fewer, thinner and smaller sheep.

The next day the truth of this would be borne in on me when we went to the warehouse, where bales of skins were piling up. The *frigorifico* had already graded them and it was known that Morlands would mainly want the best. Top of our range were rugs to lie in front of a fireplace, but from Patagonia we sought mainly boot linings. For them, size and quality were vital. I would make notes, lay down these requirements, and record the quantities likely to be of use to us. Then might come the celebration of the day. A lot of *maté* would be consumed first and then, of course, the *assado*. This was prevalent throughout that meat-loving land, though now it was a barbecued sheep instead of a barbecued steer. The other difference was that, to add to the other shortcomings of Patagonia, there was a constant strong wind blowing, so large areas of grassland were walled for almost no other purpose than these feasts.

Then it was back to the airport and on to the next *frigorifico*, Santa Cruz. Then it was Rio de Gallegos, which is the biggest one in the south that is still in Argentina. The river valleys at whose mouths these towns lay had been inhabited before the settlement of the area in the 19th century, by once cultivated, quite sophisticated Andean Indian tribes who had become severely degraded by Darwin's time; he was disgusted to see one tribesman dash his own child's brains out. The arrival of settlers, mainly from the UK, had started peaceably enough, since the settlers looked to their ports to the east and the Indians to the mountains to the west. Sometimes it happened that a Spanish fleet would come from the north to subdue the UK settlers, and the Indians would side with the settlers. But it didn't last.

In Rio de Gallegos, I met a man in the client guesthouse who might have been eighty. He had been born in the Scottish Highlands and was a victim of the clearances. When he was a young man, resettlement in Patagonia was paid for if you could prove yourself to be a sheep farmer. In reality this meant owning a whistle and two "sheepdogs", which in his case he dognapped in Liverpool before embarking. On arrival, a simple policy was explained to him. Thirty Indian right ears brought to the settlement office entitled you to a certain number of acres abutting the Rio de Gallegos a long way inland. When I spoke to him he had spent three weeks driving his sheep to Rio de Gallegos and only got to speak English on these visits. It was a dispiriting world and I was glad to move on south.

For now I was approaching the hook of Chile, where the Magellan Straits, the Beagle Channel and Cape Horn lie. More importantly for the spirit, the Andes peter out in this hook and the landscape takes on a breathtaking beauty, mountains dropping into endless fjords that are actually tree-clad, and passages peppered with islands. I was headed for Punta Arenas on the Straits of Magellan. Civilisation at last.

Although basically just another *frigorifico* port, it served a much more civilised hinterland than I had hitherto seen. Instead of windblown homesteads of desperate Welsh hill farmers, I was back in the land of gigantic, well managed *estancias*, some so big they ran their own company towns, with shops, cinemas, garages, clinics and banks. These families had become very wealthy on the meat boom, and Punta Arenas showed it. It was a stylish town in full Spanish Baroque. I had a pass to the club, reminiscent of the Edwardian Raj. Here white-coated waiters served gin and tonics and whiskey sours to the moustachioed grandees of the *estancias* in their leather armchairs. They exchanged the timeless, superior male badinage about the stupidity of others, although here it was Falkland Islanders rather than the Irish who were the butt of their condescension; they were mocked for having a permanent list into the wind.

The town was run by Companias de Exportados de Patagonia, which also owned the Puerta Natales *frigorifico* and was a kind of cooperative that was itself owned ultimately by a public company. They held most of the land between Punta Arenas and Natales, a vast area. Their quality was much more dependable and there was much less quibbling about cash flow and payment times. The operation had been set up by an English colonel, who had instituted daily orders in Gaelic and English. Porridge was called "porridgey" and a herd of sheep was a "point".

The Natales complex encompassed twelve *estancias*, with clear divisions of labour. One would be devoted to horse breeding, because horses were the staple of this world of herders. You could find 1,000 mares galloping beside you if you drove through, like mustangs in the Midwest. Another would be a machinery depot and repair station, with light engineering facilities and garages. Another specialised in breeding rams and had a library and genetics experts. Of course the main game was sheep. A grazing *estancia* might have 350,000 of them, despite the degrading land. The drovers were part paid in sheep meat and skins and would move about with the herd and live out in huts five days' riding away. Their saddles consisted of a pile of sheepskins spread on either side by short hollowed logs.

The managers were pampered by the owners, who were sometimes family members. They would live in six-bedroom houses with servants and a cook. They all spoke English and were very anglophile. The wives were bored and not encouraged to interest themselves in the business. They loved having people to stay, and at one place there was a group of students from agronomy school visiting. Eleven sheep were killed and barbecued for us.

I made friends with Carlos Menendez-Behty at one of these company *estancias* and he invited me to his family-owned *estancia* back in Argentina, on a sliver of land that still belongs to his family in Tierra del Fuego, near the Rio Grande. They were worried that lambs were being killed by foxes, so one day we rode all day to the coast, where the foxes would be marauding the penguins; we carried shotguns and chased and shot at foxes from horseback. South of them was Ushuaia, the most southerly port in the world, but on their ranch the language over toast and marmalade was English and there were polo ponies for the kids. Once we were chauffeured in a long-wheel-base Land Rover to Puntas. At lunch, a great rug was rolled out for us and afterwards the chauffeur produced a rifle for us to shoot at our beer cans as he hurled them into the river.

Natales was my next port of call, and I went by bus. As you approach Natales, the mountains gather in size until snow-covered peaks, like the Torres del Paines, are always in view. Natales itself is on a fjord with a passage to the sea that wriggles through these mountains and eventually into the Pacific, and is therefore better connected to Valparaiso and Santiago, from which many of its cargos would ultimately be shipped. The *frigorifico* refrigeration was powered by beautifully kept 1880 Manchester steam pump engines, the steam raised by a woodburner. The owners had a little steam railway to carry the cargos from the *frigorifico* to the pier head. The only problem with these skins was that the atmosphere was too damp to dry them and they had therefore to be salted, which improved them but added to our work back in Glastonbury. But the quality was so good we generally bought the lot.

You will not be surprised to learn that I tended to hurry my time in Patagonia and then linger in Chile to while away my two-month stint. Nevertheless I had another errand to run before I could return to England. It was to fly first to Santiago and then on to La Paz, in Bolivia. There was a dealer there who loved Morland sheepskin boots and thought they were just the thing for that chilly nation. Part of my duties was to report to Arica, a strange port in a pocket of complete desert at the opposite end of Chile, 3,000 miles north, with duty free arrangements conducive to Bolivia's needs. In fact it was the only port available to Bolivia, which is land bound. There was little access to it from Chile except by ship or plane. It was like an oasis, with palm trees growing throughout the dusty town, which had the only water for miles around, provided by a river from the Andes that barely made it to the sea. There was, however, a road which cut inland through dramatic valleys and gorges and up into the high sierra of Bolivia and eventually to La Paz.

Anything imported into Bolivia was subject to enormous duties which could be circumvented in a number of ways. One was to turn a blind eye to a fifth of one's cargo going missing when it was checked into the trucks that did the run up to Bolivia, whence they leaked into the black market there. Another was to bribe the government representatives there. Either way, you needed a good man on the spot. And England had such a man. He was a figure from another era. He wore a crumpled safari suit and a battered trilby and met the daily flight from Santiago with the aplomb of a man who owned the place. His office was a container with a house off the back, where he lived with a very county English wife who cooked for him and made him or his guests comfortable. If you were his client, you stayed with him. He drank whisky, moderately but steadily throughout the day, but never seemed hung-over or bad tempered. He was a good chap and had Morlands' interests close to his heart, and we depended on his good will to keep this useful contract going. On my last visit we got onto the subject of Princess Margaret and he amazed me by saying that Peter Townsend had come to stay with him there to get away from the Press fuss over his affair with her. They had both been in the RAF together during the war.

On returning from this excursion in March of 1962, I was summoned by uncle Humphrey down to Glastonbury and told my services would no longer be needed.

And it was true. I was not serving any useful purpose that good agents on the spot couldn't bring about much more professionally than I could. So there was no ill feeling and I said so. My interest in Morlands had expired.

7

New Generation

IN 1957, MY father died. I inherited a slab of Morland shares and some money. Pilcox was sold. My mother terminated the lease in Hampstead and went to live in Chalk Farm. Eduardo's studio there closed and he went to live in Chelsea and weekend in Landermere. Sue was homeless. We needed a new place. I bought a Vespa scooter from a shop in Wandsworth Bridge Road run by a high-octane, good-time chap called Keith Wilkinson, who was to become a close friend of mine. On this Vespa, Sue and I went round London looking for somewhere to live and eventually settled on 71 Castelnau.

Castelnau was not well appreciated then. It was south of the river, just over the bridge from Hammersmith Broadway, which was also not fashionable in the late 1950s. But Castelnau, like North Kensington and Wandsworth Common, had been built for rich people with servants and gardeners. It was a long avenue of detached, double-fronted villas built in the best Victorian William Morris style, mostly of exposed and elaborate brickwork. One of the fictional Forsytes in *The Forsyte Saga* bought one. The avenue had been planted with chestnuts, beeches, acacias and magnolias and at each end was a small village shopping area. Today the trees are a magnificent sight because the street is inhabited by the rich again.

In those days they were bedraggled and in need of care. Uncle Humphrey said it was a foolishly unfashionable area to buy in and that I would lose my money.

It was to be our home for the next twenty-three years.

Within a year of moving in, on finishing my training in Glastonbury, I needed to make my life respectable and marry Sue. The wedding was a small family affair at Hampstead registry, followed by a reception at Dorothy's place. That evening we had a party at Castelnau for our friends. There a musician called Ray Smith, a jazz drummer who ran a record shop in Charing Cross Road, announced that the wooden-framed upright piano I had bought for £2 would never tune. He also gave me a cannabis joint – my first. Next we were burning the piano in the garden, with the strings twanging as they broke free. It was like a Viking funeral as we danced stoned and giggling round the pyre. We barbecued a sheep *assado*-style, which I'd learnt in Argentina, and added pieces of the piano to the fire as George Melly worked his 'Frankie and Johnny' number, with his signature special effects of love, rejection and revenge. I had set up the bedroom as a roulette room and the fun went on until dawn.

I now found gainful employment at St Martin's, just north of Long Acre in central London, as a part-time lecturer and tutor. Those were its golden years. The shadow and gloom of war had at last lifted and the shops were filling with goods. Despite popular memory of the 1950s, British design was at its dazzling best. It was the time of the Comet, the Jaguar Mark 2, the Atomium in Brussels, the Norton Dominator, the M1 and its stylish cafes. And the student population was just beginning to explode. The art schools in London were bursting at the seams, anyone qualified to teach was welcome, and I needed to work. So I started teaching, no more than a total of about eight hours a week. For this I was paid £15, at a time when you could rent a Rent Act-controlled flat in Queensgate for twenty-five bob and eat your fill in a greasy spoon for two bob.

Even better than that, my fellow lecturers were the best of their generation. Tony Caro and Phillip King, for example, both became knights of the realm for their achievements. Bridget Riley was another. These were my colleagues and mentors. We roamed the West End in our free time, ate well, visited Collets and Foyles in Charing Cross Road, the antique print sellers and the jazz record shops. It was the only area of London where a remotely cosmopolitan feel could be found.

I had parted company with Eduardo Paolozzi, the sale of Hampstead having put an end to our collaboration there. But Castelnau had a big long garden and I set up a new, improved forge there of his design, where we could get up temperatures of more than 2,000 °C and resume the six-stage "lost wax" process, involving rubber, wax and plaster, to cast the molten bronze that he and I had used in Hampstead. The capacious basement of Castelnau became my studio, of a size that made the others envious.

David Annesley and Mike Bolus were part of a rising group of sculptors there who were parting company with the post-war generation I have mentioned up until now. With those two and others we developed into a group labelled the "New Generation" who were to put St Martin's in the forefront of the plastic arts in the 1960s. We all experimented with colours, materials and forms in a bid to unshackle ourselves from the traditions and tropes of the past. Little by little we acquired traction. It started when Phillip King and

I had a well-attended exhibition at the Bear Lane Gallery in Oxford. I drew some flattering reviews: the *Times* called one of my bronzes "quite outstanding" and even claimed that "Mr Morland, though only 28, has few rivals among the younger sculptors". Phillip and I became quite close, partly because of our shared love of diving. He had a place in Corsica, a ramshackle farmhouse near the sea at Ile Rousse. I went there with the family one summer. In those days harpooning fish was acceptable but very difficult. We did much better one day when the weather was stormy and we swam into a stream and a slaughter ensued: twenty-five trout.

In the autumn of 1963, a number of us were invited to show our works at the Young Biennale in Paris. This prestigious event had been set up by France's Culture Minister, the celebrated novelist André Malraux, several years earlier to showcase young creativity worldwide. There was a decent British contingent, though the only sculptors were Phillip King and me. I stayed at Jeremy Fry's in comfort. David Hockney and Peter Blake were there and some flamboyant Guinnesses, who laid on fine dining. The generous Andy Garnett, a wealthy philanthropist who I saw a lot of with Jeremy and for whom Sue worked, also gave a slap-up party for us in his office in Faubourg Saint-Honoré. He was a remarkable man who turned his hand to many things and made a success of them. In London he lived in Narrow Street, the depths of poverty in those days. He was drawn to clochards and had a strange sense of humour. He once inserted one of his unwashed tramps into the bed of his girlfriend when he found her there sleeping with a fat chap called Billy, another designer, who invented the pull top.

Our high point as a group was the New Generation exhibition at the Whitechapel Gallery in 1965. David Annesley, Tim Scott,

Mike Bolus and Bill Tucker were all there. This exemplified in one show our unique take on the use of modern industrial materials in an industrial context: tubes, levers and other puzzling expressions of human life. It is difficult to characterise the sculpture we did. Half the art world thought we were shamming fraudsters, the other that we were the coming thing. The debate was the same as it is today about the Turner Prize. You either loved it or hated it. I am no intellectual, and I did not have a thought-out philosophy. I was happy to leave that to others. I liked doing things with my hands and I liked the competition with the fellow members of this group.

As to what critics said about it, well that was way above my head. In 1963, my work was exhibited at the New Vision Centre Gallery, Marble Arch. George Melly wrote a flyer to accompany the show and in it flatteringly compared me to Brancusi, the modernist pioneer and one of the most influential sculptors of the century. Log-rolling, he went on:

> Like the dry bones in the Negro Spiritual, the discarded junk appears at the moment it is about to assume sinew and flesh. Everything Morland makes is a personage. Here they come, limping forward from the breaking yard and junk shop. Here we go, staggering past them towards the cemetery and the crematorium. Morland, with his middle class and indeed artistic background, can take no refuge in naivety linked with craftsmanship. The occasional obscenity, the huge cock on the tiny figure, is an overt reaction to the broadminded middle class aesthetic in good taste. It is an insult in passing to the gentle rebels who only drink dry sherry.

George Butcher, art critic for the *Guardian*, went one better, claiming that "Morland's sense of the multiplication of ironic reference is a key to his sculpture as a whole." So there you go.

An outdoor exhibition in Battersea Park in 1966 was opened by Princess Margaret, and I had other displays at the First Burleighfield

Sculpture Exhibition at Loudwater, Buckinghamshire, and one to myself at the Axiom Gallery in Oxford in 1969 called "Hinged and Unhinged", which was poorly reviewed. Another, a great success for us, was an exhibition partly on outdoor sites in Clifton, mounted at the Arnolfini in Bristol in 1969. At that time it was the acme of fashion, having acquired a good reputation during the Sixties. The nearby university, its art school, and the cheap accommodation for students in beautiful Georgian Clifton made the show magical, and my Rotork sculptures attracted a lot of good attention

In the last years in that easygoing era, David Annesley, Mike Bolus and I rented shared workshop capacity on two floors above a sheet metal bending factory in Kilburn. Each of us had a large space, indeed a whole floor, in which to work on our respective styles on our own. I had as my assistant a Scot, Bruce McLean, later a recognised sculptor in his own right. He was also to become an art critic. His essay in a booklet called *United Enemies* in 1968 was a cutting polemic against our generation that struck home with the dealers, some thought, and was a chord in our death knell.

For my part I now liked to work more and more in metal and fibreglass. The sight of sheet metal being bent in the factory below inspired me to a theme. Here I had the space to stretch myself and my imagination, and eventually I had a dozen large pieces, all worked from eight-by-four aluminium sheets, of which I was proud.

My chagrin was terrible when Tony Caro took Clem Greenburg, a leading critic of the time who had the power to make or break sculptors, through my space on the way up to see Mike and David's studio without so much as an acknowledgement to me, an old friend. I thought: shit, I'm dead.

There were other tensions in the air. Bill Tucker once warned me off the cylinder territory, which he claimed as his own. Phillip King was cones, Tony Caro was RSJs, David Annesley was circles and A-frames, Bill Tucker was cylinders. There was no room for two in any of those fields. Caro once condemned the two Bills, Tucker and Turnbull, for being "as good as you could get with a high intelligence and no talent". I need hardly say that there was a lot of intellectualism in contemporary art in those days, and they all published endless pamphlets about "new forms of perception" that went over my head. I just liked to be making, and thinking, with my hands.

I formed a relationship with one of my students, Stephanie Bergman, and rather recklessly took her for a week to New York on the occasion of an exhibition of Tony Caro's in 1968. We holed up at the Chelsea Hotel, which was to become a favourite of mine in my later career, and were dazzled by all we saw. The day before Tony's première, we helped him touch up and prepare his exhibits. New York was the capital of the modernist art movement, and the MoMA, or Museum of Modern Art, was its high temple. Rothko, Pollock, Nolan and Lewis were the priests. A high point for me came the day after the opening of Caro's do. Annesley, Nolan, Caro and I drove to Vermont to see the David Smith estate, which still held all his stainless steel sculptures, paraded in an avenue up to the portico of his house. Smith was one of our heroes and we felt privileged to witness such a gathering before the break-up of his estate. However Caro took a dim view of my visit to New York. To him it was a dirty weekend and he was not pleased by my adulterous behaviour. He knew and liked Sue, had often been to supper with us, and followed the progress of the two children we now had.

Not long after I got back, I lost my lectureship and had to find work out of town. This I managed, securing perfectly decent regular work at Norwich School of Art, although this meant long days, even whole periods, away from home. I had less time for my own sculpture and started casting about for other employments. The coup de grâce came when Brian Robertson departed from the Whitechapel Gallery. He had single-handedly turned the gallery into the Mecca of contemporary art in England. He'd brought Rothko to England with his "This Is Tomorrow" exhibition, had witnessed a riot there when he put on a Pollock exhibition and had launched David Hockney. He *was* swinging London in the Sixties. To have an exhibition there, let alone one that was not shared with others, was the peak of achievement in contemporary art. And he had promised me one.

I started to assemble a group of works in my back garden, and put in a lot of overtime to plug the gaps. Brian came round to view and approve them. I was ready to go. Then, almost without warning, he upped sticks and went off to America. His successor asked me dryly if I had signed a contract. No. To the benefit of my rear garden, but no one else, my exhibition was cancelled.

I was finished as a sculptor of fashion.

8

Smuggler

A ROUGH, SQUELCHY track led out into a great parkland of sunflowers, rusting and shedding their golden petals. My Citroen Pallas, with its pre-select gearbox and power steering, wallowed, its belly almost touching the ground. The stitched leather back seat was out and resting on a dry piece of ground nearby. Damien Enright and a Swedish girl called Agnetha sat on it, smoking a joint, while I worked on the floor pan, flat on my stomach in the back of the car, my long legs protruding. It was September 1966 and we were somewhere near Sedan in north-eastern France, approaching the frontier with Belgium. We were carrying a large and decidedly illegal quantity of cannabis resin. Which was why I was at work.

In the car boot was what looked like a log section cut from a tree trunk. It was in fact a section cut from the biggest single block of black resin I had ever seen. Bobby Grozki had concealed it under his bed in his flat in the Rue de la Seine, at the back of the Sorbonne in Paris. Grozki was a Brooklyn Jew, one of a group in exile from New York who Damien had befriended on the island of Ibiza. Importantly, he knew people in the Syrian and Lebanese diplomatic service who were prepared to facilitate drug smuggling. They were to become a staple of my chosen trade.

Damien came with me to Paris just to introduce me to Bob Grozki. Grozki wasn't willing to sell to me, someone he didn't know, let alone supply on credit. But Damien he knew, so if Damien wanted to take twenty kilos, he could, and payment for the balance could await sale. This was an accepted principle of distribution amongst trusted dealers, particularly if attached to a profit-sharing percentage.

So Damien changed his plans because now it was his dope and his responsibility. That being the case, he wanted us to go back not to the UK but to Stockholm, where he knew cool people who bought into the esoteric ideas of Ouspensky and Erich von Daniken and liked to get completely, but completely, out of their heads.

As did Damien, a new friend of mine. I'm sorry to talk stereotypes but Damien was a classic. A classic Son of Cork who could yarn the back legs off a donkey and have his way with any girl he met. He was short, very dark and skinny, good-looking, with a motor mouth. Damien was also a twenty-four-carat paranoia king who nevertheless had dabbled in a nervy way with drugs.

He was one of the founding members of the Ibiza set, where his perceptions had been transformed by LSD, the holy sacrament of this settlement of pioneer hippies in Europe. He was also currently on the run from Spain, having escaped over the Pyrenees after a run from Turkey in a sort of mobile caravan stuffed with cannabis came to an abrupt end at Las Jonqueras, on the Spanish frontier, where the authorities were waiting. Damien managed to slip away in the confusion and set off at a lick across the frontier car park and into the reed beds nearby. The vehicle was subsequently searched, the consignment found and his companions arrested, but Damien escaped on foot. He made it to Ibiza and then spent a hilarious – to others – number of weeks as a haggard fugitive in a semi-walled-off chamber in the Old Town, the home of his wife and children, emerging only at night and dependent on an acid-head follower of Timothy Leary and Taoism for supplies. The Taoist meanwhile took the opportunity to get off with Damien's wife.

Now he had his next woman in London, Hannah, with whom he had already added to his burgeoning squad of children. We met through a mutual friend, Tina, who had been his *au pair* before she came to me. Damien also hung out with my friend Keith Wilkinson, who lived round the corner from his place in Queensway. He swore blind to Hannah that he had turned a new leaf; he was now a writer and a stall holder in Portobello Road, and would never touch cannabis, or other women, again. Tina brought him round to Castelnau, ostensibly to see if I would fund a hippy double-decker bus to take heads to India, which Damien thought might turn into a regular travel business and might be a good way to make a few quid. I told him that was not my bag but perhaps he could point me in the right direction of what was.

For a while now, Keith and I had brought back small quantities of kif from the Mediterranean. Mainly it was for the recreational use of us and our friends. We became habitual tokers and liked to end the evening stoned and listening to both trad and modern jazz, but in particular the likes of Charlie Parker and Dizzy Gillespie, on the newfangled stereos back at my pad. Mates would regularly ring to see if we had any dope, and as often as not they were ringing up for their mates. If we could help them out we did. Eventually we could not ignore the fact that price seemed never to be a problem in our circles, or seemingly others. The money was easy, and easy money goes easily. It's the cycle that every dealer and smuggler I have ever met goes through. So you could say we just fell into dealing by chance.

Now here we all were near Sedan, with Damien on the sofa working his charm on Agnetha, a nubile but somewhat sulky blonde he had picked up who needed a ride back to Sweden. She slumped back with her eyes shut while I packed our cannabis into the floor of my car. Then Damien was off on one:

"There was this fella at school that sat in front of me in class. He would have no trouble hearing, that fella didn't. For he had the biggest ears you ever saw. They stuck out like a pair o' harps. So of course we called him Big Ears. He had like what you call a potato face. Right ugly bastard, all spotty and pitted his face was. But he was sharp as a button. Those big ears of his were always listening. You know what I mean?" Damien drew heavily on his toke and passed it to Agnetha, who stirred from her lethargy. "Don't worry about that Francis. He's work to do. Anyhows, this lad always knew the craic. And because he listened he never missed a trick. Every Thursday the priest came and spent the day attending to our spiritual needs. He hung around the classes and tweaked our ears and smacked our bottoms the way priests do, in a kind of spiritual way. He'd take the younger boys on his knees and tell them about St Patrick and that. We older boys were ready for stronger stuff than that. Tales of our terrible past, how Francis's forefathers would trample the land and take all the apples and the like. Oh, he hated the Brits, he did. There was nothing he'd like better than to take Francis by the ear and pitch him into hell. But you never could win with the English, so slippery they were."

The Morland clan. The elderly couple in the middle are John Colby Morland and his wife Elizabeth, my grandparents. I'm the boy in shorts sitting at my granny's shoulder. Far left, on the back row, is Uncle Humphrey, who ran the family firm. In front of him is my mother, Dorothy, while the moving bundle in her lap is my adopted sister Susie. The tallest chap at the back, second from right, is my father, Andrew.

Morland Industries at Glastonbury in Somerset. Founded by my great-grandfather, it became Europe's biggest producer of sheepskins, and Glastonbury was pretty much a company town.

Visiting South America on a tour of slaughterhouses for the family firm. Between 1958 and 1962, I made annual trips to Buenos Aires and various points south in the interests of sheepskin. Eventually Uncle Humphrey told me my services were no longer required.

A portrait of the artist as a young man. This was taken while I was retrieving architectural furniture for the refurbishment of my new house, by the documentary photographer Nigel Henderson, a friend.

Pottering around the Scilly Isles on Jeremy Fry's Volk boat in my striped Breton shirt. My love of the water would lead me into a life of illicit adventure. Skiing was my other favourite pastime.

Marrying Sue in Hampstead, north London. At the front, from left, are my mother, me, Sue, her sister, my sister Susie, and a friend, Paula Caucut. The world was at my feet, but I lacked ambition in the conventional sense. And that night I got stoned for the first time, a portent of things to come.

Posing at the Third Paris Biennale of Young Artists in 1963, with some of the big names in contemporary British art. From left to right: Joe Tilson, Gerald Laing, me, Peter Phillips, Peter Blake, Derek Boshier, Allen Jones and David Hockney. We were heralded as a new wave. *(Photo: Joe O'Reilly)*

A publicity photo for my exhibition in London in 1963. "Brancusi, the purest of all modern sculptors, is perhaps his principle influence," wrote George Melly in a review. Nice to be linked with the patriarch of modern sculpture.

Some examples of my work. My mother was a director of the Institute of Contemporary Arts, and I inherited her love of modernism, becoming feted as one of the "New Generation" of trendy sculptors. What no-one knew was that I was hiding cannabis inside some of my artworks and shipping them to North America.

My detached, double-fronted Victorian villa at Castelnau, the London des-res that was our family home for twenty-three years. It was here that I was arrested, for importing Moroccan resin, in 1970.

A passport photo at the time of my first arrest. I used the alias Charles Hamilton Brice, a moniker that stuck with me throughout my time in a US prison.

Nobby Pilcher, of Scotland's Yard's Drugs Squad, the hard-bitten detective who nicked me. He had previously arrested some of the world's most famous pop stars, so I was in good company.

Being visited in Lewisburg Penitentiary, Pennsylvania, by my childhood friend Harry Scott Stokes (right). While I was incarcerated, Harry invested money for me in Japan, where he lived. Sadly I lost the lot.

With Sue and our two children in the garden at Castelnau: Lee, my oldest, in the photo on the left, and Joyce, right, who would later accompany me on a smuggling run from the Med to Sweden on a trimaran. Bold girl. Sue and I would eventually drift apart, our marriage a casualty of my precarious lifestyle and too-frequent incarcerations, but we remain friends.

Back at sea. I loved the solitude and freedom of sailing, and the adventure of smuggling, so it was almost inevitable that I would fall back into that way of life, especially since my money had gone. I would continue to smuggle for the next thirty years.

Chefchaouen, the Moroccan town perched beneath the peaks of the Rif Mountains, where I was held in a tiny prison with fifty inmates to a room. I have served jail terms in four different countries on three continents, unfortunately. *(Photo: Philip Lange)*

The bay at Oban, on the remote west coast of Scotland, where I lost a yachtload of cannabis on a run that went wrong involving the tough East Ender Robert Tibbs. I got nine years in jail. *(Photo: Alinute Silzeviciute)*

It is my unwanted boast that I have been imprisoned for drug trafficking in every decade since the 1970s, save the current one. Yet I have few regrets – despite the wistful expression in this photo.

He paused. Agnetha didn't stir. But I stopped work and that's what Damien wanted to see, checking his timing. He resumed, running through a litany of Irish-sounding places and names that I'm sure were invented yet gave his tale an inherent plausibility.

"This is what he told us. Once, at Shandagerry Head, there was a church. It was the Benedictines what built it because St Patrick had run aground there in the mists, and those good monks didn't want such to happen again. And there it was for all the centuries and the monks would ring these bells whenever it got misty, and say prayers for St Patrick and all his brethren. The bells were the biggest, finest bells in all of Cork, and when they rang you could hear them in Ballyglayne and Carrigcotton. Now one day the Brits came marauding and took a liking to this fine church, though to tell the truth it was hardly more than a tower and its bells. For they were planning to land their partners in devilry close by and could see its importance as a lookout and a guide to sailors. So to that end they occupied the place and set about their rotten plans.

"The good people of Shandagarry went to work to stop their wicked ways. They cut off the water and stopped up the road so that nothing could get to those redcoats. This made them mad at the impudence of the poor folk of Shandagarry and they sent word that this was to stop. But it didn't and they shot an ironmonger from Carracloyne to teach those people a lesson. But it only made them madder and they set about firing flaming arrows at the belfry to frighten those children of the anti-Christ, and eventually it caught fire. And before the redcoats could run for their lives there was an almighty explosion and whole tower, redcoats and all, slid into the deep and there was nothing left at all to mark the endeavour. And do you know what lads? As the tower foundered, the bells rang out over the land, and a great cheer went up. So it was that God's will was done."

That justified another pause and Damien walked off into the sunflowers to have a slash. He reappeared at a quite different point and Agnetha gave a jump, before slumping back. She had swallowed a big lump of opium before we left. Damien sat down and ruffled her hair.

"Big ears was as moved as the rest of us. That summer, Big Ears became a keen swimmer, he did. He entered all the competitions there were. And there were many because the Taoiseach had said it was a disgrace that an island people couldn't swim, and everyone was to learn. And so we did. What a fine thing it was I could afford a mask and what good use we made of it for God's great purpose.

"Big Ears won the competition for staying under the water for the longest time, a minute-and-a-half as I recall it. Me, I left the underwater caper to others. And Big Ears took to fishing boats and was always out to sea on the tide and bringing home fishes for his mam, who was a widow and lived in a hovel with a potato patch.

"Next thing we hear is in church. The priest tells us Big Ears has been called by God to do his business and we are all to attend on the beach next Sunday for a re-dedication, whatever that might be. What do we find there? Fifty or so oil drums, a furlong of scaffolders' planks and twine. We are to build a great Noah's Ark, which we set about with a will, because it was God's business. It was a great raft, square, maybe thirty-by-thirty, with a hole in the middle. Next, along comes Johnny O'Reagan on his digger which he drives onto the great raft and we wait with trepidation until the tide comes in to see if it is God's will that it floats."

Pause.

"It does."

More smoking. This time he brings me a toke and he sees I'm laughing.

"You enjoying this, are you Francis? You hoping for something bad for God-fearing Irish folk, will you be?" Another pause while he got comfortable back with Agnetha on the sofa.

"Next thing Big Ears comes by in a fishing boat and tows the whole bloody raft off Shadagarry Point. The congregation attends on the scree above to see what will happen next. Reagan's digger arm disappears under the water through that hole I mentioned and next thing it comes up pulling a chain. And at the end of that chain the great bell of St Patrick's! He does it again. Two of them. A great cheer goes up from the scree to see such a sight and back we all go to the beach. Clancy Finnegan has got his Connemara ponies hitched to a great milk dray and slowly and carefully the great bells are lifted aboard and we process slowly back to Shandagarry, led by the priest on the milk dray, singing hymns and thanking the Lord for this miracle."

By now I was ready to reinstall the back seat and Damien rose without breaking his flow, pausing only to recover the joint from Agnetha and resettle in the front seat.

"For a while his mother shared her front room with those bells but then they went. Big Ears too was gone for a while. People said he'd gone to Dublin. Or maybe England. When he reappeared, it was two years later. He was in a Ford Consul. He built him and his mother a house on the main street with a builder's yard at the back. He's got a chain of builder's yards now all across the county. They sell bronze. And what was it set him up? He listened, is what set him up."

I made Damien recount this to the writer Edna O'Brien back in England. It's the only time I've seen that talkative lady silenced.

We had a number of frontiers to cross: Belgian, Luxembourgian and German. It was Damien's cardinal principle never to cross a frontier in a hot car. Each time we had to drop him at a service station or café, make our way through customs, then wait for him to catch up. He had sworn to his girl that never again was he going to smuggle drugs and he meant to keep to the letter of it. So crossing those three frontiers took the rest of the day and Agnetha started to whine, between slumps, that we need only have crossed one if we'd been sixty miles to the east. Agnetha was beginning to irritate.

That night we stayed in Koblenz and Damien got to share his double with Agnetha, despite her irritation with the frontier crossings. We were on our way to Kassel to see an exhibition of modern art. At least that's what I had told folk when I left.

At the Danish frontier we went through the same routine, then took a ship from Elsinore. Damien, security conscious, went as a foot passenger and wouldn't speak to us on the boat, so for fun I tormented him by chasing him around the ship until he found a place to hide on deck. Disembarking the boat, foot passengers leave over the same ramp as the vehicles. I paused next to him, wound the window down and called out an invitation to get in for a ride to Stockholm. He turned his head away like a Victorian girl insulted by a lewd suggestion on Ramsgate Pier.

Damien knew his way round Stockholm, and after some phone calls we drove out to a stylish, minimalist farmhouse with a log fire on the floor in the middle of the room, under a stainless steel hood suspended by a chimney pipe from the ceiling. It was also my first encounter with futons and waterbeds, which were to become ubiquitous in swinging London. Per was our host. He wore a marvellously soft and silky cashmere lambskin waistcoat, which I discussed with him. He imported them from India.

We all got very stoned. I pretended I was open-minded about extraterrestrial intelligence and Damien folded the notion into some kind of Celtic mist. Agnetha said she believed in Maharishi Yogi. Then we were told that we would see the Northern Lights and we all went outside and gazed at the cosmos while Per intoned. There were no Northern Lights, only glittering constellations to illustrate Per's toneless expositions.

I drove back alone the next morning, leaving Damien and Agnetha at Per's, and encountered a shocking Swedish phenomenon. I gave a lift to two Swedish girls off the boat to Copenhagen. They were on a Danish booze cruise, a planned day of drunken misbehaviour such as I heard said of football fans in England. They drank straight from their duty free bottle of vodka and frankly propositioned me: "English men like to fuck Swedish girls, yes, yes, yes?" I was still a little prudish and politely dropped them off outside Copenhagen.

Damien came to meet me and Stephanie Bergman, my student and lover, at the 2i's Coffee Bar in Old Compton Street a week later. He had £5,000 for me. That was big money. Stephanie was dazzled, both by the cash and by Damien's patter. Damien's news was that he'd put a word in for me with Grozki, and if I wanted to do it again I was welcome but not for less than ten kilos a time. As for Damien, he had taken his Trappist oath and was finished with the business, he was a writer not a dope dealer, and so on. Oh, yeah? In fact I was to do a number of further drives in Europe with him. They all passed quickly because of his marvellous yarns, despite the delays caused by his ultra-precautions at frontiers.

I had only just started with Stephanie, my pupil at St Martin's. She often came to my workshop in Kilburn to help me with my sculptures. She was an enchanting girl, although a little damaged by something in her childhood and prone to terrible mood swings and even to cutting herself during bouts of depression. Our relationship was to last three years and she became an important player in my drug-running deals. The thrill of picking up £10,000 in cash at a hotel or delivering a case of cannabis had an electric effect on her, waking her up and bringing her back from her bouts of apathetic gloom

Her father was a famous East End Jewish boxer, Jack "Kid" Berg, who had conquered America and become champion of the world. She often wore his stencilled boxing dressing gown. Her parents were then living comfortably in retirement in Sussex, but had no children other than her. She felt they wished she were a boy. Still, there were advantages to being an only child. There was some money set aside in trust for her and at my urging she obtained the release of this money and bought a house in Wellesley Road, Chiswick. This both facilitated our relationship and provided me with an excellent base away from home for my accelerating excursions into dope trafficking.

I was not secretive with Sue about my affair. Her line was that it would pass and she trusted me to put her and the children first, in which she was not far wrong. I explained to her that it was impossible for a sculptor and St Martin's lecturer in the middle of the Swinging Sixties not to want to visit gardens other than my own. But actually it went further than visiting. After a particularly tense period in

Castelnau, I moved in with Stephanie. Twenty-four hours later it was clear it wouldn't work and I moved back.

Meanwhile Stephanie and I would drive to and fro to Paris. There we dealt with Grozki's right-hand man, Jacques, who had a flat with his girlfriend in the 14th arrondissement and would put us up overnight. I would release the rear panel of my beloved DS, in what looked like a wheel replacement job. I would take the panel indoors, secure ten or twenty kilos to it, and the next morning bolt the panel back on in full view of rush-hour Paris and set off back to the UK. The innocence of the age is well illustrated by the fact that I once took the family on one of these Parisian excursions and did the packing of the cannabis while Sue and the family spread a classic French picnic in a wood in Picardy.

THE DRUG SCENE in 1965 was, in truth, very small. It had started with the arrival of Caribbean immigrants in the mid-Fifties. A principal ghetto grew in North Kensington, particularly around All Saints Road. This area of London, now characterised as Notting Hill Gate, had been built in a grand and planned style in the 19th century and was aimed at the middle-class professionals and business people who had proliferated with the Industrial Revolution and the expansion of Empire. The houses were up to seven floors high, stuccoed, in late Regency London style, and gave onto communal gardens. They had separate dining rooms and servants' quarters. The bottom floors had big rooms, twelve feet high with decorated plaster ceilings. Nowadays the richest bankers and oligarchs inhabit them, but at that time the development had failed and fallen into multiple occupancy by students, the poor and Caribbean immigrants. The American beatnik movement made its mark on the students, and the world of jazz, largely based in Soho, popularised cannabis smoking amongst cool clubgoers who flocked to Ginsberg's shows and read Kerouac like he had written the Bible. Soon the psychedelic era was joining hands with the hipsters, something that was particularly evident if one went to Ibiza. This was the main axis that I was aware of in this rapidly expanding dope scene. There was of course also an explosion in rock music, bringing with it a virtual requirement to get out of your head if you went to open-air festivals like the early Glastonbury shows – if only to escape the horror of the mud and the rain constantly distracting the turned-on mind from Jimi Hendrix and Grace Slick. But my generation slightly missed out on this side of the scene and I recite it only to illustrate the rising demand for cannabis.

In my first years, it was to the Notting Hill market that I delivered. I had a Transit in my garage lockup in Barnes, and thirty kilos stored there would take up to a month to dispose of. I'd be called up by Keith or Damien or John McDonald and told to go to a person they knew in, for example, St Luke's Mews, off All Saints Road, and deliver, say, five kilos. I doubt many importers were distributing in greater quantities at that time; if they were, I never came across them. I am guessing that the whole London market was not much more than a ton a year at that time. I must have been bringing 150 kilos a year from Paris, which certainly exhausted the contacts Keith and I had and perhaps accounted for a tenth of the whole market. The great hippy trail to Afghanistan and Nepal was well under way by this time and I'm guessing the single kilos that various longhairs sent or carried back supplied a good half of London's needs. My own mum once came back from Morocco in the Fifties with a titchy lump to see what it was all about. But I was never aware in the mid-Sixties of anyone bigger than us in organised importations.

Keith was friends with John McDonald, a ballet dancer and a Scot. He'd had a good run in a very successful ballet called *Man of La Mancha*, which was based on the story of Don Quixote and which made the song "Impossible Dream" famous. He lived comfortably with his wife in London, but the musical had had a long and successful stint on Broadway and John, whose wife was a native New Yorker, knew a lot of people there. It was he who set in train a new profit avenue for me and Stephanie. Lebanese and Moroccan dope sold for a lot more in the US than the UK and the market was much bigger, so it was well worth the extra effort of getting it over there.

On returning from my trips in the DS with Damien or Stephanie, the cannabis went to my studio in Kilburn. There Stephanie and I made sculptures, my sculptures in my style, composed of hollow fibreglass tubes and boxes. Inside we would carefully pack ten or twenty kilos of fine Lebanese cannabis resin and then have the sculptures picked up by a specialist fine arts shipper, who would put them in crates and ship them to their depot in New York. A representative from "Harrington Modern Arts" – in reality a friend of John McDonald – would pick them up.

These specialist fine arts shippers mainly worked for Agnew's, Christie's, Sotheby's and other top-drawer galleries in Bond Street. It was a very gentlemanly and unhurried world, most unlikely ever to attract the attentions of Her Majesty's Customs unless they suspected grandees of shipping out national-treasure paintings to avoid the painful taxation of the rich that occurred then. Modern sculpture would barely raise an eyebrow, except perhaps in mockery. Using such art to hide my smuggled dope was a good method and one I should have stuck to, but I feared the paperwork, which has never been my forte.

I insisted that the sculptures be returned to me after unloading. I still had my pride. The top half of one, called *The Kiss*, crossed the Atlantic twice in this manner, on one occasion returning with $40,000 packed in the same sweet concealment spot. I suppose I got greedy. Not only did I not like the paperwork involved but I also thought the method would be noticed eventually. So Keith set about recruiting couriers, who instead would take the dope in their luggage, to be met by Stephanie or Gretchen Buchanan at JFK in New York or Dulles Airport, Washington. Gretchen was another feisty girl, perfectly well off with her civil engineer husband but who just loved the thrill of airports, hotels and wads of dollars.

John McDonald was also a friend of Charlie Radcliffe. At some point after my debacle with the Drug Squad, John went to live in Paris and he and Charlie developed a line of their own from Paris to New York. Keith Wilkinson remained an associate of theirs and introduced them to our excellent Arab contact, Khaled, who in due course they took full advantage of, making Charlie in particular one of the more significant traffickers of the Seventies. Later I fell out with them over this. I didn't know Radcliffe personally, although he married Tina while I was banged up inside. After I left prison I started up again by moving cash around for their operation, but then fell out with them. But that was all in the future.

Back at the very beginning Keith, who because of our efforts had been able to afford a place of his own in his spiritual homeland, Ibiza, astonished us by turning up one day on his scooter, having come the whole way from Tangier. Stowed in a saddlebag was a kilo of Moroccan grass. Inspired by this, Stephanie and I drove out one Monday, met some Americans in Tangier on Wednesday and went to stay with them in their completely bare, recently bought villa outside Tangier. We were taken from there by an Arab contact of theirs on a two-hour journey to a farmhouse, owned by a man called, predictably, Mohammed, and came back with two kilos of grass and two of hash, which we had back in England by Friday. That was how one became a drug baron in those days.

THAT FIRST trip was a learning operation. We found that nothing, not even cling-film, could conceal the smell of grass, which is also very bulky. However, we gathered that in the Rif mountains, the great cannabis-growing region of Morocco, they had recently been shown by an American the technique for making resin, or hashish, an essential precondition of making it big in international markets. So that was the destination for the trip that followed: the small town of Ketama, already described. Stephanie and I did two of these runs but the quality did not compare with Jacques' resin from the Lebanon. Nevertheless I now had my own separate channel to Mohammed's farm in Morocco, which became an important standby later.

Jacques also gave my name to a gentleman called Khaled Mouneimne, a Lebanese businessman with good connections to the Syrian regime who travelled regularly to Rome and London. Sometime in 1967, Khaled telephoned me out of the blue and we arranged to meet at the Daquise restaurant in South Kensington. He was clearly well educated and spoke Arabic, French, Italian and English fluently. He dressed like a prosperous businessman in shiny suits and had a belly to prove it. He was also a very patriotic Arab and wouldn't tolerate any pro-Israeli talk in his presence. He liked to imply that sending us Lebanese hash was his duty, to weaken the West. Maybe, he hinted, he worked with the Palestinian Liberation Organisation. Certainly he seemed to live in hotels on the back of an American Express card, very chic in those days, provided by his government. He wanted someone reliable in London to sell on fifty-kilo-plus quantities of dope. Since I now had an American clientele, this was doable.

So it was that, with Khaled on board, Paris faded from the picture, and the quantities increased.

Khaled was to become a very reliable supplier. This was by no means his only business. For example he had set up a large importation channel of Patagonian half-grown lambs throughout the Middle East, where demand was enormous. The brothers who financed this fell out, but the strangest thing was that he was dealing with people I had once dealt with in Puerto Natales. Needless to say, like any good smuggler he also moved gold and cigarettes around, using a wretched Nigerian diplomat laden so heavily with his gold that on one occasion he collapsed with an asthma attack whilst lumbering to the loo on a flight with Khaled.

Another of Khaled's recruits was Fulton Dunbar, who worked in the Liberian embassy in Rome. He and his wife had medical problems that could only be expensively fixed in London, and we were willing to help them out in return for his services as a courier. Fulton took to flying from Beirut to both Rome and London with our goods. Eventually he spread his wings and flew on to Montreal and New York for us. Keith and I were more than happy to take him fruit and flowers in hospital in the Cromwell Road and settle his bill.

Khaled also recruited two Ghanaian embassy officials in Rome, a Mr Ankrah and a Mr Tamaklos, who did useful work for us.

Another person at our end was Pat Newsome, a friend of Keith's whom Damien liked and trusted. He was used by us to deliver money, particularly to Khaled in Rome and Beirut. He was unusual in our circles, being smart, reliable, well organised and straight looking; right up Damien's nervy street. He also had a fling with Keith's wife despite having a wife of his own in Lisbon. He was South African and had done his military service there. Pat was a useful man to send into a bank or hotel, or to deal with paperwork, but not to do mule work. This we farmed out to students and tourists.

It was a smooth operation, particularly with these diplomatic passports in the mix – until the arrests started, in 1969.

One of our runners, a lad called Abdul Aziz Mohammed, was caught with twenty-one kilos of Khaled's Lebanese at Heathrow Airport, and got an eighteen-month jail sentence at Middlesex Crown Court. There was nothing we could do for him, as he had been apprehended with the gear.

Nor could Khaled save Keith's mother-in-law, Mimi Reynolds, from a terrible fate. She was sent by Keith to Beirut to collect a load from Khaled. Perhaps information had leaked, because she got no further than Beirut Airport when she was arrested. They submitted her to the painful indignity of the *bastinado* and held her for the best part of a year. Despite the general corruption of Lebanese society, Khaled had no influence with them at all. Mimi, however, was a feisty woman who complained bitterly about her treatment until it got into the Beirut Press. She was eventually repatriated to the

UK and left a legacy of some reform in the treatment of women in Lebanon, of which she remained proud to her dying day.

Even more alarming was the arrest of Cherry Thompson, also in Beirut. She was nothing to do with Khaled but was a typical find of Damien's, a chirpy good-time girl up for any adventure. We had a stringer in Kabul, the capital of Afghanistan, who we called "Stringy Taffy" because he was Welsh and wasted-looking. He kept sending messages about what he could get there, so we sent Cherry with a return ticket. Taffy was always short of money and up to tricks to make a little more so that he didn't have to return from his life of idleness on the hippy trail. He persuaded Cherry to cash in her return ticket and to go back via Beirut, where an Aeroflot flight to London would be safer than coming straight from Kabul. He kept the difference.

When she got to Beirut this all turned out to be baloney and she found herself stranded. She was a plucky thing. She put her case into left luggage and went off to the casino, picked up an Egyptian playboy who backed her on the tables, spent the night with him and returned to the airport with the money she needed. When she went to collect her luggage, however, she was nicked with sixty-four kilos.

It was all ending in tears. In late 1969, Stephanie lingered in New York to see an exhibition at the MoMA, where one of the St Martin's crowd had some pieces to show. By the time she reached Dulles Airport, accompanied unnecessarily by Gretchen, they were too late to watch our courier arrive; the incoming passengers had all gone. So Stephanie and Gretchen made their way to the home of the courier, a female American student, not realising she had been busted on arrival. They'd have seen this if they'd been at the airport on time; in those days you could see the customs bench from the Arrivals lounge. At the courier's home they found some weeping and bitter parents and a phalanx of ICE agents. They were ultimately both sentenced to three years in a federal women's prison. When I found myself in an American prison two years later, I got to hear that Stephanie had been a big figure behind bars, teaching wild black girls to handle clay ("Never lifted nothin' heavier'n a dick or a dollar bill").

THE ARREST OF Stephanie and Gretchen made me rethink my approach. Airports seemed too risky; the sea seemed to be the thing. I loved sailing and still did some when I went out to Essex. I kept a boat there at Landermere and would sail out to Skipper Island, shoot some rabbits and maybe catch some mullet on the way back. I'd visit Eduardo and Nigel and look at their little factory and we might have lunch in Thorpe-le-Soken. The game came back with me to London for supper, Tina would get Pat and Damien or Keith over to join us, Sue cooked, Damien rolled joints and yarned and so life went on. But it was a strain. I was going to Norwich to teach two or three days a week. The rest of the time I was to and fro to the banks and money changers, the Harrods depository, the airline offices and the airport. I didn't really enjoy this; it was hard to sustain my sculpture.

And now all these arrests.

What I wanted to do now was to pick up big-time and deliver. One or two really big scores would be better than lots of smaller ones, preferably in our own boat. And so it was that while poking around the yards and marinas of Gibraltar in the summer, looking for an ocean-going boat, Ken Nagle, Harvey Bramham and I met Bob Palacios. Marinas are funny places. A day's sailing inevitably leads to several more of fixing. Stay bottle screws need replacing, batteries are not holding charge, water tanks are leaking, water cooling circuits are bunged up. It never ends. So sailors are always asking for favours:

"Got any masking tape?"

"Got a metric spanner?"

"Can I borrow your soldering iron?"

And so on, amidst the clattering of rigging slapping a hundred anodised masts along the pontoons.

I knew Harvey from Ibiza, and somewhere along the line he had met Palacios, an American in his late twenties who was always popping about in his catamaran, eager to make new friends. There was something of the abandoned puppy about him, wagging his tail and trying to get his new European buddies to foster him. He was over-keen to give advice about the boat we eventually found – the *Beaver* – and all its problems, of which it had many. In fact I found him a bit of a know-all and insufficiently respectful of the ten years I had on him, but then he was Californian – and he was a competent sailor. Although we never explicitly told him why we wanted the *Beaver*, he no doubt made an educated guess, of which we did not disabuse him.

The *Beaver* had been sitting in Gibraltar for years, occupied as a houseboat by a gay retired colonel. He was getting old and his Moroccan boyfriend/housekeeper/crewman needed to think about his future. In fact we were offered him with the boat, which we declined. She wasn't fit to go to sea and we had to make a long-term plan for her. We expected to take a year to make her fit for the transatlantic trade that was to make our fortunes. In fine weather we took her on day-long proving excursions up the coast to assess what was needed. What was mainly needed was money, and the investment in buying her had stretched our means. Bob would always volunteer to escort us in his *Letitia*, accompanied by his sister who had joined him from California. She was a classic Beach Boys blonde and quite a draw. I found it mildly irritating being shadowed by them, but Harvey liked having a support boat in case we got into trouble.

Tangier was and is famous for its festivals of jazz and film. There are several of them, attracting big European followings. We decided to take the *Beaver* over and pig out on the Méchoui going on there, a great fair of food and drink, Arab and European bands, dope smoking and *flânerie*. It was a great, colourful city for that kind of fun. This time Bob didn't even ask us; we just found him tagging along off our stern and tying up on the neighbouring berth. I was a bit sharp with him.

"You again."

"Cool it, man. I'm just looking out for you."

"Why do we need a lookout?"

"You can always use a good guy riding shotgun."

"Why would I need that? I'm not going on any stagecoach."

"Hey, easy. With this kind of draw you'll know I'm your pal."

And he did indeed produce for us a perfectly made, Californian-style funnel to pass around as we meandered among the displays of saffron and aubergine, radiccios, peppers and peaches, as the late summer sun beat down.

That night, on the deck of the *Beaver*, as we chewed into our pulled lamb in naan bread from a wood-fired oven, I made an offer he couldn't refuse.

"Look, Bob. You obviously want to get involved. So here's the deal. You front five thousand dollars, I'll front three thousand. That'll get us two hundred kilos of hash. You take it to the UK, I will sell it for eighty thousand dollars and you can have half of it. Call it proving yourself."

It wasn't that good an offer: his risk and his money. But the guy didn't need strong-arming; he nearly bit my hand off.

"Cool, man! Let's go!" They certainly have get up and go, those Californians.

What we had agreed to undertake would be the biggest movement of cannabis I had ever done. Two hundred kilos was a huge amount for the London market; I doubt that many bigger importations were being done at the time. Who would want to? Nothing is worse than having stock on your hands. Storage and slow distribution was what attracted attention. In reality most of it would have to be moved on to America, for which I was not yet ready. But it was my hope that this would be the last time that onward distribution in the UK would be my responsibility. My aim was to hand that over to the home team: Damien, Pat Newsome, Mick O'Shea, Keith and Tina. From now on I would do boats.

So I closed my workshop in Kilburn. I still had a garage, where I had been using my fibreglassing skills to restore Rolls-Royces, but it was not going to make me a living and I decided to wind that up, too. In a perfect world I would crew the *Beaver* for runs to Jounieh or Al Hoceima, and from there to Stockholm, Fishguard, Oban, New York, Providence, or wherever. Pass on the dope and back to sea.

On October 6, two days after Bob Palacios, his *Letitia* and the cannabis arrived in Cowes, I introduced Bob and his sister to Damien and Pat Newsome at a dinner party at my house. Annoyingly Damien was distracted from the business in hand by the attractions of Bob's sister. Still it was agreed that Damien would send Mick O'Shea to collect the load. At that time, I was thinking Bob could repeat his UK run and maybe even crew the *Beaver* for its first US excursion. He had certainly proved himself. I could bow out of storing and selling the dope on from lockups in the UK. We would be "consultants"; Damien, Tina, Keith and Pat could handle the finicky delivery end.

Many have come a cropper chasing that simple dream. And so it was to be with me, with my arrest that October and all that followed.

In the meantime, Khaled had been leading a colourful life in Rome. He was kidnapped by the much-feared Israeli secret service, Mossad, and held by them in a room in the Rome Hilton for a short while. It was all to do with his links to the PLO. The Italians gave Mossad first bite at the cherry; they used the lever of our impending arrests and the likelihood of him being charged with serious drugs offences in an attempt to "turn" him. It was during this episode that he managed to get down to the hotel reception in his dressing gown and ring me on a public telephone, the call I received while the Drug Squad were trampling through my house in Castelnau. Khaled wanted to warn me, but it was already too late. Later during his enforced stay at the hotel, he bribed a callgirl they had laid on for him – that was the sort of thing they did, apparently – to smuggle in some clothes so that he could escape. It was wasted effort: he was immediately arrested by the Italian police, on October 22, for an earlier drug seizure at Rome Airport, when the couriers Dunbar and Tamaklos were caught. Even our diplomats were being arrested, albeit they were subsequently released. But Khaled's contacts were impressive. Much later he got access to our Interpol file and reported back the identity of the traitor in our midst.

We were always doomed, for it was Pat Newsome who was the informant named in the Interpol report. Newsome was indicted for the 1971 conspiracy, and realistically the Drug Squad had no choice about that, despite his cooperation, because it was his comings and goings to Rome that proved the Khaled connection. However, he was in Rome when I was busted and sensibly escaped to Portugal, where his wife lived, before he could be arrested. Although a warrant for his arrest was issued, it was quietly withdrawn by the Drug Squad three years later.

Damien Enright managed to escape the whole mess, disappearing back to Ireland where he put the scene behind him. He went on to make his mark as a nature writer and journalist and penned an engaging memoir about the Sixties, *Dope in the Age of Innocence*, which is an apt description of the times. In the eyes of the law, however, my innocence had gone: Francis Morland was most emphatically guilty.

PART THREE

1971–2015

9

Lewisburg

SLABS OF ICE floated down the Hudson as our bus crossed the George Washington Bridge. The New Jersey turnpike was fringed with two feet of grimy snow as we headed west. My whole family had come over, including my mother, to see me off. Huge numbers of dollars had been given to lawyers to achieve not very much. And here I was, on my way to prison.

There were about thirty of us, handcuffed in pairs. We had been collected at the break of day from the holding pen in the West Street detention centre in the Bronx, where we had lived and slept in groups of thirty bunks in huge cages that dotted a large warehouse. I'd been held there since my arrest the previous August and now it was January. I was looking forward to some privacy. I didn't know any of the people on the bus, and gleaned only that we were going to Lewisburg, Pennsylvania, a five-hour journey with one handcuffed pee break.

"It ain't so bad," a character called Johnny "the Trick" Manolo told me on the way. "You'll be with the crème de la. Take it slow. Don't make any pals you might regret. Like, take your time, watch, remember. Most important thing, get on the right wing. With people you can get on with. Don't do nothing in the first week. Guy asks you a question, you answer polite. But brief. You won't be asking him no questions. Why would ya? You're not short of time. There'll be guys say they can get you jobs in the kitchen or the stores. Just say you'll take your time. You need to get your bearings."

The bus's windows had grilles over them, like police buses at demos. Each time we crossed a district line we were joined by a fresh police car with its home town named on it. Like that, we knew where we'd got to.

A guard stood at the front of the bus facing back towards us. This being America, he had some kind of shotgun across his chest.

"That's good advice you're getting, Hamilton," he called out to me. "Now listen up."

He then gave us the welcome lecture to "the federal correctional facility of Lewisburg", like he was proud of it and wanted all of us to have a good time as his guests. He talked like we were one big happy family, with maybe a trace of sarcasm.

"There's fourteen hundred of us in eight blocks. There are two floors and four wings on each block. When you leave reception, you'll be in one of these wings. Some of the wings are freer than others. Depends on your conduct and why you're here. Some of us are kidnappers with homicide, some are traitors, some obscenity artists, some revolutionaries, some are drug smugglers like Hamilton here. He's English in case any of you wanna learn to speak good."

I gave a little nod and there was a round of sarcastic clapping.

"Each wing has its cells, the good guys get one to themselves generally and they're open most times to the rest of the wing. Others get sent to the Jungle. You'll find a day room with TV, shower and washrooms. It's not so bad. You leave the wing to eat and to work and to recreate but you'd better get on with those guys on your wing. You won't be partying with the rest of the guys much else of the time. Lock up, 8 P.M. Lights out, 10 P.M. Reveille, 6 A.M. Any questions?" Then there was an issue of cigarettes, one packet per head.

The Trick took this up after the introductory talk was over.

"So you're in the narcotics game, huh?"

"Well, cannabis. Do you class that as narcotics?"

"Sure I don't. That's this hippy dope, right?"

"Right."

"And what you pick up for that?"

"Eight years."

"Eight years! You kidding? Must have been a whole lot?"

"They got seven hundred kilos of it."

"Kilos? Don't give me kilos. Heck of a lot anyway, huh? Up from Mexico, maybe?"

"No. By sea in a yacht into New York."

"Yuh sailed it in? From where?"

"From Europe."

"From Europe. The Common Market of Europe, no kidding." While I'd been away General de Gaulle had died and the UK had joined the Common Market, which interested Americans a lot.

He called out to the bus: "Hamilton is with us from the Common Market of Europe. He came join us in a yacht with a stack of cannabis from the Common Market."

"Cannabis!" They all yelled and whooped in disgust.

"And you?" I asked.

"Rackets."

"What's that?"

"Hey, Hamilton. You forgot my advice already. Don't you go asking the questions till you know where you stand."

Actually all the time I was at Lewisburg I was treated with respect. This was partly because I was English and partly because cannabis in America was still a cottage industry with very few big players. I wasn't treading on anyone's toes and I made a change from the usual inmate, with my good manners and diffident English style.

Pennsylvania, as the name implies, is heavily forested. It rolls gently and beautifully up to and over the Appalachians and onto the Great Lakes. Areas have been cleared to make endless, prosperous farmland, a lot of it dairy, but there's corn and rape and barley too. It's as lovely as England but goes on forever with its small market towns. Near Kelly Town, on the Susquehanna River, is the prison. It was a great big hulk of brick-built blocks astraddle a central corridor, the control building, put up in the 1930s with little expense spared. It had a running track, cinema, gym, library and basketball court. Best of all it had tennis courts, two of top quality clay, and nobody used them. They were built for the prison by a Wimbledon champion called Falkenburg. It also had a library, into which they were happy to induct me when they heard that I was a craftsman willing to sort and bind their books, a block transfer of Mills and Boon-type slushy novels from a dull US Air Force base which needed a lot of weeding. I did mornings at the library, then broke off after lunch, when the governor was happy to let me play tennis all the afternoons that the weather, when it improved, permitted. The winner stayed on. I was a university-class player so I got very fit.

Nice though all this sounds, it was, of course, surrounded by a high wall and machine gun towers, floodlit at night and patrolled by dogs on running leashes. This was where the next three years of my life were to be spent. Later we had some Watergate convicts pass through on their way to the open prison at Allenwood, also in Pennsylvania. But the guards there were apparently so jumpy that some inmates applied to come back to Lewisburg, where the security was more relaxed. The main currency in prison was cigarettes and a carton of those got you a session with one of the sissies. You paid their minder, who was never far off.

THERE'S NOT a lot to be said for prison. But one compensation is that you meet people who have led the strangest lives and done the weirdest things. In the refectory you queued by race: blacks, Latinos, whites. I would join the Black Panthers and the Nation of Islam cons because I didn't know any better and they got spare ribs. I met the likes of Huey Newton and Ishmael X. Once Ishmael X came to me in the library and asked me if I'd rebind his Koran. He'd been good to me in that queue, so sure I would. It was in a terrible state because he gave readings from it every prayer time on his wing. This book was part of a kind of cult issue from Elijah Muhammad, leader of the Nation of Islam, or Black Muslims; he enjoyed free labour on his big ranch as tribute from his following. They also had to buy a journal of his, *Elijah Muhammad Speaks*.

Then I noticed something. His accent was familiar and I asked him where he was from. St Croix, would you believe. We chewed the cud about the island, he in a polite, diffident style. I didn't like to ask him why he was inside. One didn't. But I found out. He was Ishmael LaBeet, one of a group of black civil rights activists who had invaded a golf course in St Croix and shot repeatedly at a group of privileged white tourists, killing eight of them. Many years later, this polite man hijacked an American Airlines plane and diverted it to Cuba.

The Panthers had a strike one day in the furniture department where they worked. We all went on sandwich and Kool-Aid rations and prison lockdown, to the delight of the screws, until the whole prison except the Panthers voted to get back to normal. After that we never saw the Panthers again.

Everyone moans about the food in prison and Lewisburg was no exception. Actually the food was much more acceptable to me than what I had had in Brixton, which was all gristly stew and lumpy mashed potato. Here there were burgers and French fries, still a novelty to me, albeit combined with a slice of pineapple and other such weird combinations. I was saying this at lunch one day when Kenny intervened. Surprisingly he too had been in Brixton:

"Couldn't eat nothing there but biscuits and chocolate."

"You were in Brixton?"

"Sure. Pending my extradition."

"Extradition for what?"

He told me as the others cleared away. "I was in Vietnam and retired early with a disability pension. We were on a river in a rubber when some gooks started picking on us from a hill. They punctured the boat and it started going in circles so we swam for the shore rather'n get truly wasted. Somethin' bit my leg and that was OK for a while. But it swole right up and the grunts with me left to get help. Next morning fuckin' Uncle Sam napalms the neighbourhood and I get a whiff. Now I'm in a state. They copter me out and give me a pink chit. On the house from now on in."

This was a far cry from my national service.

"Back in New England I got the brass band treatment. It all seemed nice for a while, what with not having to work and sitting in bars talking to other vets about wasting Reds. But then it's kind of boring too. Girlfriend got tired of me and my pals. Every Thursday I'd go down the Providence and Something Credit Union where these nice old ladies used to cash my cheques. 'How you doing, Al? Shouldn't you be saving some of this?' and all that.

"I noticed the safe. These trusting old ladies used to leave it open during working hours. Not always, but often. We're talking small town, New England. I'm going a little mad, I guess, cos one day I blow up some telephone poles, I go in there with a gun and tell those kind ole ladies to clear out, I'm going for the safe.

"'Don't do that Kenny. You can have a good life. You don't need to be a bad guy,' cried the ladies. My balaclava had been a waste of time. Course they were right. My little pension was generous enough and although I limped and was a little short of breath I could have worked. But I was feeling a little crazy.

"'I'm comin' over!' I cried. 'Clear the way.' Over I went. There was more'n a hunnerd thousand dollars in that safe. I stuffed it into a shoulder bag and I was on my way."

"Where'd you go?"

"Down to the river, where I had a canoe waiting. Now this wasn't thought out good. It was late afternoon in winter. It was real cold and parts of the river where it ran fast were too shallow to float over. I fell in a couple of times and had to drag the boat over the shallows. Then it got dark and I headed over land shivering to death till I got to a road. Man, I was out of my mind. One time I found myself staring into some headlights and threw myself onto something furry and warm. It was the biggest fucking bear you ever saw. I was so mad with disappointment I kicked it. But hey, it was dead. Reckon it had been shot by some bounty hunters. It was still warm, and that was something. How come? Shot looking for me?

"I was delirious the next few days but had a little money. Must have been picked up by a truck going south. Next thing I clearly remember was waking up in a convent in Mexico. Hell, I was being nursed by nuns in Mexico! How did I get there?

Anyhow, I recovered and made my way to Europe. Bummed around. Finally did some hanging in Ibiza. I was cool with the money and banked it for when I had a good investment idea. I liked your Triumph motorbikes, particularly the one called a Trophy which you don't see in America a whole lot. I was going to buy four of them so that me and my hippy pals could go to India. I went to Jersey because I could get them tax free and ship them from there.

"Jersey was kind of boring. One day I went to weigh myself on those penny machines that speak your weight. I'd put on a lot. But I didn't believe what it told me and spent another penny. Same weight. I got so mad I punched the glass in and cut my finger. There is not a lot of crime in Jersey. They put the dogs and their FBI onto this little outrage and followed the trail back to where I was staying. Then they did an Interpol check. They had me. For some reason all that had to happen in London, which is how come I got to know your Brixton Prison."

I didn't see Kenny again because we got cleared to different wings. Although we all ate communally, it was along an endless corridor hall connecting the wings. You got to see people from neighbouring wings but not the distant ones. Violent prisoners tended to be segregated away from us white-collar types. I met Jimmy Hoffa, and hung out with Guido, a big time steel union boss. He was educating himself in the "Mafia structures of Renaissance Italian city states", believe it or not.

Then there were some radical monks from the anti-war Berrigan brothers group, who had succeeded in wiping a lot of FBI information with magnets. They went on hunger strike, making out that they needed Zen food or some such nonsense. Kantzler, the deputy governor, put them on kitchen duty, cutting up meat.

I eventually got onto the "honour" wing and got to meet Major Glenn Thompson, otherwise just known as "Spy". I used to play a lot of chess on my wing. One of the inmates was in a federal prison because he had stabbed an officer in another prison for confiscating a jug of hooch. And he had been in that prison because he'd shot his grandfather, who had shot his dog. Not a typical federal inmate. Anyway, I beat him twice quite easily and was playing him a third time when this handsome, composed, smart-looking man, maybe ten years older than me, put a coaster under my mug of coffee. Next time I picked it up, I saw he had written the single word "lose" on it. Sound advice.

This "major" was in the neighbouring cell and when the wing was redecorated he doubled up with me. He became my best friend in Lewisburg and he was a remarkable man. This was his story as told to me.

"I was born in Vladivostok, one of twins. My mother was Russian and my father was German, an engineer. He'd been drawn into the Civil War as a Red sympathiser. When I was six, there were terrible floods in the Far East and my brother and I were swept down a river.

I was holding his hand as I pulled myself by a branch on a tree out of the river, when I lost him. I never saw him or my family again.

"I was brought up in an orphanage and then at the age of fourteen moved to an army cadet school because I could speak German and Germany had invaded. They trained me as an engineer and I taught German to army intelligence officers. At the battle of Kursk I commanded my very own tank. I was only sixteen.

"After the war I was sent to Moscow to KGB school and was trained in all the arts of spycraft, including English and homosexual seduction. I qualified as a lieutenant in 1947. I was taken before Beria because I had come out top, at his large villa near the Kremlin. In his office he sat at a desk on a plinth and came round to put his hand on my head from above. He was a very short man and the incarnation of evil. The hackles of my shorn head rose.

"I started out in Leipzig and married Sylvia, a citizen of the German Democratic Republic. When I was recalled to Moscow she wouldn't come but I promised I'd be back. A Latvian lady had returned from California to her homeland after her son had died, to bury him. She had all his identity documentation. The KGB got hold of them, don't ask me how. That is how I became Glenn Thompson. I was given these and sent by Polish boat from Gdansk to Cuba. There I was appointed engineer on a Cuban freighter bound for Montreal. Nobody on that boat apart from me, the captain and the navigator had a clue what they were doing. And the reason? The whole lot absconded on arrival, including myself.

"I made my way to California. I ceased to be Gregor Best and became Glenn Thompson and eventually had my own garage in Los Angeles. Then I joined the US Air Force. I was a major eventually in charge of the technical needs of sixteen Sabres. I pretended to do a course in Russian and passed with distinction. We were a rare breed, I can tell you. I was transferred to Forces Intelligence and stationed at our air base at Templehof in Berlin. Would you believe it? I was in the office that coordinated allied military intelligence for central Europe.

"When I reported to the KGB in East Berlin, they took a lot of convincing. No-one had heard hair or hide of me for ten years. Sylvia was impressed that I kept my promise and I demanded a flat for her in East Berlin. We lived together for much of the time I was there. She had a beautiful flat off the newly built Karl-Marx-Allee. She's still there in that flat to this day, waiting for me. Eventually I convinced them and to their amazement I took to copying our reports and carrying them on the U-bahn to General Milche in person.

"For my work I had an Order of Lenin and a Hero of the Soviet Union commendation and, more important, funding for whatever I wanted when I was eventually retired back to the USA. This happened in 1959. Next I was a full salaried CIA operative, following a training period at Langley conducted by the FBI. This was the most agonising three weeks of my life, waiting for my security clearance. But finally it came through. Once again we were all congratulated by its head, Edgar Hoover. It was like being back in Beria's office fifteen years earlier. Another short man exuding evil.

"All this allowed me to set up a home with a new wife and a supply fuel depot in Babylon in New York State. Once again Sylvia would have to wait for my retirement, for which I had plans. I continued to pass the gossip to my KGB handler, though to tell you the truth I was just telling him what I had read in the papers. Unfortunately the FBI got wind of this from a Soviet double agent, probably Oleg Penkovsky, and I was arrested handing some pap to a man from the Russian consulate.

"Anyway they deceived me. I pleaded guilty on the understanding that I was a Russian spy who would be the subject of an exchange for Gary Powers. At the last moment they announced that I was actually an American and therefore a traitor. And here I am doing thirty-five years."

Gary Powers was a CIA pilot whose spyplane had been shot down over the Soviet Union and who was jailed there for espionage. He was eventually released in a spy swap for a KGB colonel.

Greg was outraged by his treatment and was already learned in the law. He even got a legal qualification in prison. He was consulted by everyone about their appeals and claimed to have saved 150 years of imprisonment for his flock. I was one of them. With his advice I got two years cut from my sentence. He was much loved by all, including Kantzler and the screws, who knew his story and accepted he had been cheated. If Kantzler had known the brilliant mimic that Greg was and how he creased the wing up with his impersonations, he might not have had such a high regard for him.

He loved to make trouble for the authorities and then appear to fix them. Once he needed a rivet to fix his watch and found himself working the interfed supply network, which employed early IT technology which Gregor understood. He cheerfully logged an order for a whole ten tons of these rivets, which duly arrived and had to be buried out of sight to save the governor's face. Later Gregor fixed the problem and had them reassigned.

Payment for his advice and fixing was often in gifts of tasty food. Once he was given a magnificent piece of rump, but faced the problem of how to cook it. Well, he was an engineer and had access to the prison boiler room. He rigged up a tin oven there and somehow directed a water overflow outlet, raised by him to be very hot, so that it sluiced over the oven without getting inside it or causing a flood. During the time it took us to watch *The Gang That Couldn't Shoot Straight* in the cinema, this slab of fillet slow roasted to a T and four of us had a post-show feast. We also celebrated the shame of the Italian contingent, who had irritated us with a show of strutting after we had watched *The Godfather* the previous week.

Greg was released after me in another prisoner exchange with the Communists and returned to Sylvia in East Berlin. I called on him there later when I was trying my hand at running furniture from Eastern Europe to the UK, and nagged him about his autobiography, which he had promised me. He seemed rather broken and faked a burglary, I think, as an excuse for having done nothing despite his promises. It may be that he was still beholden to his old KGB comrades and feared to tell his story.

Another surprising encounter was with Mike Griffin. He too was a sailor and he, too, had sailed the Atlantic, in his case to Miami, with a large load of cannabis, albeit from the Lebanon. The first time, he made so much money that he and his brother John both bought Ferraris in Miami and lived a jet-set life for six months, before shipping the bling back to Europe. Then he did it again. Something went wrong and they started sinking. They limped into some kind of harbour, ran the boat onto the ground, and after one thing and another, the shipment was found. We vowed to meet up after our release.

Every summer I was there, my family came to visit. They would hole up in a motel in Lewisburg, spend time at the leisure centre and the shopping malls and come to see me in the visitors' centre, either all of them together or Sue alone, for two or three hours at a time, or sometimes all day. Sue was getting by. She had escaped the fallout of the Castelnau bust with a £500 fine for unlawful possession, though really she should never have been charged. Most of the money Harvey had got back to England was now heavily leveraged by my cousin Harry Scott Stokes on gold in Tokyo, where he was working for the *Financial Times* writing a biography of the Rothschilds. It was quite clear that the children were disappointed when my sentence was reduced to six years and cheerful when they heard my first parole application had been rejected: nothing in England could make up for the soda fountains and drug stores of rural America. Its prosperity, its huge fridges and cars, and TV all night were still astounding to Europeans and a delight to children.

I did get parole and in the summer of 1974 I was transferred by Immigration with twelve others to Pittsburgh Holding. It was a dreadful place where we slept two to a bunk in our cells, despite many being empty. People screamed all night because nothing is more to be avoided for most deportees than their return from the Land of the Free. I made a huge fuss, and when they looked up my story I became a bit of a novelty *cause célèbre* – someone who was actually looking forward to going home! So I was taken shopping at Sears by the guards and even given a joint to while away the afternoon and asked for my autograph. Finally I was flown to New York, where I spent another ten days in a similar facility. Some of the deportees there were hobbled with two-kilo, lead leg shackles to discourage them from running for it before being put on their flights. Then I was driven to Kennedy, marched across the tarmac, and handed over to a Pan Am air hostess. My passport was returned. For a few hours I was free.

At Heathrow, I emerged into arrivals to see my family there to welcome me. But so were the police. They had not forgotten me.

A MONTH LATER, in September 1974, I was at the Old Bailey, being reminded by prosecutor John Matthews of the facts of my activities with Bob Palacios, Keith and the others four years earlier. The Press lapped it up, making much of my artistic background and peripheral connections to Princess Margaret. "'Margaret's Set' sculptor jailed," was the headline in the *Daily Mail*, while "18 months for 'Snowdon Set' drug smuggler" was the *Telegraph*'s version. The *Express* went for a heavy-handed play on my sculpting background with "Downfall of a chiselling drug-runner". Very droll. I pleaded guilty – I could hardly do otherwise – and Judge Abdela took into account the three years I had served in America, handing down a comparatively lenient eighteen months. Then I was packed off to HMP Northeye, near Bexhill. I might have gone to the open prison at Ford if it were not for the fact that Detective Sergeant Nobby Pilcher, who had come to my door in October 1970, was there himself, serving a prison sentence for faking evidence after another of his drug sweeps.

So I was back in England. Back to the dismal world of my national service: Nissen huts, eight to a dormitory, military discipline, roll-calls at inconvenient times during the best TV shows, a two-ounce of rolling baccy chess prize immediately confiscated because you "are not allowed, Morland, prisoner two-one-eight, as you well know, to carry more than one ounce at any time on Her Majesty's premises".

Visiting compared unfavourably with Lewisburg. There were endless VOs, or visitor orders, more paperwork and interminable waiting, all for an hour and a half once a fortnight. The work was depressing too, packing and attaching some medallion concoction to Tommy Cooper perfumes, but we did have dreary little vegetable patches that we worked on half-heartedly and association was unrestricted outside work hours.

After nine months, I was released. Sue met me and we went to the best hotel in Littlehampton. You can imagine: the build-up, the rubber steak supper in the empty dining room, weird corking ceremonies over Spanish vinegar, the waiters hovering for you to finish, the disappointment of freedom. And then this as a killer of conjugal rights: "Harry's sorry. The market's gone against gold. It's all lost. In fact you owe him."

10

Back to Work

THE BASEMENT AT Castelnau was still my studio, although the children had invaded it in my absence. I did what work I could find down there. When the phone rang, I was studying some rushes that Keith had filmed on the canal. Keith had a film business called Mobius, with a studio in Paddington. Corporate training films, and yoga, and cooking and lifestyle, were the coming things, though this did lead to something more interesting. David Grant and David Sullivan were taking "glamour" away from its 1950s meaning and decisively towards porn, whilst the titillating likes of Raymond's Revue Bar and *Men Only* were passing themselves off as cultural. Jay Murdle, who had helped out in my big bust in London by rescuing some cannabis from a car not spotted by the police, was by now a very professional special effects photographer, and he worked for all these new arrivals in the nudity business.

And British currency had been decimalised. I needed time to adapt.

Then came the phone call. It was Mike Griffin, who had just got back from Lewisburg Penitentiary.

"Mike! Where are you?"

We talked awhile about the folk back in prison. Gregor was still king on our wing. There had been a small riot with the National Guard called out. Things like that.

"What are you doing?" he asked.

"I've been converting a warehouse in Narrow Street. Wapping. On the Thames"

"Fuck. Who'd want to live there?"

"Andy Garnett. You're out of touch." I reprimanded him. "It's cool. He can wave to Lord Snowdon across the river. His bed is on a plinth so he can see the shipping on the Thames. Wapping great room," I joked. We laughed.

"Sounds a bit lonely."

"Not at all. Philip Pound and Dan Farson have places there. And the scoff at the Grapes is good. Dan has a motorboat to go to work in."

In those days everyone knew of Dan Farson, a writer and broadcaster with a taste for the seamy side of life. He'd been in on the start-up of ITV, and had shown pictures of naked girls onscreen for the first time. He also wrote books about London Docklands including, needless to say, one about Jack the Ripper, and had a pub somewhere thereabouts. The boat bit was not strictly true. A week earlier I had watched in horror as a loaded barge settled on the falling tide on the stern of Dan's James Bond-style motorboat and crushed it.

"Who are they?"

"Designer-type people."

"That's right. I haven't forgotten you're into sculpture and things. Good place to land some dope?" he joked. I laughed a little falsely.

"No good at all. They closed the docks to shipping while we were away. But it's dead quiet. What about you. What are you doing?"

"I'm on a Baltic trader in the Hook of Holland. Come and join us. We're taking it to Littlehampton."

That would certainly beat sitting round the house. I did not feel at home at all. Sue ran the house her way, she was working as a teacher, and my reappearance was not going to change things, not unless I earned some money.

I had tried. I'd even gone down to Glastonbury, where those good Quakers at Clarks shoes had invited me to apply to work at an arts centre their welfare people had. This might rehabilitate me, was the idea. The Morlands were perfectly friendly but there was an awkwardness. I was the black sheep in the sheepskin factory. "A natural," was my comment about myself when explaining my recent past, a term not lost on them, as it was the trade description of a sheepskin with black hairs in it and therefore defective.

Mike and his brother Jake were working and living in Littlehampton, on the Sussex coast. I took the Harwich ferry over to Holland to join them, and arrived the next morning. I was really pleased to see Mike again, who introduced me to Jake. I was not so pleased by his boat. It was in a very poor state. No life rails, no masts, piles of sawn teak lying on the deck, no radio, no lights.

We stayed up late that night talking and got on to wondering what to do next. We were anxious to avoid crime but would have liked to do something with boats.

Eventually we hit on the idea of my favourite occupation, diving. We had found a suitable boat to take to the Red Sea and decided tourists would pay us big bucks to go diving and harpooning. Maybe we'd run a diving school in tandem. Jacques Cousteau had made scuba diving fashionable and it was a boom industry, in which training was becoming more and more compulsory.

Mike had found this Baltic trader 96, the *Zeba*, cheap and had moved it from Denmark to Holland. Now it was to move to

Littlehampton. Off we set. It broke down in mid-Channel. It had a two-stroke, air-cooled diesel with a vast flywheel to enable one to start it. The shuddering when it started up forced Sherstin, his wife, to put on a bra. Jake was a good mechanic and eventually fixed it but in the meantime we had no power and we wallowed in the busiest shipping lane anywhere, in total darkness, near the Sangatte lighthouse. Luckily we had a car on board, so I did a three-point turn on deck – actually more like a twenty-point turn – so that it was pointing forward. We idled the engine and put the headlights on full beam. At least we could see ahead and be seen.

We had bought a huge amount of duty free booze and because we were good boys now we declared this in Littlehampton, but said we were going to move it all off to the Red Sea in due course. Britain being a maritime nation with a big empire, there was provision for this: the booze was Customs-sealed in a forward locker and once a week the Littlehampton representative would appear from somewhere up the River Arun in his little cutter, board us and inspect the seal, allowing a rations issue of two whiskies and a carton of fags per week, followed by resealing. That the locker also opened from the top didn't seem to bother him. We played along and replaced bottles of whisky that had been drunk with cold tea. His expertise was seals, not whisky colouring. Mike told me they also sent a diver to inspect the undersides: they clearly had suspicions about what Mike and I were up to.

It took us a while to refurbish the *Zeba*, in fact the best part of a year. This we did in Hillyards yard in Littlehampton. Hillyards made boats for sailors who loved boats: no glass-fibre resin for them, but pine planks on oak frames and minimal, galvanised-only metal. The uppers were mahogany and Hillyards' signature was a canoe stern. They were also agents for the sale and re-sale of secondhand boats, which they refurbished for the market. It was a really nice yard where you could work on your boat and use their services as and when you needed them. The Griffin brothers lived aboard the *Zeba*. I was made very welcome and often went for a week at a time, contributing carpentry to the refit.

The rebuild included replacing the absurd diesel with the Rolls-Royce of marine engines, a brand new Gardiner. The keelson was cracked and a replacement thirty-five-foot length of oak came with the boat for substitution. Also masts had to be made. It took a long time. One of my most pleasurable experiences was working with master shipwrights in the mast shop. There we glued a lorry-load of two-inch, twelve-foot pine planks in overlapping layers, making up an eighty-foot length held by G-clamps from all the yards in the area. Now we had a stepped square which needed to be carefully power-planed to the final rounded and tapering shape of masts. Then the booms, and finally the great day came. The crane was mobilised and the masts stepped into the *Zeba*. This great restoration project had reached fruition. It was ready for its maiden journey from the Hillyard yard to the Channel Islands to replenish the Customs stock, and back.

Then Mike and John had a fall-out over the future use of the boat and it was sold.

I was flat broke and in no position to restart as a smuggler except at the bottom. The bottom is the mundane need to carry large sums of money for others to and fro. Travel to the Middle East was particularly hard work for currency smugglers because of terrorism there, just as big a deal then as it is now. Lebanon had sunk into civil war.

The "raw material" of a money courier – the cash proceeds from sales within the UK – always seemed to contain a lot of Scottish notes. The only virtue of Scottish currency was that some of their banks issued £50 notes whilst English banks were confined to £20 notes, so more money took up less space. Otherwise they were about as recognised abroad as roubles, which is to say, hardly at all. Dealers within England liked to dump them on suckers like me who had the job of moving them abroad. This involved a thankless tour of bureaux de change to change them into used English notes, which I then had to take to banks such as Allied Irish to turn into packs of new English. For all this there were charges.

My line was that I was an antiques dealer going to cash-only auctions. I burnished my credentials at the Allied Irish by pointing out a genuine Adam fireplace at their sumptuous offices in Bruton Street. I got quite good at the job but it was hard work. Mike Griffin was at Castelnau one day when I was just back from the bank with £50,000 stacked in what look like bread loaves, and he was impressed. The banks had been cautious about me before; now I was gaining in credibility.

For whom was I doing this? Well, whilst I had been in prison Keith Wilkinson had resumed operations with Khaled, who had only spent a year in prison in Rome and was now working with John McDonald, Charlie Radcliffe and Peter Jordan. I was a bit of a pariah at this time, associated with the disastrous end of the Sixties. As a result I was not privy to the transactions for which I was to be their gopher.

Khaled had moved his base of operations to Damascus in Syria because of the civil war in Lebanon. He needed to be paid there. I was a good candidate because I knew him and was tasked to move a whole half million in sterling to Damascus for the Radcliffe-McDonald team. This was going to take five different trips.

In the meantime, I sorted a suitcase of assorted currencies into twelve wine boxes, by denomination and by bank, Queen's head uppermost for their counting machines. There followed a week of the Scottish-to-English routine described above to turn them into packs of new notes suitable for suitcase linings. I learnt the hard way on the first run, when they gave me a case of soft toys packed with unsorted money, including Scottish. This gave Khaled and me major headaches, given the full searches all passengers on MEA and Syrian Airlines, departing to and arriving in Damascus, were subject to, something I had not foreseen. Khaled and I then had to present this vast assortment of currency to a shoe shop in the souk in Damascus, and watched as they re-sorted them into shoeboxes stacked at the back. What happened if you went in asking for shoes, I don't know.

It was hard work, mitigated by the good humour of a city bank one of whose directors, an American, watched the transaction in amazement when he came across a Clydesdale £5 note with a picture of a slave in chains.

"Hey, Francis. I'll keep that for myself. They won't believe this back home."

As for all this cash, all he could say was, "Hell, its good to be reminded what banking's all about. I haven't touched cash in years."

I'd done my good deed for banking.

So I was miffed when, having done this hard and risky legwork, Charlie and John declined to pay me. They seemed to think the two per cent that Khaled had paid me was all that was due; it wasn't they, too, who owed me two per cent. And what I did get had anyway to be shared with Keith, who had subcontracted the task. This was doubly annoying as I was the one who had originally found and cultivated Khaled. My relationship with John and Charlie did not recover from this, and a slight rift opened up with Tina, now Charlie's wife, who had been such a good friend of our family. I dare say they say I am stubborn and mulish about small things.

Then I heard again from Khaled, who was back living in Beirut. He wanted to talk to me about something and offered me an MEA ticket to visit him there. He lived in a sumptuous apartment full of gilded Lebanese Quinze furniture and pictures of naked, dusky maidens. I met lots of his friends, went to many kebab feasts and was introduced to girls who wore high-heeled shoes and shiny lipstick. No way were they interested in coming diving with me, and my jet-set small talk failed me. Pity.

One day he took me to meet a Palestinian family in the Bekaa Valley. They appeared to be the owners of a large vineyard and wine press, all surprisingly modern and high tech. Later Sarwar, the proprietor, drove me and Khaled up into the hills above the valley, along a dirt road among the pines and out onto a cultivated plateau. I recognised immediately what was growing there: my old friend *cannabis sativa*.

So this was the home of Lebanese Gold.

WE DRANK tea at a dilapidated farmhouse and watched the crop being cut and tied into sheaths, sacked and carried, ten to a donkey, to a threshing shed nearby. Here was the problem: the arrival of hundreds of thousands of Palestinian refugees in southern Lebanon had set off a simmering civil war between them, Hizbollah here in Bekaa and the Christian-dominated government in Beirut. I had actually heard gunfire and explosions in Beirut at night. The old way of smuggling cannabis out of the country on MEA flights was no longer so viable. It would have to be shipped out from a beach, out of sight of the Israelis who patrolled the coast. There had been a long hiatus. The product was accumulating in barns unsold and needed to be shifted. It was never going to be cheaper, the troubles would end soon. Was it right that I was just the man for such a job?

It seems I had a reputation. I was flattered. Go for it. I'd sold our house in Birkirkara, in Malta, that summer as the children were now teenagers. So I had a little cash to invest. That night we stayed in a hotel in Baalbec and the next day Khaled drove me in his Chevrolet over the line of mountains that is the backbone of Lebanon and down to the coast. There he showed me a headland near Jounieh that overlooked a beach he thought suitable. It offered an expansive view out to sea and you could make out shipping up to twenty miles away. Below was a sheltered beach with very few buildings nearby, which was rare given that most of Lebanese life was on this coastline.

Back in Beirut that night, I rang the Griffins and explained the proposition. Half a ton could be delivered by lorry to the beach near Jounieh. Khaled would put up a third of the money, the three of us another third and the remainder was on credit. The big money was to get it to America but we were too well known there. It would have to be Canada, and as I was putting a bit more into our third than they were, it wouldn't be me on the boat. They liked the idea. That would set us up nicely for our business venture in the Red Sea, by which time the *Zeba* would be ready. As for a boat, the easiest thing would be to buy one in Athens, which was no great distance. We could be ready to go in weeks.

I went to Athens to meet Mike, who had found a forty-two-foot Hillyard. It had been so long in Piraeus and its undersides were so fouled that it housed the biggest octopus I've seen in a long history of diving. Mike wanted to take it to Malta and slip it, but I persuaded him we needed to strike while the iron was hot. So Mike set to work making the boat seaworthy, told Sherstin, his girlfriend, to join him and I went back to Beirut, though not before going into Piraeus to buy a ship-to-shore radio for the boat and two handheld receiver-transmitters to go with it. They were beginning to come in in1976 and were just about affordable for the leisure yachtsman, though they were very limited and I moved later to the Citizen Band radios used by lorry drivers, which were cheaper, more reliable and had a longer range. They were to prove invaluable in due course. Meanwhile I had to fly out our money.

I persuaded Khaled to get a fishing boat in Jounieh to go out to meet Mike and Sherstin with the dope, while I watched the whole scene – the arrival of the Hillyard, the departure of the fishing boat, the meeting of the two boats and the trans-shipment – through a pair of binoculars from the same headland I had visited with Khaled a few months earlier. All the while we spoke to each other over Channel 16, which was a bit risky as it was a public, twenty-five-watt channel. As soon as the deed was done, I told my gopher, Jim, who was with Khaled in Jounieh, to take him to our hire car and hand over the balance of the money. Jim and I flew out that night. I don't think MEA flew much longer after that, as the civil war gradually engulfed the whole of that once serenely wonderful country for the next five or six years.

Jake Griffin was meant to have gone to Gibraltar, hired a boat and sailed out to replenish Mike as he and Sherstin passed through on their way to Canada. He did all that but three weeks too late and missed them; he had been delayed by some acting part he had in a film. So Mike and Sherstin had to cross the Atlantic on starvation rations. That may have been one of the reasons the brothers fell out.

They managed to get to Sable Island, off Nova Scotia, where they buried the load just as I had at Fallen Jerusalem, checking in to Halifax to recover. There they got hold of Jake, who was still in Gibraltar, and he came out to join them. They sailed back to Sable Island and collected the load while Sherstin remained in Halifax, then sailed to Port Hawkesbury, where Jake was eventually left behind to do the business. Sherstin joined Mike again after that.

However, they were rattled by an unexpected visit from the Mounties, and left Canada in a hurry, again with inadequate provisions, for Littlehampton. This time they hit a three-day storm and were badly thrown around. The autopilot failed and the helm proved too heavy for Sherstin. She was badly shaken and never went to sea again. Jake, however, was able to deliver to buyers in Montreal and Quebec as and when they could be found.

Meanwhile I went back to Malta and bought *Trimala*, a trimaran whose special feature was that the outrider floats could be retracted. This meant that she was suitable for fast ocean-going sailing but could also, with floats retracted, negotiate the European canal system. Yet another advantage was that she could be sailed right up onto a beach. I took her first to Ibiza to deliver Pauline Davies, a family friend at the time who had helped me make *Trimala* seaworthy, to Keith and Jean in Ibiza. Then I went into Marseilles and through the canals of France, using a road map to Le Havre and back to Littlehampton.

This was not without incident. It was very cold, and near Chaumont, waiting for the locks to reopen next day, I cooked chicken on my charcoal grill. It was so cold that I took the grill into the saloon to warm it before going to sleep. I fell asleep and awoke choking and vomiting, with a headache I thought would kill me. This was my introduction to carbon monoxide poisoning which is a regular killer of sailors.

Back in Littlehampton, we had quite a fleet: the *Zeba*, the *Trimala* and the Hillyard. Life was good again.

Jake had stored all the money we had made in a safe deposit box. He and I went to Toronto to get the box and took it to a room at the Holiday Inn there to count its contents. There was $600,000. Two young men from a Swiss bank, on the instruction of Banque de Rives in Geneva, came to collect the cash from me. No receipt was given: it would not be necessary, they were kind enough to inform me. I had opened an account with them on the grounds that when Mike had been busted in Florida, they had on their own initiative cleared his dollar account in New York and remitted the sums there to a bank account in Geneva. That was our kind of bank.

A Quaker restraint meant that I was never showy, even when I had money. When I went with Mike to Geneva to collect our money, I took my normal RAF grip whilst he had to have Gucci luggage to take into the bank's leathery ambience overlooking the lake.

I guess memoirs of drug runners generally include Ferraris, five-star hotels, hookers and drug-fuelled partying. That all faintly disgusted me. I can confess to only one real extravagance in life: my boat *Katanavik* some ten years later.

Now I could put an extension on Castelnau and get an updated Citroen.

11

Sailor Ted

LEE, MY OLDEST, was sixteen, Joyce fourteen. Sue was a respectable teacher of neighbourhood English to immigrants, who loved her work. Her job and the income from renting out the flat upstairs at Castelnau meant she did not completely rely on me. I was glad of that. My friends now were people who liked sailing rather than people who liked art. Pop art had left me cold and I no longer saw my old St Martin's crowd, who had largely adapted to teaching. And of course some didn't want to be seen consorting with a convicted drug smuggler. Nigel Henderson remained my closest friend. Sue and I had become semi-detached, but Malta and a family sail on *Trimala*, along the same route as I had first brought her to Littlehampton, re-cemented the family as a unit. And the bursts of money that my boat projects from time to time injected did much to keep her sweet and tolerant. We would get by.

One of Sue's tenants was a chap called Philip Sparrowhawk. By one of those weird coincidences that beset one in life, we were once in his flat checking his provenance. He paid us in wads with a fold-over, and he had a lot of visitors. His girlfriend Cindy always went out in taxis. In his room was a Bangkok telephone directory and the

ABC of international airline timetables. Seemed familiar, this. On the other hand, he had an invoice book that sort of satisfied us.

Then one day he knocked on my door and invited me up. He had learnt that I had been a drug dealer in my time. Well of course, so was he. Howard Marks, for whom he was working, knew my name. Marks was at the time a kind of non-person. The Press had it that he had been kidnapped by the Mafia, or KGB, or somebody, to stop him revealing something at a trial he was meant to have faced. In fact he had gone on the run to Italy, until life in campsites drove him mad. Then he simply came back to England and carried on as though the world was his oyster. Which I suppose it was, now that I have read his book. I've also since learnt that my son Lee used to go upstairs and play liar dice with him in the flat.

Anyway, Philip and I levelled with each other, and although he trusted me we agreed it was essential he move out. It took a week or two for him to find a new place, and in the meantime we talked. He told me a typical tale of the trade. He had picked up a consignment in a crate coming into Heathrow. Stopping on the way back in his car at some traffic lights, he took the opportunity to look into the crate, because he had already smelt a rat. His fears were confirmed. There was a kilo in there but the rest was bricks, most likely meaning that HM Customs or the police were onto him and had removed and substituted the drugs. He guessed he must also have a tail. So he went to my old alma mater, St Martin's School of Art, in Charing Cross Road, where he knew you could walk in one side and out the other, and abandoned the car outside. It was a close escape. I also introduced Philip to Uncle Eddie, my personal supplier. They did some business, I gathered.

It was about this time that I realised that Howard Marks was a kind of overlord of a business that had become huge during my absence, and that he had sucked people like Charlie Radcliffe, Peter Jordan and John McDonald into his orbit. My return to the business via smuggling currency for them to Damascus was doubtless ultimately under Howard's umbrella. If I had once been the biggest single figure in the cannabis game, he had now taken that mantle, and in a far more purposeful and organised fashion. Good luck to him.

A few months later, the police came for Philip and Howard, but too late. The birds had flown. For a while the law hoped that though they had missed one or two targets, they had bagged another in me, and we were kept under surveillance. Nevertheless this period of prosperity continued for a while, and two further projects with the Griffins ensued, one of which ended badly. But they were not my only partners.

I had sailed *Trimala* back from Littlehampton to the Mediterranean in the autumn of our first Lebanon-to-Canada run because no-one wanted to cross the Altantic in winter and the Griffins were reluctant to smuggle to local waters, since they imagined they were on the UK Customs radar. I was not so bothered. I knew the French canal system pretty well by now and *Trimala* was part of family life, the nearest substitute to the farmhouse in Malta. Lee and Joyce both loved these canal trips and Joyce loved Ibiza. Her close friend was Liza, Keith and Jean's daughter. So Ibiza, where Keith had a flat near the old town, was a natural destination. The children hung out in Ibiza Old Town and went clubbing in the evenings. It's a great place for the young. There's a fortified hilltop that looks down on the harbour, and inside and all around its skirts are narrow, cobbled streets of two-storey, white-painted houses, most of these streets being closed to traffic. General Franco was still in charge in Spain but hippy hedonism and a thriving sailing community meant that there were full shops, seafood galore and an atmosphere of endless, affordable holiday.

I pondered projects with Keith whilst Jean and Sue cooked up paella storms and barbecues, which drew in every local expat and his wife. If the weather was nice we took picnics out on the *Trimala* and pottered round the prettier coves of nearby Formentera, or even made excursions to Valencia, which had a magnificent sandstone yacht club that welcomed all yachtsmen to marvellous food in its grand dining rooms. For some reason Franco had hugely favoured the sailing world, although in those days the surrounding towns and countryside were still shockingly poor.

I spent a lot of time in the marina mucking about on *Trimala*, devising better boarding ramps, installing sound systems, mending water heaters and so on. One day I was doing this kind of thing when Keith came along the pontoon, accompanied by a tall, skinny man in his fifties with a mass of thick curly hair beginning to turn white. He wore long canvas shorts of the kind hot-weather Tommies in Aden would have worn in the Fifties, and a shabby kind of painter's smock. He had the leathery, suntanned face familiar from yachting marinas the world over. You could see he lived on and for the sea.

"This guy knew Philby," Keith opened. Kim Philby had defected to the Soviet Union in 1963 and was still there, having been revealed as a member of the traitorous Cambridge Five ring of spies.

"He wasn't a friend," said the stranger shyly. "I only did him some boating favours."

"He's been telling me about high jinks in the Adriatic," Keith rattled on. He could be most embarrassing.

"There's some cable cover tubing on the dump," said Keith's friend, "which makes perfect anti-chafing tubes for the mooring ropes. The sections have collars." He was commenting on my seamanship, which interested him much more.

"Are you going to introduce us?" I said, wiping my hands and standing up.

"Ted Falcon-Barker," he said simply. "I'm on the *Moon River*, there." He pointed to a sloop further down the pontoon, which I had already noticed. Ninety per cent of boats in marinas never go to sea. Some are kept immaculate; some are permanently for sale, their teak decks green with verdigris and their hulls with fouling, reeking of abandonment and disappointed dreams. Ted's boat fell into a separate category: the permanently working home of a lonesome sailor, worn with work not abandonment; endlessly patched but robustly seaworthy.

We took him back to lunch with us, and although he was shy and reticent we gradually learnt about his strange life and times. His voice sounded public school English.

"Actually I'm Australian, really. And a bit French. My mother was French and we lived in Antibes before the War."

Keith's mother-in-law, Mimi, had joined us. She had a flat nearby, already knew Ted well and was a drinking buddy. It was she who had introduced him to Keith. She was relentless at trying to get shy people to open up.

"But you speak English like a gent, like our Francis here," she prodded.

"My father was English and I did spend five years at a boarding school in England. But then I went to Australia."

"Like, your parents emigrated?"

"No. I ran away from school."

"To Australia?"

We all looked at him, as it began to dawn on us that this was a real curiosity of a man. But we couldn't get much more out of him that day. He preferred to talk boats. He was no bragger and it took a while to piece his life story together in our minds.

He proposed a flotilla excursion to the other side of Ibiza, where Pat and Mike, a couple I knew, had a large finca and pool. We thought Tina and Charlie Radcliffe were there, maybe even Harvey Bramham, although that gang were a bit sniffy towards us, thinking Keith and I were flaky. We agreed to go, and it was the beginning of an important friendship.

So off we set one spring day, Keith with Ted leading the way, me with Joyce and Sue and Lee as help. Little by little we gradually gathered Ted's strange life story. He had been living on one boat or another since 1965 and was an expert diver. He had explored a buried Roman ship, lived with sharks in the Red Sea and written many books about treasure and ship finds and other underwater archaeology. These books had sold quite well but he was always hard up, as his patched-up boat and gypsy-like interior lifestyle made clear.

At the finca, Keith and I rolled up joints and we all got merrily stoned, including Ted, who had never smoked dope before. Nor did I ever see him smoke again. Eventually he guessed exactly what our game had been, while we got to know more about him.

He had run away from school at the age of fifteen, got to Australia and joined the army at sixteen as war broke out. This got him back to England, where he was co-opted into the Intelligence Corps and sent to the Middle East. He'd been in Crete at the time of the German invasion but still found time to get to Santorini and take his first peek at the ruins of Thera, parts of which had sunk into the sea. For a long time he seemed to have been a spy in Damascus, and learnt more about archaeology. He was fascinated by Roman remains.

Next he was parachuted behind Japanese lines in New Guinea on some kind of insurgency work, which he would not be drawn on. He was much prouder of a club he had opened for Australians in London after the War. Somewhere along the line he had also joined the Communist Party – to spy on it – become a good photographer and learnt to fly. It seemed clear to us that he had joined MI6 but he would never admit it and changed the subject when we tried to pump him about Philby. He seemed to regret ever mentioning this to Keith. Keith had only got him onto the subject because he had found a newspaper account of Philby's unmasking and escape to the Soviet Union on board Ted's boat, heavily underlined and annotated. On another occasion, when proposing a smuggling route, Ted told me he knew people in Albania.. No one in those days knew the first thing about Albania; he had actually been there.

We did a number of excursions together that spring. He showed me oyster beds off Formentera and we had a barbecue feast on the beach. Keith, the actress Maria Aitken, another grandee of the times called Nathan de Silva, and countless children joined us with a huge hake and a very good time was had by all. Actually too good a time: Keith, Jane and I had been having supper in the Old Town and walked home through the market, where I had gathered up an abandoned sack of lemons suitable for lemonade, but had added a hefty dose of vodka to stop it fermenting, in accordance with good naval practice. At our picnic the children got very boisterous and giggly and started falling about; they had been swimming out to *Trimala* and helping themselves to citron presses.

Another time I was walking through the Ibiza Old Town with some shopping bags when I saw Ted sitting outside the Zoo café, in company with an older-looking man. Ted beckoned me over and I joined them drinking hot cocoa. His companion had a big sombrero, a moustache, dark glasses and a collar-up coat, and seemed to shiver a lot, occasionally interjecting in the conversation with pre-War expressions: "Oh, I say", "Crikey", "That must have been a bit sticky", "What a cad", and so on.

At one point Ted said, "Francis comes from the family that make the Morland driving coat."

"Oh, I say. I've got a lot of those. You chaps are always sending me them compliments of the house."

"Really?" I said. That didn't sound like Morlands.

"Yes, yes. You chaps keep hoping I'll wear them in the flicks."

Finally I realised it was the marvellous Terry-Thomas, with that gap in his front teeth, the bounder who made all those Ealing comedies go with such a zing.

"I'm in bloody awful health, to tell you the truth," he said. "Might have to go back to the good lady I've been such a rotter to."

She apparently lived on Majorca, not far away. But Ted was having none of it:

"You stay right here. You've got plenty of friends to look after you."

"Thing is, I'm a bit strapped for money," he said. "If you lot needed any sailing done for you, I'd be very willing to help out. Do you know what I mean?"

I did.

IN IBIZA ONE day, Ted came on board the *Trimala* as I was preparing it for a run, and made some tea for me.

"The thing is, I've lounged about the place a bit too long," he said. "And I've got a bit strapped for cash. People are jolly nice to me but it's time I bought a few drinks."

I knew what he was talking about.

"Okay, Ted. You can go to Morocco for me. I'll arrange for a hundred kilos of cannabis to be delivered to the beach and you can take it to England, where I'll pick it up."

I never thought he'd agree, but two days later he came back and shook hands with me. And so I acquired one of the best, most reliable, and most self-sufficient of sailors for my schemes. If they had all been like Ted, I wouldn't be where I am today, one of the most oft-convicted cannabis smugglers in UK history.

What we did first was go over together to Al Hoceima in convoy. I took him up to Ketama and introduced him to Mohammed. We then returned to Al Hoceima and put back to sea. The weather was perfect. I ran *Trimala* up onto the beach at Pointe des Pêcheurs, loaded up, the muleteers pushed me back into the water and I met Ted ten miles offshore. On a flat, moonlit night, we transferred the load onto *Moon River*, and he was off. I left *Trimala* in Gibraltar and returned to England by air to await his arrival. I still had my ship-to-shore handhelds. He was to land the load on Skipper Island, in my childhood dreamscape of Hanford Water.

Actually, when the day came I had an unbreakable appointment at the doctor's and so sent Lee, then in his late teens, to go to meet him. I arrived the next day and Lee, who had stayed overnight and been watching the island through binoculars from Landermere, reported that there had been three sloops that fitted *Moon River*'s description there. Despite pelting them with mud from the island, he could raise no response.

Then I got a call from Nigel Henderson's phone. Ted had actually gone to the King's Head and made friends with Nigel; he was so resourceful. He was anchored out of sight off Skipper Island and had not yet reported to Customs. He now lifted anchor and arrived on the high tide, just as it was getting dark at the wharf. Lee and I unloaded quickly and sent him back to Skipper Island to the anchorage. It was a short walk for us to the nearest place to park a car and we trudged to and fro carrying fishing gear to disguise our purpose. I did slightly dread meeting Nigel and having to improvise a story to explain the weight of our luggage. I have no doubt he'd have guessed the truth whatever I had said, given the coverage there had been of my troubles in 1971. We did meet, but he discreetly asked no questions and had us in for a drink. I learnt he had fallen out with Eduardo and their business there had closed.

A good example of Ted's resourcefulness came on another occasion when he made a pickup from Jounieh for us but broke down on his way back. He got himself to Athens, where he persuaded a merchantman to lift him on board and put him down at Harwich – with 200 kilos stashed. This had everything going for it: no Customs and all done in seven days.

Keith and I were not Ted's only employers. As he met more of the people in the trade, he proved popular for his resourcefulness and reliability. But it goes wrong even for the best of them. Much later he was forced to put into La Rochelle when his Baltic trader 80 started to sink in the Bay of Biscay, his keelson having split. He had a big load on board but put the boat into a dry dock and got repairs underway. He had retired to a nearby restaurant to wait when he heard a loud, drunken argument break out between what turned out to be policemen and Customs officers. His French being perfect, he gathered that the police thought the Customs idle and inefficient. He then heard it said, "And that boat there has never been searched." He hurried back and warned his crew to scatter but rather nobly remained with his ship as the inevitable unfolded. He was busted, serving time in the same French prison I would later get to know.

I was to have many more dealings with him, but Ted was not the only specialist sailor that Keith and I used. There was a whole community of boatmen for hire. Philip de Bere, an ex-artillery officer and a gentleman, was one. He learnt to sail with Special Boat Operations in the army. He had a bald pate and wore a toupee all the time. His wife was called Squirrel, and kept house for him in Mortlake in a very old, untouched Tudor pile. She was dotty, and committed herself from time to time for mental treatment. Philip too was paranoid, took too much cocaine, and once dumped a load of Keith and John McDonald's cannabis after some drunken shenanigans in the Med; he was doing the run on his own in his own boat and thought he was being followed by a NATO armada. Maybe the load was "fuming", or leaking vapours. He was wrong about NATO; it was merely on an exercise.

Anyway, *Trimala* had proved herself. She was ideal at getting the load away from the beaches and moving round the Mediterranean, but she was not fit for the Bay of Biscay, let alone America. Getting her to the UK or Sweden meant going through the canals, which was pleasant but slow. So that became the formula: the Griffins or Ted offshore, *Trimala* at the beach, and for a while all went well.

But all good things come to an end.

I had met someone we called Uncle Eddie. He was actually my local dealer if I ran short of a smoke in Barnes. He was a low-life Cockney, a small-time local dealer really, and different to the types we had used at the UK end hitherto; they tended to be art-schooly, alternative-culture types. Uncle Eddie, although white, had built up a clientele in the black street community in Wandsworth whose tastes were informed by ganja, or grass. He did not want resin; he wanted grass. I warned him that the grass we could get was Moroccan, which might not compare well with the Caribbean or Mexican weed his clients liked, but he would not listen. He smoked, considered himself to be discerning, and thought he could be crafty and selective with our grower if he had an introduction.

We compromised. I would meet him in Tangier and take him, along with his girlfriend and a rugged chap called David Paterson, up to Mohammed's. There he could negotiate the deal himself, get his girlfriend to try the dope, and pay for it. And that is what we did. My guys and I were just the carriers, with no other stake in the load whatever happened to it. David Paterson was ex-SAS and apparently laid out one of the muleteers on the way down for insubordination, which left them very impressed.

Meanwhile the Griffins had sailed the Hillyard down to Gibraltar and we cruised again, in convoy, to the beaches with which I was so familiar. I got to the sand and there was the usual scene: Mohammed's boys in their typical jumpy state, in bad need of the melon and cigarettes I had bought them. Although it was daylight, they rushed to load the great bags of grass onto *Trimala* before heading off into the bush. I hurried back out to sea.

The Griffin brothers were getting jumpy too on hearing of this daylight delivery, and a comic scene ensued where I was having to chase them out to sea while they kept sailing north to see whether I was being pursued by the forces of law and order.

I wasn't and the load was eventually transferred. Back it went on the Hillyard to the south coast of England. There, for some reason or another, they landed it on a beach and buried it in sand dunes, while we discussed how to get Eddie to pick it up. Eventually some team arrived to collect it and were greeted by the sight of a group of children with buckets and spades, digging and playing more or less where this consignment lay. They waited nervously on the beach all afternoon, watching this scene, before finally the family day on the beach ended. At last the bags of chaff were collected and brought to London.

Eddie said I would have to keep it until he'd sold it and I stupidly buried it under the terrace at the far end of the garden in Castelnau. Eventually Eddie came to collect, when I was out and about doing something in Putney. Lee, who had helped me bury it, was in the house alone when Uncle Eddie arrived to pick it up, and took him to the end of the garden, where Eddie disinterred half of it and left.

Predictably it was the usual low-grade grass you get from Morocco, little liked by the man who wanted to get high. So now Eddie was in trouble with his backers and his clientele. They all got angry with him and some sort of row rumbled on in Bristol and Notting Hill. Bad deals attract bad attention. For one thing the distribution tap remains open for far too long as the seller struggles to divest himself of his stock. For another, voices get raised and the ripples eventually get to the police. There is no sweeter revenge on a dealer who has conned you with a duff deal, when good money has been parted with, than to point the police in his direction. And so the news had got to an ambitious detective sergeant called Carol Bristow, who arrived shortly after I had got back home and went with the unerring eye of the well informed to the end of my garden. She had bagged Uncle Eddie no more than an hour earlier and he had thrown in the towel. I was done for again.

I wasn't the only one. Charlie Radcliffe and his crowd were tapped in a separate Customs operation while bringing a yacht with a ton-and-a-half of cannabis into an old smugglers' cove on the Welsh island of Anglesey. The operation rounded up not just Charlie but the yacht crew, the shore team and the London distributors as well. Charlie, who was portrayed in court as the "paymaster", got five years in prison.

Then the law caught up with Howard Marks too. He had been on the lam for four or five years, running the caper that he was enjoying some kind official protection because he "knew too much". Customs and Excise were not impressed. They watched Howard's London team, and ambushed a monster delivery of around fifteen tons of Colombian which had arrived in Scotland but had then been warehoused in three separate locations, including one stash in Essex. The evidence was exhaustive and damning, but this did not deter

Howard. Someone who had been with him at Oxford, and then went to work for MI5, had once asked Howard casually what he could tell them about a certain Jim McCann. McCann was a wild Provisional IRA man who controlled Shannon Airport in the Republic, which had been very useful to Howard, allowing him to fly cannabis into there, then use couriers to ferry it by car to the UK. From then on, Howard was an "MI5 agent", and he now claimed at trial that he had been lent to the Mexican Secret Service to encourage and penetrate international cannabis smuggling gangs. It was a ludicrous defence but just ludicrous enough to be believable.

Jeremy Hutchinson, the silk who represented him, was a showman too. He called an alleged Mexican secret agent with a Zapata moustache and a strong stage-Spanish accent to testify about the help Howard had given them. The man was not at liberty, of course, to identify himself or give any details of his work. The nation's gaiety and the jury's entertainment at this spectacle was tremendous and Howard was rewarded with an unlikely acquittal. I am not cut in that stamp, but until this day the "what is the prosecution concealing from us to do with secret intel about the accused" line has been the mark of many a drug trafficking defence.

In 1980, at Middlesex Crown Court, I had no such good fortune. Judge Suzanne Norwood gave me four years. It is typical of my luck in life that those who actually owned the drugs got lesser sentences. Then again, you might comment, I did appear to be incorrigibly drawn back to a trade I was supposed to have learnt my lesson about.

Ironically my demise was mitigated by the usual honeyed words. I was said to have huge tax bills following an assessment on my past criminal career, which was true, and that therefore I could not escape the treadmill of returning to the only way of earning I knew. This lay ill with the suggestion that I came from, and brought shame on, a wealthy family whose name was a household brand.

Hardly a year later, the third of the great Thatcher austerity, Morlands collapsed into bankruptcy and Glastonbury into mourning.

12

A Family Affair

HMP LEYHILL, Gloucestershire. What a long shadow the War had cast over the UK prison estate. Yet again I was housed in prefabricated huts, line after line of them banked up a hillside overlooking the heartland landscape of west England. Surrounding us was a small wall which had not been there when this had been a clap hospital for American soldiers thirty years earlier. But there was no barbed wire and the entrance was still the original swing pole across the road and a small guardhouse with a bus stop nearby. Leyhill was a Category 4, low-security prison, with some emphasis on rehabilitation of the not-too-wicked, such as we drug dealers. There were a lot of us types who, it was hoped, might reform the lifers.

Pretty good confusion had surrounded drugs policy up until 1976. Not much was known about the prevalence of drugs or their consequences that was not largely anecdotal. Every now and then, the Court of Appeal weighed in, purporting to take a judicious and well-informed approach to sentencing drug offenders. In fact they tended to give vent to *vox populi*. They pontificated in one celebrated case, *Regina v Aramah*, that the "Class A" drugs, heroin and cocaine, were the worst imaginable scourge on society, and they set suitably heavy sentences, whilst with cannabis a certain tolerance was acceptable.

Drug sentencing had been a bit of a lottery up until then, one judge with student children of his own handing out suspended sentences, his brother judge in the same courthouse claiming to be fighting the source of all crime in his area with mercilessly long terms. *Aramah* was an improvement in one sense in that at least the dealers knew where they stood.

As with the more recent hysteria about sex offending, the authorities liked to blame supply rather than demand – "trafficking" rather than consumption – so we cannis sailors were still subject to half a ton of bricks under *Aramah*. Still, four years in a Category 4 prison was not backbreaking. What I had not anticipated was the number of my fellow offenders. I had been the lone drug runner in my last two sentences. Now we were a whole community. The prisons were starting to act, to some degree, as employment exchanges where fellow craftsmen can be found all in one place, instead of randomly discovered in the marinas of the Mediterranean. I met several there whose fortunes I was later to follow from time to time in the papers.

There were about twenty of us to a hut in curtained-off cubicles in single dormitories. Each hut had four cells but they were for the lifers, not for us. Each hut also had a washroom complex, so that for long periods we were free to associate with each other in semi-autonomy. Later Gordon Goody, of Great Train Robbery infamy, would be brought to Castelnau by a girl we knew and he amused us with tales of Leyhill in the Sixties. He and his fellow train robbers drank whisky with the screws and subscribed to a manly disgust for drugs. But when they heard from the likes of us about six-figure sums recovered from mattresses, the attitude of our fellow villains changed.

There were no parades, only counts in the billets, and we ate in a communal refectory, helping ourselves from a servery and sitting with whoever we chose. So we got to know each other and formed into flocks of birds of a feather. You can guess who I spent my time with. A lot of it was with Peter Jordan, a fellow sailor who had worked with my old associates Charlie Radcliffe and John McDonald, and eventually for Howard Marks. Peter had lost his boat at his trial, just as I, in theory, had lost *Trimala*, although it was still in Gibraltar awaiting auction to pay the harbour dues. We fantasised about the ideal boat, the best sources, the best landing places and anchorages, and all the other things sailors talk about.

Unlike my previous incarceration, I was under no illusion but that I would return to my hard-learnt trade. It was the only way that bankrupts could remain at sea. Peter, on the other hand, intended to, and did, go straight. We both enjoyed the America's Cup, the world's top competition for twelve-metre yachts. In 1983, America and Australia battled it out in the most exciting contest for decades. We were rooting for Aussie Alan Bond to break the USA's 132-year hegemony in the event, and kept promising to willingly add weeks to our sentence if only he would win. He won. We owe the Prison Service at least another month if they want to claim it.

Peter and I shared a lot of memories. He too had loaded off the same beach near Jounieh that I had used with Mike Griffin, and his experiences echoed mine. You are told that the fishing boat will meet you three miles off, where you dutifully await him. Of course he's late and invariably lures you, for his own convenience, much closer to the beach than you would like. Why? Police jurisdiction rather than Customs? Quick escape to shore if things go wrong? Who knows. Peter had found himself, to his alarm, just 100 metres from the beach in the dark, transferring 100 kilos of cannabis. After a while he became aware of a crowd on the beach, apparently watching him. Gradually his eyes became used to the dark. People were sitting in serried ranks to watch him at work. Then it dawned on him. It was an outdoor cinema show on the beach, with the screen backing the sea. That excursion of his, that so mirrored my own, was conducted for his then principal, Howard Marks.

Smugglers such as Peter were not my only associates. Prison is full of comedy and weird life stories. Ernest Saunders, a leading figure in the famous Guinness share-ramping trial who attracted universal derision for escaping imprisonment by claiming to have premature Alzheimer's, had kindly commissioned an education block at Ford, where an adventurous programme had been instituted. This mood of re-education had reached Leyhill. I was a great adherent of this opportunity to pass the time and spent a lot of time on various courses.

One of the men on my painting course was clearly very talented and a bit of a favourite when the prison inspectors came. His name was Jim Gilbert. He was very tall and unfortunately very violent and liable to lose his temper, which spoiled his favoured status for parole. He was in prison for stealing two Purdey twelve-bore shotguns, made in the 1920s with exquisite craftsmanship, from a country house. At trial, it turned out they were worth £12,000. Quite a cool burglary, you might think. Not so. Having no idea of their value, Jim had stolen these guns for a squalid robbery on a chemist, and to that end he sawed off both barrels! The money in the chemist's till was a few hundred pounds; it was the drugs that were the big draw. Ah, the folly of man. Jim promised to take me along as consultant on his next country house burglary, so as not to make the same mistake again. He became a useful decoy for operations I did later.

There was a very keen drama group, popular particularly because it had a link to an outside group that included women. They put on a fast French farce called *Up the Bedouin* or something similar. There was a prisoner we called the "Dirty Dentist" who hated his wife and studied poisons in the prison library. He became entrapped by the *News of the World* by a fake sheikh type posing as a contract killer, whom he would meet up with on the playing fields at dead of night. He was actually arrested for conspiracy to murder his wife after the first act of the main performance, in front of a busload of old age pensioners. He was hastily replaced by a black prisoner who had understudied all the parts a bit. Great was the confusion and mirth.

I enrolled on pottery courses and an excellent teacher came in two days a week from Bristol Art School to give us lessons. He actually remembered the Arnolfini exhibition in the Sixties, where I and other New Generation sculptors had had the apogee of our success. He took me up and fired some creations of mine at the Art School facilities. Finally he persuaded the authorities to allow a group of us to go into Bristol once a week to make use of their state-of-the-art kilns and wheels, but above all of their skilled adult fellow students. It was most enjoyable and I learnt a lot of what I know today in the company of those students. It certainly rekindled my interest.

But I blotted my copybook. I was also a cleaner at Leyhill and therefore allowed to carry a set of keys to get at the equipment and get in and out of cupboards. In one of the routine searches, a canny old officer spotted a key that was not native to Leyhill. It was to a locker at the Art School which was available to the students. It was searched and a bottle of wine and a cheque book were discovered there. They were pretty harmless, but against prison regulations. That was the end of my stay in Leyhill. I was on the next convoy out, initially to Bristol gaol. I'm an idiot sometimes.

"ABANDON HOPE all ye who enter here." This chilling inscription is carved into the stone lintel above the entrance to Dartmoor. It was mid-winter when our batch arrived. The moor was snow patched, the air freezing, with occasional volleys of sleet and hail. I was entering a different world, where actual bats hung from the rafters in the dim hallway that led to reception.

We had dressed in civvies in Leyhill. Here it was boilersuits with "HMP" on the back. There it was a dormitory, here it was a cell to yourself, made of stone erected by prisoners taken during the Napoleonic wars. There it was the gentle forested landscape of the Avon, here an endless barren rocky heath, dotted with marshes and ponies. There it had been unhurried free movement around the campus, where the screws lived and let live. Here it was endless lockdowns and echoing, shouted orders. There you walked with your chosen mates from admin block to education block to refectory. Here you walked slowly round the yard in front of the screws, albeit dressed comically in Gannex raincoats from the Harold Wilson era, talking only to the person in front and the one behind. So cold was it that we wore our towels round our necks and pairs of socks over our hands, which we blew at with steaming breath. It was a scene reminiscent of the retreat from Moscow.

As for work, there wasn't much. That winter I was assigned a table and sewing machine in the so-called engineering block, and after a twenty-minute training session was launched into stitching pre-cut rectangles of jute-like sacking into, yes, this is not a cliché or exaggeration, mailbags. After three hours of that, it was back to the cells for lockdown until the next event. This was announced by the unlocking of the door and a shout of "Dinner!" or "Exercise!" or "Restitution!", as one ironic warder denominated work.

It was a great relief to be assigned to "quarry". This may once have meant what it said, but now it designated any work outside the prison. That meant maintaining the hedges and verges of the small town that goes with Dartmoor, called Princetown, which had once housed the prison support staff. The screws were better off now and all had cars, so most of them commuted from Plymouth or Okehampton. Princeton had become a sink estate for single mothers and the unemployed.

On another work detail, we would maintain the French and American graveyard that the wars had left behind. This was preparation for an annual American commemoration ceremony. But it was not strenuous, the work, and quite quickly we would gather in the cricket pavilion to while away long tea breaks. It was on one such break that I befriended a Swede who gave me the contact details of a big distributor called Kentar, in Stockholm. Kentar was to provide a useful outlet for my wares after my release.

I vaguely remember that there was a farm there, but what it supplied to the kitchen escapes me. The moor, across which we sometimes took roundabout return journeys, seemed only fit for the occasional sheep or pony. Like a minor public school, the prison had its slightly artificial traditions. Two hunters were kept there, and at any one time two of the screws would solemnly parade around the prison perimeter on them in case of an escape and the subsequent hue and cry. There was also the prison cat o' nine tails, which was produced by a screw and combed through his hands when he deemed that we were becoming unruly, as though flogging was still occasionally permitted by the prison regulations. The prison chess sets – and as usual in my prison stays I played a lot – were of bone, maybe human, and crafted by an earlier generation to sell and thereby to feed themselves.

We had visits of course, although they must have been a nightmare for the families of inmates to organise to such a remote part of England. Joyce visited me once. The girl had certainly grown up. Ibiza was a second home to her now and she knew all the associates Keith and I had known. So I was not surprised at a turn the conversation took.

"Dad, you're so reckless and disorganised. Three times you've been caught, always because of making simple errors in planning."

"It's harder than you think, you know. People arrive out of the blue with drugs. You have to get rid of it quick. You have to rush around. You know."

"And you are too trusting. And you always give up."

"What can you do?" I pleaded. "You need all the friends you can get, and it's the police who can make the biggest difference at trial. Lawyers and friends are useless on the day of sentence." I must admit that has always been my philosophy. "With my record, they only need to see me coming and it's a nick," I continued. "And one that they can make stick. After that, it's passing the attitude test."

"Well, things are going to change," said Joyce. "I've been in Ibiza with Liza and the Wilkinsons. I see a lot of Philip de Bere and Nick

Seary and I've seen how they do things. They're so much more careful than you. You're getting a bad reputation. That's why the Radcliffes and John McDonald cut you now. You're not professional."

I shrugged. Can the leopard change his spots?

"Next time we do this, I'm going to supervise," said Joyce. "Okay?"

We? The cheek of the young.

"Next time? I'm penniless and don't have a boat," I said.

It was true, I was penniless. I had lost a lot on a dumb leveraged-gold-futures scheme dreamt up by Banque de Rives, which they had drawn me into. But Joyce had an answer.

"Ah! That's the thing. *Trimala* didn't make the reserve at auction. I've bought it under the counter for eleven hundred quid. But it's in a very poor state because a bunch of junkies have been living on board. I've thrown them out."

Wow. The girl *had* grown up. I told her what I had heard about Kantar, the Swede. At least I wasn't known in Stockholm. Now we had a plan. That was that for the moment.

I settled back into Dartmoor, which in the end was fairly painless after the first horrific induction. Most surprising of all, there were very few rows on our wings, although there was another world there, that of the nonces, or sex offenders, who would appear on a segregated balcony when we attended the prison cinema. Their arrival would invariably trigger a great cacophony of whistling, catcalls and abuse from the stalls. It may be that one of the Krays was also held in segregation there for a while, although I was never aware of him during my stay.

One day I was called to reception, my clothes were returned to me with a warrant to travel from Plymouth to London, and I was told to go. I was free again. Rebirth.

MUCH HAD changed in the world. There had been the Falklands War and the Miners' Strike. Morlands was no more. Metrication had even come to the drugs world: you could get dope in grams. But at Castelnau things stayed the same. Sue had her own life and I was in the way. The children were grown up. Lee was at university. The queues for the bridge were interminable. I started a campaign to sell the place and move to a flat in Notting Hill. Sue was not agreeable.

So it was a relief to join Joyce in Gibraltar. She had met a boy called Ron who was living on a fishing boat he'd brought from England, which allowed Joyce and I to get to work on *Trimala*. One evening Ron launched a verbal class-attack which annoyed her and made her think again about the fishing business that they had had in mind. After a sail with him and his mates to Ibiza, she jumped ship. Joyce is a bit of a feminist and had taken offence at the way Ron and his friends cut her out of any conversation about their tiny cannabis deals. The conceit of it! After what she had seen!

Perhaps to teach them a lesson, she did a run with Philip de Bere and Nick Seary, who had a route from Morocco to Benalmadena, in southern Spain, followed by a car delivery to Barcelona for a handover to a German team, who then took the consignment to Hamburg. Apparently Philip always posted a lookout 300 feet above for their arrival at Benalmadena. Jim Gilbert, the ex-Leyhill inmate who was now working with them, saw police in the vicinity, so Nick in the BMW did his usual runner, leaving Joyce and Philip on board. It was a harmless patrol and Joyce fended them off, but I think she liked Philip's caution.

Meanwhile I had got *Trimala* ready and finally the two of us did our first and only number together. It was from Pointe des Pêcheurs to Port St Louis, at the mouth of the Rhône, and then through the canals to Rotterdam, the Kiel canal, the Baltic and finally Stockholm.

Here is Joyce's recollection of the trip:

It was 1984; I was twenty-one years old. One year previously I had been carving my way in the world in California as a Cordon Bleu chef and had been offered the chance to open and manage a café in the most prestigious part of Santa Barbara, called Montecito. I was being asked to design the menu for the owners when a letter arrived from my father inviting me to join him on his yacht that summer to cruise around the Mediterranean.

Homesickness and the temptation of the beloved Mediterranean Sea and sailing lured me back to the UK, only to find within two weeks of my return police suddenly appearing in the garden at Castelnau and approaching the house from the rear, as others walked into our dining room, arresting myself, my mother, my brother and a friend who was visiting at the time. We were carted off in a police van to Shepherd's Bush Road police station, where we were shut in separate cells, and then escorted to Richmond, where we were held overnight before being questioned the following morning. That is how I learned that my father had returned to his life of crime, and two weeks after I had rejected my future prospects as a café manager in America, my father had been arrested for the third time in my life.

By now my brother and I were able drivers and we shared the prison visiting orders, taking turns driving to Leyhill to visit my father on our own, so that he was never deprived of visits. My mother, my grandmother, my brother or I would drive down and sit with him for two hours once every month or two.

On one such visit, after he had almost completed his three-year sentence, I had this gut feeling that he was planning to return to what he described as the only thing he knew, other than being an artist and he'd blown all of his chances in that direction. I could not understand how or why anybody in their right mind would want to risk their freedom in doing such a thing and I challenged him. I can remember saying, "You're going to do another number, aren't you? Well, if you are going to do it again, I want to come with you this time. I have to see for myself what the hell it is that attracts you, and perhaps if I come along too, I can help stop you from getting caught by offering some female cover."

Not long after this conversation, in May 1984, I was given a bundle of cash to take with me to Gibraltar and instructions that I would find the *Trimala* in the marina. I was to stay in a hotel the first few nights because the boat had been abandoned for three years and had had squatters living on board, who had ransacked it for every valuable item and left it in the most squalid condition. It took two days, sixteen hours of cleaning, four binbags of black, soggy, rotten clothing that smelled like sewage water and various bottles of cleaning fluids before I checked out of the hotel and into the *Trimala*.

I was instructed to get it taken out of the water and have it scraped and anti-fouled, and that my father would join me one month later. I was on my own and had been given just one point of contact from someone my father knew. Why on earth this point of contact was supposed to be helpful to me I don't know, all I had to go on was a name and a location: "Find Willy at Bar X and tell him you're a friend of Dave's." I found Bar X and within found this huge, blubbery, Gibraltarian greaseball, introduced myself and said, "I am a friend of Dave's and he told me I should say hello."

I was there a while and had various adventures.

Dad eventually arrived by car and we went to Ceuta by ferry, to then drive up to the mountainous marijuana farmland territory of Ketama. I remember the winding hill road leading up there and a boy shouting, "Hashish, hashish," waving a block of hash the size of a giant matchbox at us. We drove on, to what looked like an empty mountain road with an old, closed-down petrol pump at a small turning, where some bored-looking teenage Moroccan boys hung around. We stopped and Dad asked them where we could fill up with petrol. One boy said he would show us and got in the car with us. As we continued, with a view of mountaintops stretching as far as the eye could see, I spotted a farm tucked away just to our left. The boy said, "I live there."

A little further on, we filled up the car and turned round to take the boy home, and he invited us in for tea. I noticed that our car was brought inside their farm courtyard and then hidden from the roadside view, and before long I realised we were able to do business here. My dad began all the negotiations; they took us long into the next the morning. We had been given beds for the night and were fed copious amounts of sweet mint tea and a fantastic lamb tagine, followed by eggs coddled in half a pint of dark green olive oil that I thought at first was horrid, but would love to try again.

We stayed in a hotel down near Ceuta that night before returning to Gibraltar, and before long we set off again for Morocco, only this time Dad sailed *Trimala* to a little marina there while I took the car to Ceuta to join him. We needed to be able to get up to Ketama and see the hash producer a few more times to finalise arrangements. Meanwhile a few riding trips on Arabic horses in the Moroccan foothills took our minds off things.

We left the car behind, and set off to pick up the 200 kilos of hash that we had ordered and paid for. I learned then that Mohamed, the hash farmer, would be bringing the hash down to the coast by donkey, meeting us at night. The only visual point of reference we had would be their torchlight, plus the bearings Dad had been given. It may have been 1 A.M. by the time we saw their torchlight on the beach; I think we had been there for hours waiting. Then the hash was brought to the boat in a small dinghy that took more than one trip.

We set off into the night heading towards Ibiza as a stopover, without a breeze and on engine power, when a loud, repetitive thud started. Dad quickly shut off the engine. Something had hit the propeller in the night and broken off a blade, so the engine was out of action until we could replace the prop. A change of plan meant us sailing into Alicante, where there was an airport. Dad could ask Lee to buy a propeller to give to someone flying to Alicante, and we could meet them at the airport. However, we had no engine, no wind power, and were drifting at sea with 200 kilos of hash on board. Next the electrics cut out, so we had no port or starboard lights to warn other ships of our presence. We did have a couple of fold-up bikes on board, and Dad used their torchlights, strapping the red bike light to the port side with sellotape and covering his green handkerchief over the white torchlight to use as a starboard light. We took turns to keep watch for other ships and boats during the night, and had to jump up and turn on the port and starboard torches whenever we saw any, then turn them off again afterwards to save the batteries.

I was on duty and fell asleep on my watch. I suddenly jumped up to look outside and saw that we were in the middle of a vast fishing fleet. I leapt outside to turn on these feeble little torchlights. I can't think of a time when I felt more vulnerable. They probably all had radars and had detected us and were giving us a nice wide berth; nevertheless my pulse rate was through the roof.

The next day we had a fair wind and made good progress towards Alicante, sailing past the Costa Blanca towards an isthmus that we needed to tack around. But as the sun was setting, the wind dropped, and without power we began drifting backwards into the night. Then at about 2 A.M., when I was on watch, I saw a bit of a breeze and quickly got busy, tacking left and right round the isthmus, which took until dawn, before we could sail directly once round the headland into the harbour mouth of Alicante and straight for the Club Nautico swimming pontoon. Our inflatable rowing boat had been strapped to the side of the *Trimala* but wind and sea had ripped the bottom so that it no longer served, so we had no choice but to make a crash landing rather than anchor in the harbour and row to shore.

So there I was, having been winching and tacking sails all night long and exhausting myself in the process, crash-landing into the Alicante Club Nautico swimming pontoon just as some Spanish lady had come out to get some sunbathing done and was applying her cream. She began complaining to me in Spanish that I could not then understand, but her gestures and tone of voice were enough to let me know she was unhappy about two crazy people crashing into her swimming pontoon and lashing the *Trimala* to the only available spot we could find. I found myself screaming back at this woman in English, "Can't you see what we're doing, you fucking idiot," or words to that effect. She stormed off, to return with the Club Nautico harbour master, who happened to be the ugliest man I had ever laid eyes upon. I had looked up "broken" and "propeller" in my Spanish–English dictionary and had no sooner explained that both the propeller and the ability to row ashore were "roto" than he turned to the fuming Spanish lady, shrugged his shoulders and walked away.

Later we somehow managed to get a tow across the harbour to a shipyard and had *Trimala* pulled out of the water again, this time to have a new prop fitted. We went to the airport to meet the person Lee had given the prop to and returned to the shipyard.

I became horribly ill with some sort of stomach virus that gave me a raging temperature, with the stone shipyard in August at forty degrees acting like a furnace. All I could do was drink water and stay very close to the lavatory while my rear end frequently exploded. Dad used this time to build a hidden chamber for the hash, which he covered with fibreglass in one of the holds, creating a false bottom effect for the mainsail storage space.

With the hash now sealed, we continued on our journey, bypassing Ibiza and heading for the Gulf de Leon. The plan was to take *Trimala* through the French waterways and on through Germany, Holland and Denmark, then to Sweden, where Dad had a contact. From Alicante we took another couple of days to reach France. With a strong tail wind, we approached the Gulf de Leon and began to head inland. Dad wanted to drop speed by changing the large jib to a smaller storm jib, only the halyards had not been tightened off thoroughly enough and had wrapped themselves around the mast steps at the top of the mast. This meant that nothing could be done except to climb up to the top of the mast and unwrap the tangled stay lines.

We were charging along at high speed. Dad said he would climb the mast but needed to turn the boat into the wind to stop her speed while he did this. "You're mad!" I said. If he turned the boat into the wind it would rock back and forth like a bucking bronco at a fairground, which would be far more dangerous. I said, "I'll go up the mast as we're moving along." Dad said, "No, that's far too dangerous," and went inside to get his life jacket on, but I knew I was right and was up the mast before he had come back outside or could do anything to stop me.

I remember how high up it was, and how scared I felt gripping the mast between my thighs, clinging on for dear life while I unwrapped the tangled stays from the foot rails sticking out of the mast and climbed down again. We were able to continue without stopping, dropped the jib immediately and headed towards what was supposed to be Port Saint Louis – only Dad had misread the map.

We had entered a river with boats along it and a low bridge blocking our path, when Dad said, "Hang on, this doesn't look familiar, I'm sure there wasn't a bridge there before." Instead of checking his map, and because we could not go further without taking the mast down, Dad decided to use the bridge, some rope and his winch to lever the mast out of its foothold. The only trouble with that was, he hadn't used *Trimala* for over three years and the aluminium mast foot was almost galvanised into the foothold. As he stood by to grab the mast foot, I was to do the winching, which is normally easy enough. But something didn't want to budge, and the winching went from gently pushing a lever back and forwards to putting my feet up against the wall, putting my whole body weight behind me and the winch lever, and then pushing with all my might, again and again and again. Nothing was happening, and Dad said the boat was being levered out of the water by my efforts, when suddenly, with a bang, the mast jumped out of its socket about three feet in the air. Dad caught it and we lowered it down on to the deck.

In the morning, when I found I could barely move my arms or legs, Dad learned of his mistake by looking a little more carefully at the map. We only had to motor across to Port Saint Louis, where there was a crane on standby to help lower your mast and a sea lock to provide access into the Rhône and our highway through France. At least I had saved the crane fee.

No sooner do you enter the Rhône than the whole experience of sailing is removed. You are now boating through France, pulling into and mooring in the heart of every charming town or village along the way. *Trimala* was very well adapted for sailing, where you would sit down to man the tiller, but for boating along waterways, where the guiding and tiller movement requires constant vigilance, it is better to be standing and looking over the cabin roof to the waterway ahead. My dad cast his eye about him on our first day of travelling up the Rhône and spotted a builder's plank of rough wood that was long enough to rest across the life rail at the stern. He lashed both ends of the plank with rope to the handrail and lashed a cushion onto the plank in the middle, where he now had an elevated perch and could steer the tiller with his foot and see a good distance. He also found a discarded beach umbrella that he erected so as to protect himself from the August midday sun.

If this didn't look strange enough to the eye of anybody passing, the next object that caught Dad's eye was half-buried in mud on the side of the riverbed at Arles: an antique, wooden, horsehair-lined chair. Dad ran the *Trimala* aground so I could hop ashore to salvage this thing, as he thought he could lash it on top of the plank in place of the cushion. I don't know why, to this day, and I soon became aware of a crowd of people gathering to watch me trying to wash the mud and silt out of a horsehair fucking chair, just so that we could look like the oddest fucking boat on the waterways, just desperate to attract attention to ourselves. Questioning the sanity of my father, and irritated with the whole situation, I snapped and, scooping up a handful of mud and moulding it into a cricket ball, hurled it at my father. I am not a great shot but this mud bomb hit him right in his balls.

Dad started the engine and set off without me, leaving me on the river bed. I had to wash all the mud and silt off me first before I could start to plan my way back to London without any clothes, money or passport. Fortunately Dad quickly returned and we said no more about that one.

At Avignon we had to stay for a week with a broken gearbox. We were lucky to find a German mechanic on a neighbouring boat, who helped my dad to fix it. This also meant taking the train to Marseilles and having a nice seafood lunch before collecting a part for the gearbox. I had a rather hot and steamy romance with a married Frenchman called Serge for just one weekend, as Lee soon arrived with his girlfriend. They were driving through France and thought they would just check the riverside, not expecting us to still be there.

Then the boat was fixed and ready to go. Dad wanted to visit his old friend Jeremy Fry at his place in Grand Banc, so he took Lee's car and left me and Lee to take the *Trimala* on our own, saying he would meet us in the following day or two. Dad duly returned with Lee's car and we proceeded on our way.

We were then joined in Lyon by my mother, who had brought a friend's daughter from the States with her for a holiday. The first night they arrived, we went for a meal to a well-known three-star Michelin restaurant, Léon de Lyon. Both Mum and Dad had forgotten their reading glasses and were holding the menus at arm's length to see the writing better. The waiter swiftly arrived, holding a tray piled high with assorted reading glasses. I liked Dad's policy when dining out, which was either to eat for more than £50 a head or for under £5. We generally ate very well on low-cost set menus, with the occasional culinary treat.

At this point we parted from the Rhône and entered the Saône. The land steepened and the locks became more frequent as we headed towards Epinal, where my mother and Katy departed by train. We had no mishaps and nobody else knew of the cargo we carried. We were, after all, supposed to be holidaying through Europe and needed to be seen doing that.

From here on, we were heading due north. Summer was closing in on us, the weather was changing and we needed to press on and do as many miles as we could each day. As soon as we reached the border of Germany, I presented our passports at our first crossing. We were told of a wine festival at Bernkastel that we could make if we kept up the pace for five days.

At Bonn we joined the main part of the Rhine, which was a whole new ball game. This river flows, and the weather was a bit misty first thing in the morning, but mist doesn't put my father off, so we set off all the same from a foggy town centre. No sooner had we got out on to the Rhine proper than we were tearing along, assisted by the current; not only that, but we couldn't see two feet in front of us. Suddenly we came within touching distance of a huge tanker, as large as those ships out in the Mediterranean. We stopped rather shakily, had a cup of tea and waited for the fog to lift before setting off once more.

Heading through Frankfurt was perhaps the most awful day of the whole journey, in that it was just all day long breathing sulphurous green air from factories spewing their chimney smoke out into the atmosphere. I had a handkerchief over my mouth all that day, but luckily we had passed through it by nightfall and the following day the scenery improved.

Another time, we approached a major town with a vast bridge crossing with at least eight huge pontoons, and a vast number of gigantic cargo ships that made me feel as though the *Trimala* were made of matchwood. As we approached the bridge, with several other ships heading in both directions, we ran out of fuel and began spinning around in circles, such were the current and river eddies. Before Dad could get the funnel into the engine and pour the spare diesel in, the German river police had pulled up alongside us to assist. We were both amazed by the speed of their response, and very grateful.

We still managed to arrive at Bernkastel in time to catch their wonderful wine festival. The firework show was unforgettable. Using the old castle, which was itself dramatically lit with spotlights, to launch the final display, they created a river of golden lava that flowed out from between the castle parapets down into the Rhine.

When we reached Holland it was noticeable that boats changed, from expensive fancy launches to anything that could float and have an engine attached, such as a caravan on a raft with an outboard. We came out at Delfzijl, which was heavily industrial, and moored up against some gigantic tankers. Then we sailed across the "Riddle of the Sands" waters – is any book more loved by he or she that likes to mess about in boats? – to an island called Norderney, where Dad wanted to get some navigational maps for the North Sea.

We had no idea what this little German island would be like. All I can say is it was very strange, a place where it seemed only people aged over sixty, with plenty of money, came on holiday. It was very flat and beautifully laid out, with pretty street lights and garden paths and walkways. The hotels had mixed sauna baths and we were very much in need of a bath, so had a sauna and massage ourselves. We learned that this was a place that people came when having an affair. Most of the couples there were in extramarital relationships and all seemed open and jovial about it.

I forgot to mention that *Trimala* had no washing facilities on-board, only the head, or toilet, to use. In the Mediterranean and coming through France, when it was warm, we had a five-litre plastic canister that we painted black so it would absorb the heat. This was then poured into a watering can, which one of us would then pour while the other showered. By the time we had reached Germany and Holland, it was late September and our only chance of having a proper wash was in public facilities. So the sauna at Norderney was seriously appreciated.

We pressed on, got through the Kiel canal and I had to jump into the sea once more. I asked Dad to heat up the kettle and prepare a warm shower from the watering can, as I was about to leap into the Baltic Sea to untangle the shaft. Thinking the water would be freezing in October, I was amazed by how warm it seemed at eight in the morning.

After this we sailed non-stop for Sweden. It was cold and we both wore double socks, a jumper and waterproofs on top to keep warm. Heating the kettle to make tea or coffee warmed the cabin and galley up but produced droplets of condensation on the ceiling. We approached Karlskrona and could not see any towns, just hundreds of tiny, tree-covered islands. I spotted one yacht sailing towards us and made arm signals for help. The yacht approached and I called out, "Can you tell us where there is a marina?" The man turned around, said, "Follow me," and led us straight into a tiny sheltered marina with shower and sauna facilities. It was heaven.

By the end of our first day, we had found a place where we could have the boat taken out of the water, had hired a car, unloaded the cargo into the boot of the car and had been to visit the customs. Dad and I sat there and were asked why we had come to Sweden at this time of year. I decided it best to do the talking, and told the man that we had been on holiday, intending to explore the Swedish archipelagos, but had taken much longer to get here than expected, so we wanted to leave the boat here over winter to come back for her again next summer. As I spoke, I could see our hired car outside in the car park with the boot filled to the maximum with hash. The officer said something about needing to arrange for a loan to cover the VAT until our return, then off we went to get the paperwork done, returned to the customs office, then headed straight for Stockholm to meet Dad's contact.

The contact turned out to be a factory worker and we met him at his workplace. We were then directed to an apartment on the outskirts of Stockholm, where we were invited to stay while we found somewhere suitable to hide the hash. We chose a spot in some woodland nearby and Dad got the necessary tools to bury the hash, presumably because he had brought rather more than his Swedish friend could deal in one go. The decision was then made to head back to the UK. Dad would come back later and dig more up as and when he needed it.

Actually Kentar, my contact via Dartmoor, was doubtful about my appearance. I had gone to meet him in the canteen of the factory where he worked. He'd had two Englishmen approach him previously with elaborate and clever-sounding proposals of this kind, together with devious financial wonkery, neither of which had come to anything. So he listened to my offer sceptically.

"Oh yes?" he said. "And how will you get it into Sweden?"

"It is here in Sweden."

He went rigid.

"Where?"

"In the boot of that red hire car over there." I pointed to the factory car park.

Kentar found us a flat in a village outside Stockholm while he sold off twenty kilos to get us started back to England. I would return from time to time as he released the rest of the load. Sweden was riding a wave of public spending on social care at the time and the sports centre in this village would have done Marbella proud.

We made a lot of money out of this excursion. Joyce got enough to buy a house in Ibiza and settled there. She married a local electrician called Lorenzo, by whom she had one child. For my part I was set up, for a while at least.

I left *Trimala* in Sweden and went back to the Mediterranean and met up with another sailor, Peter Catlow, in his thirty-two-foot sloop. The idea was to do another run to Sweden, but I foolishly did not attend on the beach in Morocco, and Pete was unable to link up for the delivery. I had gone to Gibraltar to ready the Stockholm end. As a result we had to replace it with a load that was going begging in Benalmadena. Another 200 kilos proved too much for the Swedish market and Kentar got bust halfway through the sales. No-one got paid and I was beholden to the Benalmadena folk: Nick Seary, Philip de Bere and Jim. They would bide their time and ultimately help themselves from my cash pile at Castelnau the next time I was arrested.

So it was that I fell in for a while with the Benalmadena gang, until their German team got bust. Philip de Bere had a forty-two-foot steel ketch, an Endurance 42, but although he was a good sailor he was prone to panic, and from time to time I walked out on him. For example, we bought in a load to Benalmadena and Philip wanted to transport it in a little rental car from the marina to his lookout area, a café with a car park, where it was to be transferred to a big BMW for him to drive to Germany. Each time we were about to do the transfer, he ran away from the café car park where the two vehicles were, saying he'd spotted something untoward. Eventually he lost the keys to the BMW. That meant it had to be towed to a garage so that they could fix up a replacement set. The load had to be transferred back to the rental. To and fro we went, Philip gibbering away all the while. Then he lost the keys to the rental. It never ended. I walked out on him in disgust. No wonder Khaled had said he would not pick up from the Lebanon again unless he was accompanied by someone with much more calm.

Next, he and Seary were buying Hermann Göring's old yacht, flying the double eagle flag, which was insane since it attracted attention wherever it went. Why Joyce had admired these people over my calmer nature beats me. Anyway, they were all I had for the moment and I was important as a master of the Moroccan end of the operation.

It was a busy time and I was involved in various cannabis operations. Every deal had its own structure, with different financiers and different methods of transport: air, land, sea. There were different boats, different outlets, different divvies of the proceeds. From time to time there were busts and the losses lay where they fell. I should say these were considerable and very few of us ever ended set up, once and for all, rich.

As a rule of thumb you could say this: if a unit of cannabis in Lebanon cost £1,000, and sold at the retail level in the UK for £10,000, the profits would be approximately £2,000 to the man who took it out from the farm in Lebanon, £2,000 for the man who took it into the UK and the remaining £5,000 to the distributors in the UK. Bear in mind that the risk of being caught with one kilo was nearly the same as being caught with 100. That is one of the principal attractions of bulk. He who takes all these functions under his wing gets the lot.

13

The East Ender

NOW LET ME tell you about Robert Tibbs. Tibbs was a member of a family of Cockney hard men from the East End of London. Their world was scrap metal, boxing and muscle, and Tibbs grew up in the era of protection rackets and wage snatches with sawn-offs. The digitisation of money transfers meant that the latter was a dying trade and some moved into drugs. Tibbs, who had served a jail term with his dad and brothers for his part in a brutal gang feud in the Seventies, had a villain's villa in Estepona, complete with swimming pool. Despite having an absurdly expensive hide furniture suite, he kept the plastic covering on to preserve it. I saw the place after his demise. It had been looted down to its marble floors.

He appeared on my horizon through a prison contact of mine called Philip Escott. Philip came to be in prison with me because of a dazzling crime of his own. His family were coal merchants near Newport, in South Wales. He had managed to divert whole trainloads of coal destined for the steelworks there into the family yard, which he then sold off. This went on for four years. The judge had never seen anything like it but it had to be treated as theft, for which the sentence was limited.

My first meeting with Robert was in a car park at Membury service station with Philip. He wanted a load of his brought in from Morocco.

"You Francis? I got seven hundred ki in Morocco. You want to sail it over?"

"How much?"

"A ton per kilo."

I looked puzzled.

"Hundred quid, mate."

"Okay."

"Done. Philip'll sort ya." He turned heel and got back in his car.

I got Philip de Bere to do this one and later he and I did similar runs for and with Robert, but with us handling the supply end. On one of those, I sent Philip to my Mohammed for a load. After a lot of delays and setbacks, it was taken out to Philip's yacht on a speedboat from the beach and sailed to the Shannon estuary in the Irish Republic. There Tibbs had an amusing route for the dope to get to London: in a horsebox with a wild stallion.

I did the next one. Mohammed was doing well and his dad was building a mosque somewhere. He had his eye on Nirvana, a villa in Tangier. For once everything went smoothly on the beach and we loaded using the big Avon that Philip had as a tender. Tibbs had arranged to deliver the load to Newport. It was only the second time I had been out into the Atlantic and it was just me, Philip and Tibbs's man, who proved to be a very good cook. It was a hard slog without stopping for six days. Off Plymouth, I was on watch when a helicopter checked us out and flew back. No way would I tell Philip this and Robert's man agreed; he would have panicked and the load would have gone overboard. We went into the Severn estuary, where we expected to mark time near an uninhabited island called Steep Holm until there was a high tide at night, when we were to meet a fishing boat crewed by a single recruit of Tibbs's called "Evan the Boat", whose eponymous boat was kept on a tidal estuary, the Usk. I had been introduced to him by a friend of Tibbs the last time I'd been in the UK. Despite what I had told Evan, these instructions for the meet had gone through a reprocessing of Chinese whispers between Tibbs's landlubbers and had become a low-tide, daylight rendezvous. Evan was sensible enough to know this must in fact be high tide and came out regularly for two weeks to look out for us, but only in daylight. We had no way of forewarning him of our arrival. We tried Channel 16, the open, twenty-five-watt channel that allows everyone within twenty-five miles to hear you, but we couldn't raise him; he was recovering at home from his failed excursions.

All day and night we waited. High tides came and went. We sailed round the island looking for a beach. There was one patch of sand with derelict buildings and an iron staircase climbing the cliffs behind. Finally I unloaded, no easy matter on Steep Holm with just an Avon Scow dinghy. The tides are very fierce there and an anchor could barely hold. Then we went empty to Evan's berth on the Usk, again when the tide permitted, to find out what had gone wrong. But nothing was wrong. He was there making ready for sea. Bring on mobile phones! He followed us out back to Steep Holm and I now had the task of again getting into the Avon and shifting the load to his boat, struggling with the five-knot current. It was a pretty bad nightmare but all was well in the end.

For once I had money to spare. Some of it went on refurbishing Castelnau to ready it for sale. I had prevailed over Sue and in 1989 we parted with this wonderful house we had had for twenty years.

Yes, yes, I kick myself today. Who was to know that simply living in a fine house in 1990s London would earn more than I ever could floundering around the Mediterranean, throwing cash around on running boats and flying about the place at standard, on-the-day single flights?

Camper and Nicholson was an ancient yacht builder for the rich in Portsmouth, more English than Greenwich Palace, more gentlemanly than the Duke of Devonshire. They built simply the most beautiful yachts in the world, streamlined beauties that lay low in the water, narrow as a pencil, gracefully rising in the bows to fade at the stern over a slimming extended counter. The central wheelhouse would be beautifully slaked to look as though it were just peeping over the deck, into which it was sunk, at its contemptible rivals. It was the E-Type of yachting style, almost always finished in Oxford blue, black or white.

I wanted one. And now I could afford it: the Nich 48 ketch *Katanavik*. She was my only extravagance in my whole life. My pride and joy.

I found her at Aquileia, near Trieste, and she cost £75,000. I sailed her to Benalmadena and did some minor repairs. She was well equipped, with depth finder, speed log, wind speed and direction and so on, with Eberspracher heating, a seventy-five-horsepower Ford engine, removable roof, bow and stern cabins each with their own head and a lot of dry room in the bilges. Six passengers were comfortable, eight could be accommodated at a stretch if the saloon berths were merged with the table.

Alas, I was to get little personal use out of *Katanavik*, because circumstances overtook me.

I also caught up with Harvey Bramham, with whom I had done the epic Atlantic crossing back in 1971. He had eventually been run to ground in a Welsh commune and extradited to America for some aspect of our US run. He had served his two years and no-one had seen hair or hide of him since. Now he had a boat in Newport, south Wales, on which he lived alone. He had changed a lot from his young, carefree days and had sacked his girlfriend in a fit of paranoia that the police were onto him again. Even I thought this was incredibly unlikely, since he had not at that time considered making any nefarious use of the boat; they were hardly likely to assign full-time officers to watch him in case he returned to his Sixties ways.

He filled me in on the missing years. He had lived well for a while, driving a Bentley Fastback, but then had to go on the run when I'd been imprisoned. He had found life on the lam a nightmare. Yet now he was planning to get down to the Mediterranean to re-launch himself in the drug business, solo. His music career had not revived. I reminded him of the way he slept like a log, even on watch. Get the girlfriend back, I advised.

He did sail off in the end, disappearing completely. He never came to collect his guitar, and nobody has seen him since. This was confirmed for me by mutual friends, Pat and Mike, who lived in Ibiza later. Poor Harvey; he was probably asleep at sea at some disastrous moment.

Meanwhile I was not the only beneficiary of this flowering of prosperity. Peter Catlow, a mechanic at one time in Keith's shop and a very competent sailor, bought a boat and did a run on his own to Stockholm, probably contributing to the general over-supply at that time. His run was successful and enabled him to buy a bigger retirement boat in Florida. He invited Sue and me to go for a Caribbean cruise and so we joined him in Venezuela and cruised a while among the islands in those parts.

Peter was, however, unseamanlike about detail. He allowed the rowlocks on the tender to come unglued and failed to vulcanise them back on. The two lengths of anchor warp had been connected by a double shackle which snagged when the cable was running out. This sort of oversight could have bad consequences in a crisis, and eventually we were in one.

We were sailing near a group of islands called Las Roques, chopping along one evening in a stiff breeze. It was his watch and I was asleep. I awoke, perhaps alerted by the unusual sudden calm, and looked out the cabin window. Palm trees! I raced up to the wheelhouse and found Pete asleep. I cancelled the autopilot and threw over the helm but it was too late. There was a crunching judder and we jammed on a large rock. We gunned the engine, backed the sails and so on but nothing would move us. That meant we would need to kedge off, which means putting an anchor on the tender and paying out the cable as the tender motors away from the yacht. Then, having dropped the anchor fifty yards off, and providing it holds, one can use the powered anchor winch on the yacht to drag the boat off the rock. I did all this at high speed, but the double shackle on the anchor chain jammed as it paid out, jerking me to a violent halt. The dinghy stopped dead and I fell over, pulling the safety key out, which I then could not find. I chucked the anchor overboard and started to pull myself back by the warp. Meanwhile Pete was winching the cable in under the spreader lights, which meant it was dragging my arms under the water and the rest of me too unless I released my grip on the warp and found myself drifting off into the night. There were no oars stowed, so I was helpless. Luckily I was blown ashore. There was nothing to do for it except dig myself a sand berth against the wind under a mango tree and wrap myself in rubbish bags I found lying about against the endless droppings of the booby birds above.

Daylight revealed Pete's boat upright but stranded on the reef to which his hauling on the anchor chain had brought him. However I was in wading distance of the boat once Pete had brought me some shoes and, even luckier, the island was occupied. It was a Venezuelan army base, and they had their own fishing boats which eventually came by to pick up their pots. They rescued us and took us to their base. Pete's cup of misery ran over when they told him that they would eventually pull him off but we would have to await the passing of an imminent storm.

It turned out to be quite a big base, with about 500 soldiers encamped and dependent on a big Israeli desalination plant and the fish they could catch. They welcomed us into their refectory for a much needed meal and to await events. The storm came, roared away for a day and then blew out. We were taken back with sinking hearts. The boat had indeed been blown further up the reef where, after a short inspection, we realised it was a write-off. We had to hire a plane to come and collect me and Sue, leaving the wretched Pete to contemplate the remains of his uninsured dream.

I got Pete to crew my beloved Nich 48 to do another run from Pointe des Pêcheurs. There was the usual panicky scene on the beach while loading the Avon, which I supervised. We ended up drifting with a fouled outboard on the Avon, towing a life raft with the dope. We floated westward all night while I tried to free the outboard.

Pete and *Katanavik* had gone back to sea. Next morning we fetched up on another beach, where some locals helped bury the contents of the Avon. Now I had to relocate *Katanavik*, which after twenty-four hours I did. We had moved a considerable distance west out of Hoceima province.

This was a pity. I had only just made a moving presentation of a specially ordered tea set from Asprey's, which had cost me £1,500. It was to a specification of Mohammed's from one of their catalogues. Needless to say it was hideous gilded rococo kitsch, or Lebanese Quinze as some call it. This I had presented to the district judge of Hoceima province in the hash storage shed at Mohammed's farm, to his delight. A worthwhile investment was about to be wasted.

So here we were, in the neighbouring province, with some locals, replacements from somewhere, who helped us reload. They demanded our outboard engine in payment. Jim Gilbert, who had come with this load from Ketama, suddenly deserted me without warning or any coherent reason. If it was to get the car, I had forgotten. I was alone on the beach in just my swimming trunks; there was no sign of my clothes. Pete had retired over the horizon. Then a soldier and a policeman appeared on the beach, from different directions, and for a while appeared to mind their own business. I waited there helpless in the broiling sun. Occasionally I swam. Were they waiting for the return of the others?

At about midday, with it getting hotter, one of them came up to me. Did I have my passport? No, my clothes had been stolen. How did I come to be there? Was I alone? And so on. Eventually they asked me to go with them and walked me up the valley to Jim's hire car. This did not look good. Jim was there. He had lost the keys.

There was another long wait. Then we took a bus. On it, a passenger slipped me my passport. Weirder and weirder. We got off at a stone lookout post with one bed in it and were left in the custody of the sentry there.

There was another long wait. The sentry made us lunch and brought us cups of chai. Finally we were collected by an officer in a jeep, who mysteriously had my clothes. We drove down to a small town and were held in a stifling police station in the outskirts. Next a number of villagers were brought into custody until they had identified us. Great was the wailing of their womenfolk outside. From there we were taken to Chefchaouen. In a nutshell, we were busted.

They hadn't caught us with anything. Still, after a five-minute hearing, I was sentenced to ten months, Jim to eight. They knew what we had been doing from the villagers whose arms had been so swiftly twisted.

THE FIRST prison they put me in was in Chefchaouen, a lovely and mysterious town of white and pale blue buildings surrounded by stone walls. The prison was rather less lovely. It was small, and we were confined to and slept fifty in a room, on bunks. My bunk mate had taken vengeance of some sort on his wife's family. She had died and the family had repossessed the donkey that was her dowry. This had angered the old man, who had taken the law into his own hands and was serving, like most of us, a short sentence. The daily issue of bread was more than that abstemious old fellow needed and he stored what he didn't eat under his sheet. The room boss didn't like this. He slapped the poor chap round the face and confiscated his little store, which had virtually become his bedding.

On the whole the food was execrable: a dustbin of boiled lungs. A daily rooting through and clearing the rice of the rat shit it had picked up in storage made it bearable only to the most wretched. Almost everyone ignored this disgusting fare and ate food brought in by their families. Here the gracious hospitality of Arabs towards guests asserted itself. Their generosity in sharing their food with Jim and me was unstinting. Friday was a day of feasting on all that had been brought in on that day's visiting period. By Sunday we'd all be starving or eating prison food.

After a while we were moved to Tetouan, a city, where there were other Europeans. Here the generosity was just as marked. We had only summer clothes, and winters can be cold and damp even down by the coast. One of my new roommates solemnly unpacked a parcel with two *djellabas*, the traditional long robe of the Berbers, and went through a ceremony of trying them on, followed by a grave announcement that they did not fit him and would we do the honour of taking them for ourselves. Later a Berlin taxi driver, in for smuggling Mercedes cars stolen in Germany, explained that the elaborate face-saving ceremony we had witnessed was to spare us the humiliation of feeling beholden to him. Incidentally the car smugglers were in for having false documentation rather than handling stolen goods, so that the cars did not have to be returned to their rightful owners in Germany.

One day there was a new arrival in our twenty-man cell. He was a large, prosperous-looking man who exuded power. The cell boss immediately conceded his bed in the corner furthest from the latrine, and all showed him respect. He was there for five days before he departed with equal style. I learnt that he and his friends could close Tangier port with a command. On such occasions, whole lorry loads could transship in perfect safety, mainly going to Amsterdam. It was clear that over time I and my friends no longer featured in the premier league.

Life was very hard. A single open toilet was poorly connected to the sewage, through which rats could emerge into the cell at night. A plastic bottle was meant to block the hole but that didn't prevent me being awoken one night with a stinking rat sitting on my forehead. Nevertheless such is the preciousness of freedom that we Europeans all agreed that this kind of suffering over a year was preferable to the dreariness of three years in an open prison in the UK.

At last my day of release came. I was picked up by a policeman. Apparently there were four days of procedures to be gone through before I could be repatriated. Or there was a quicker way. What was that? Four hours, at a cost of £20. I went for that.

I was driven to the Ceuta border and seen off with an embrace and a kiss.

After my release, there was some good news. Pete Catlow had made it back and there was money in the kitty despite a raid on my attic, where I kept a big float, by Nick Seary, who had been admitted to the house by Lee. This taking advantage of people who get bust to settle old debts is a hazard of the trade. Nick was claiming for his load which had gone down in Stockholm, in my view breaking a rule of the trade that losses lie where they go down.

For a short while there was peace before the storm. I linked Pete up with Ted to take *Katanavik* back to the Med for another run for Robert Tibbs, who now favoured Oban, in Scotland, as a landing site because it looked quiet on a map – a fatal error. Meanwhile

I was at Keith's place in Ibiza with my family, admiring the new house he had built for himself there. We had that expat habit of getting the London papers, airmail edition, from town. Keith came in and casually started reading out a story. It went something like this: "Customs made a dramatic raid on a forty-eight-foot ketch as it arrived in Oban in Scotland yesterday. On board they found a ton and a half of cannabis, worth three and half million pounds. A fifty-seven-year-old mechanic from Kendal was on board. Further customs action led to the arrest of Robert Tibbs and two others, who were remanded in custody by the Oban sheriff."

"Anything to do with you?" asked Keith.

"Fuck it. They've got the *Katanavik*."

I waste too long thinking. I couldn't rescue my lovely boat but I might get to my money, and so I took the next flight to Barcelona and thence back to London. Too late. My deposit account had been frozen, so there was nothing for it but to return to Ibiza.

It's a cardinal rule with me to avoid being tried with others. The pecking order in a so-called conspiracy is best examined in the absence of others and so we carried on in Ibiza, trying to have a good time until autumn. Then we returned. Castelnau had just been sold and I had been thinking of settling with Sue in Ibiza. We had helped Joyce with her house there, and bought three ruins in the Old Town. Spain had recently become fully democratic and a member of the European Union. Great was its reward. Motorways mushroomed and Malaga became a boom town, with huge swathes of speculative development going up in its hinterland. Welcome to dreamland. At the door ushering me in was Edward Crawshaw. He was buying up fincas cheap in a lovely valley there and making them cute for holiday lets.

Edward was typical of the era. I met him through a cousin of Philip's. He had a restaurant somewhere in Notting Hill just as it was entering its golden era and was an early investor in Westbourne Grove, whose heady road to Bond Street/Notting Hill hip was beginning to open up. He had an art gallery on the triangle there and a desktop publishing business that cost him his house in the dotcom crash and would have cost him his gallery too if I hadn't bailed him out with two of the fincas as collateral. So he owed me.

For a while Sue and I lived in a flat above Edward's gallery. In due course he bailed out of Westbourne Grove and disappeared to Mexico. Needless to say we lost our money. But for the moment we had that flat.

One day an ex-girlfriend of Lee's rang for him, and I foolishly answered. She recognised my voice.

"Francis. You're in London. I thought you were on the run."

Fuck.

I left that day and went to live in a bed-and-breakfast in Monmouth Road, nearby. I still returned to our flat from time to time but could feel the net closing in on me. One time I went round and saw a man in a car parked outside, reading his paper. On another occasion, the phone rang but nobody spoke.

I survived a week. Broke and desperate for company, I arranged to meet a friend for a drink and we went to the Castle pub in Ledbury Road. They struck. We were about to go in when two men came round the corner and I was grabbed.

Apparently HM Customs had been onto us for three years, in what they called Operation Beagle. I went guilty before Guildford Crown Court in January 1991. My reward was nine years' imprisonment.

Robert Tibbs, who was portrayed in court as the driving force behind the operation, was originally jailed for twelve years but appealed and got a retrial because of faults the first judge had made in summing up. He then decided to plead guilty rather than face another jury and was given a reduced sentence of eight years, though he was also ordered to pay £200,000 under the Drug Trafficking Offences Act. Customs had watched him go to Morocco six times to negotiate deals. Peter Catlow was jailed for twelve years, at the age of fifty-seven. Philip Escott, then aged forty-three, got five years and another chap who was supposed to pick up the Oban shipment got six.

Philip Escott's adventures would continue. On his release he managed to get to a liquidation sale being conducted by the National Coal Board and for a song bought centrifuge equipment worth hugely more than the NCB appreciated. This he sold to a diamond mining group in the Congo. He supervised the shipment himself. As his party made their way up country and paused at a rest stop, a gang of bandana'd militia pulled in to seize the load. A burst from an AK47 injured one of Philip's group, and he returned to the UK much shaken.

14

One Last Punt

I TURNED SIXTY in the second year of my sentence. Jo Boothby, my barrister friend who has put these words down on the page, is always astonished that I never reflected much on the way my life had panned out. It's true that I live from day to day. I don't, on the whole, muse about the past or where I am going. This may seem surprising, given the amount of time to oneself that prison provides. But oddly I think more about the nature and effect of imprisonment and enforced idleness than I do about what got me there.

That is because I always want to do something, not think. Sailing is doing. Every hour at sea takes five of preparation: obtaining parts, making repairs, dealing with marina offices and yards. Dope running is as much going from bank to bank collecting or depositing cash, flying to one place or another to deliver it, waiting for phone calls in hotels, as it is actually collecting and transporting loads. The reader should not be misled into thinking otherwise merely because I have not spelt out these details, which would make dull reading.

Dope. I have been smoking it regularly ever since the day of my wedding. But I am no "head". I rarely smoked during the day and certainly never when I was working or needed a clear head. I do think cannabis is harmless. Not totally harmless, what is? Food, alcohol, cigarettes, even sex, can all be harmful in excess. But a few joints in the evening have left me at age eighty fitter than a lot of people I meet in their sixties. That's partly luck and partly because I have always been active. Now I have returned to sculpture and pottery. Would that that had been all I had done.

Harmless though I think cannabis to be, I have never subscribed to the philosophy that a lot of my fellow smugglers propound: that because it is harmless, it should be legal and therefore it is wrong that they have been imprisoned. That is senseless. If it were not illegal they would not be loading it into yachts, sailing it into ports and selling it for gigantic profits. Our profits are, in a sense, the other side of the coin of imprisonment. It ill behoves us to complain.

However, prison is dead time and I hate it. I have always moaned about it and sought to persuade the authorities to "reform" us inmates with useful activity that might change our ways. When I was out on bail back in 1971, I had even given an interview to the *Guardian* about it when I was out on bail back in 1971, disputing a Home Office claim that remand prisoners were not locked in their cells for twenty-three hours a day. They certainly were. Remand inmates in Brixton at that time couldn't even have a radio, a privilege reserved for convicted prisoners.

By 1990, a more reformist mode of thinking was gaining traction. Barlinnie Special Unit, in Scotland, was mould-breaking in its time and so was the Special Custody Unit at HMP Blantyre House, near Maidstone, Kent, to which I eventually persuaded the authorities to send me. On arrival, I lost my precious phone card; I must have dropped it. Later, outside the dining room on the noticeboard, was a notice: "Phone card found. Apply to CO." Right then I realised I was entering a very different kind of prison to those I had hitherto known.

Blantyre House was just that, a house. Well more like a big school, an ex-Borstal with playground and sports field and some outhouses for workshops. It is situated deep in the Kent countryside, near the handsome town of Goudhurst. However it is obviously a prison and is surrounded by a high fence topped with barbed wire. This may go against the spirit of the place, which I will describe to you. But bear in mind the criterion for admission. You have to be bad, very bad. I'm not actually that bad a person. I'm not like Winston Silcott and Kenneth Noye, who were there in my time. But I tick all the right boxes. I'm a recidivist criminal who has been deemed to merit long (more than four years) sentences. So I doubt that I am quite what they had in mind when the Blantyre House experiment was developed.

I'm no intellectual but the thinking behind it was courageous and I applaud the brave beliefs of its director, Jim Semple. Criminals were people with no sense of responsibility towards their fellow men. This was because of bad upbringing and being treated as born bad all their lives, in care homes, foster homes, special schools, Borstals and prison. If you treated them as fellow human beings and trusted them, gave them respect and so on, they would change. They would respect others and want to earn their way decently.

This was indeed a sharp contrast to the short, sharp shock regime of high Thatcherism that had been practised at Blantyre House in its Borstal days. One of the screws there told me they had once, for the benefit of the new boys, faked a shooting of an inmate who had completed his time. These novices were launched on a cross-country run and the graduate was told to wait by a trench for the approach of the running party, at which point the screw fired a starting pistol at him. This was a signal to fall into the trench, to the terror of the runners.

Now it was run like I imagine a small public school is. There were only about 100 of us. Once past induction, we slept one per room, with no locks or eyeholes. There was no period when you couldn't visit other rooms. The screws were in civvies, like teachers. Most of your time was free. We were responsible for cooking, housekeeping and organising our time. There were educational facilities of all kinds: art, drama, reading, writing, building, carpentry. We were expected to do something better with our time than keeping fit and running round the track. Many in prison thought gym was the be all and end all of life. Prison is full of bodybuilders.

There was no parading or roll calls. You had pretty much free use of the public telephone boxes. In fact you were free to go, though you'd be caught and sent elsewhere if you did. People did indeed go missing, as you could come and go pretty freely, if you had a good, constructive reason for doing so, once you had completed six months. It was allowed if a written explanation was given to the director. Those reasons were either work or education.

The SO asked me politely to smoke my joints down at the sports ground.

The son of Ginger Marks, or "Rent a Psycho" as the Press called him, was only there at weekends. He had a job as a scaffolder in London. One of my friends there went off and trained to be a mortician. Another of my mates swept the underground tunnels at night.

The results were very good. Only eight per cent were reconvicted within two years of release, instead of the usual fifty-seven per cent. It is of course true that we were volunteers who had been selected by the governor, but I did not detect that he chose the goody-goodies. There was a rumour that there may have been some bribery to get in. Although a Category C prison, it was much freer than a D Cat. One of the principles behind it was that you only went there for the last part of your prison sentence because the aim was to release you a better person.

There was a six-hole golf course. There was an excellent library, open all day and night like the education department, and I read a lot there. There was a chicken enclosure which Kenneth Noye managed, as farming was close to his heart; at large he had a house with quite a lot of land around it. It was a considerable risk having him there. He had actually stabbed a police officer dead, which made him a bit of a hero with hardened criminals, but that's not why he was there. He was acquitted of murdering the officer. He told me he was defending his property and thought the copper was an intruder. The officer was actually there to do surveillance linked to the Brink's-Mat gold bullion robbery. So Noye cannot have been popular in police or prison officer circles. He was nearing the end of his sentence for smelting some of the gold from that notorious robbery and after his release he was quickly nicked again, this time for stabbing a man dead in a traffic argument. It was always said that it was a road rage incident, which surprises me. He seemed a quick-witted, self-controlled individual who always knew what he was doing. He was a generous character too. Once he paid for a travelling fair to set up at Blantyre House for two days. On the first day it was free for all for the charity Mencap and their flock. We did a lot of work with Mencap, taking them on excursions to the coast. The next day we were the beneficiaries of this fair. Wives and children congregated en masse, loaded with provisions for our kitchen. I think it cost Kenny the better part of £10,000.

How well behaved were we? Not that well behaved. On New Year's Eve, a lot of alcohol got smuggled in and everyone got rat-arsed. Then a gang turf row broke out in the early hours, and knives were deployed – there were no searches in Blantyre. Two people were hospitalised.

Another time, the video player in the common room was nicked. Kenny organised a whip-round to replace it. I set up a fund to buy a new kiln for the art department, which was very productive. One scheme allowed us to be driven in to Goudhurst to sell our art works from a stall at the Saturday market there. It became well known and a place of pilgrimage for people who wanted to see what lifers looked like and check whether they were just misunderstood. I am sorry to admit that we eventually ran out of product to sell and took to selling the stylish, solid oak chairs we sat on at the market, of which Blantyre had a ready supply after the refurbishment of the chapel.

Blantyre was a great success for me, relatively speaking. It confirmed my love of pottery and I did, for the first time in my life, resolve that I was going to change my ways and leave sailing and cannabis behind me. However, as usual, I blotted my copybook.

Sue was living in the flat at Westbourne Grove above the gallery. We only had a four-year lease there. Ted Crawshaw's money problems continued to deteriorate and he wanted to sell it. This was a double worry. I wanted my money back, so I took advantage of our freedom to go up to London to confront him. Nothing was achieved. He was trying to sell the gallery but nothing was moving and so on. I made it clear that Sue was not moving out until we got paid, or he could give us the flat. But I was spotted at Victoria and reported. Jim Semple was very disappointed in me, despite the success of the kiln fund, and I was out and back to Maidstone Prison, where I had started.

Old lags, like I was becoming, get to know how to work the system, how to get food and fags and telephone cards, a cell to yourself, a good work detail and above all a transfer. That's how I got to Ford, a Category 4 open prison but nowhere near as easygoing in its way as Blantyre House.

And it's also how, in 1994, I got to Berlin.

SOMEHOW GREGOR Best, the KGB spy, came back into my life. I had a letter from him, giving me a number in Berlin, and I telephoned him without admitting I was in prison. It was good to talk to him again.

The Berlin Wall had come down, Russia was in chaos and innumerable chancers were trying anything to come up with a new way of making a living. Amongst others, Gregor had been approached by some Leningrad chemists who were proposing to launch some miracle addictive recreational drug on the West and thought that Gregor, with his contacts and his English, might be able to help. But he was well into his seventies and too old for ventures of this sort.

I thought I detected an opportunity to help with my parole applications, the first of which was not far off. I wrote to Detective Inspector Stevens, who had masterminded the Oban ambush as a result of which I was incarcerated. He was interested and came to see me in Ford. As it happened, he had moved to the National Criminal Intelligence Service, which was already interested in Russian crime, so I had struck a chord.

After a suitable delay, I was encouraged to make further contact with Gregor, which I did. I was to go and see him as though a free man and say I was interested in what his chemists might offer my contacts. I was to make out that I was interested in an importation. This did not actually fit with what Gregor had been offering but I played along for the sake of an outing.

I was on home leave by this time and met Stevens and a German liaison officer and another NCIS operative at Victoria. We went to Heathrow and flew to Tempelhof. There we booked into a hotel, but not without a drive around Berlin during which we passed Spandau. That, I was told, was where I would be staying, although I spoiled the joke by my enthusiasm to make history.

The next day they allowed me to go unaccompanied to meet Gregor. I met him outside our hotel in his car and we went to a restaurant on Stevens's expenses. It was a delight seeing him again. He was very well and had found a little business that kept him going. He photographed Old Masters, projecting them and painting over the projection, then selling them as decent reproductions. I confessed to him that actually I was in prison and was here with the police, but it would help me if we could help them out. He was amused to hear that I had not changed my ways. I guess he didn't like the sound of all of this but he agreed at least to come and meet Stevens the following morning, more, I think, as a favour to me than to get into any ambush scams.

Stevens, Gregor and I met the following morning in the coffee shop of the hotel. Stevens was very nervous. Gregor frankly related his Berlin history but said he could no longer help with any introductions and could give no current information. The chemists' emissary had returned to Russia and to trace him now he would have to go to Moscow. The whole thing spluttered out in the sand.

The NCIS operative wanted to get his money's worth for this wasted excursion. "You've crossed the line, now," he said. "Let's talk about the things you know about, Francis."

"I've not crossed the line. I've tried to help you with something nasty coming from the East."

"Drugs are drugs, Francis."

I disagreed.

At my parole application, I tried bringing this episode up but they were ready for it. They had a letter from an NCIS superior saying I had been no help to his officers. I'd probably done myself more harm than good with this wild goose chase.

A walking buddy of mine was Darius Guppy, a stylish, handsome young man who had pulled off a scam on Lloyd's of London, who had bankrupted his very rich father. Darius staged a jewellery robbery in New York to claim insurance in what was supposed to be revenge on Lloyd's. It came unstitched, partly because rope had been used to tie him up, which was a giveaway: this is not the method of choice used by professionals in New York, they use duct tape.

I remember Guppy once being last in the prison chow line for the latest container of battered fish, and getting rather a small one as a result.

"Bit small," he said, peering in disappointedly.

"Saved it for you, mate. It's a guppy." A lot of chortling.

I have subsequently learnt that a great-grandfather of his did name this species.

AS FREEDOM loomed, my financial situation at least looked sound. My infinitely long-suffering mother died not long after my release and so there was about £100,000 of inheritance in the kitty. I am indebted to Dorothy for her patience through all the sufferings I had caused her. She had led a good life and I had not. She had collected, I had squandered, but at least I didn't have the usual excuse when I was released that I had nowhere to turn but back to crime.

Sue still had the properties in Ibiza; that was her condition for selling Castelnau. They were largely derelict but gave her a place to stay and be near Joyce, who had restored a villa in the country with a pool and terrace, where she lived with her partner. Later, as we all got poorer and Joyce split up with Lorenzo, she moved into the Ibiza town buildings, did them up and sold them. Keith too was ageing. He and Jane moved back to England to send their daughter to a school that did the Baccalaureate. The move was quickly followed by the break-up of their marriage in Cambridge, where they ended up living close by each other. Ibiza was no longer part of our lives.

Sue and I led semi-detached lives but to her credit she never washed her hands of me. I had nowhere to go when I came out, so I joined her at Westbourne Grove.

I feel, writing this, as though I'm bringing the curtains down. And if I was the type to take a bird's eye view of my life, as I am having to do now, I would conclude that that is indeed what was happening. I no longer thought that I must immediately return to the Mediterranean. In hindsight, I was running out of steam.

It did not feel that way at the time. My love of ceramics, of making things with my hands, absorbed me more and more. I owe this to imprisonment; it's the only good thing I have had out of it. I took a share in a pottery studio under the Westway in west London with a lady called Barbara, bought a wheel and materials and threw myself into the ceramics business. I turned out domestic pieces, bird baths, amphora and jugs in a simplistic style with minimal decoration, reminiscent of my Sixties sculptural *oeuvre*. I remained very drawn to pieces that would be sculptural and outdoor rather than kitchen-based. Punting them through stalls and shops in the Portobello Road, I did acquire a small following. My sisters were very supportive, always praying for my redemption. They both married doctors and one of them, Susannah, remained throughout her life close to Hampstead Heath, our childhood playground. All my life we have had Sunday lunches and Christmases there and to this day they have a number of my ceramics in their garden and house. They've been to our place in Malta for holidays and once to the Scilly Isles with us. Her husband once compared my life to my diving. He said, "You'd never know, when Francis was about to slip overboard from the picnic boat, when he would reappear or from what direction." He told Sue she would have to live with this habit of mine in our real life, away from holiday boating.

The flat in Westbourne Grove was too small to have the children, and Crawshaw would not give it to us. It was becoming clear that he too might be going down the tubes, with only his gallery to support him. So here I was: semi-detached marriage, little income, insecure accommodation, getting older. More than anything, I was restless.

Time for one last punt. Here were the problems:

1. If it was going to be my last operation, it had to be reasonably big. No way could I start a routine of driving to and from Morocco

to get twenty or thirty kilos a time in a car, crossing endless frontiers in a short space of time. It had to be about a ton, and in one go. That meant a boat.

2. I couldn't afford an ocean-going yacht. Even if I could, I couldn't sail it alone out into the Atlantic. I'd actually only done that twice and the second time, with Philip, I was with a professional.

3. Not only were my sailing co-fraternity getting older, wiser and more settled, but none of them would touch me with a bargepole. My reputation was now appalling. I was always getting caught. Once or twice was one thing, five times in twenty years was another. I was on my own.

4. It needed to involve minimal numbers of frontiers. If my name was dirt with smugglers, by the same token the authorities could see me coming from a mile. I had to come up with something that was not copybook and obvious.

This was my solution. I bought the biggest trailer sailor available. A trailer sailor is a sailing boat that can be put on a trailer and towed. You've no doubt seen people towing boats of all kinds around the roads of Europe. Some of them are just day cruisers, Avons, speedboats, small fishing boats and so on. Well, there comes a point where a car cannot safely tow them. Still, big powerful 4x4s were now commonplace and the limit of what they can tow in the way of boats is about twenty-eight feet and a weight of two tons.

I bought an American trailer sailor with a retractable dagger keel for £19,000. The ingenious aspect of this boat is this: boats have to be bottom heavy if they are to sail in heavy seas. In most, this is achieved by loading the keel and the depths of the boat with ballast, the weight of which keeps the boat upright because the bottom is constantly dragged down by the greater heft below water. That's why boats generally right themselves even if turned upside down. This trailer sailor solved the problem of being too heavy to tow with ballast by having a floodable hull below floor. So it was towable at two tons. When you put it in the water you then flooded the chambers in the hull below the deck with another ton of water.

Only it didn't have to be water.

The other advantage of a trailer sailor was that you had caravan accommodation wherever you went; no hotels, restaurants or sleeping in cars. Still, I needed help, and for the reasons I have already given, the quality of the assistance available to me was not great. I found a young man called Edna – yes, Edna – who was anxious to earn a quick buck, just like me. He was a small-time dealer, well spoken, who ran a supply line from London to Nottingham. Reassuringly, he held a yachtmaster's offshore certificate.

I bought the boat at Dell Quay, near Chichester. There and then we cut a hatch in the ballast tanks and attached bolts so that it functioned safely in default mode. Then we set off. I took a perverse pleasure in serially side-swiping and damaging the barriers of the *péages* on the motorways south through France. You paid your money and the barrier lifted, but because of poor design the barrier then started to close when it had detected that the car had passed, and caught the boat as it followed. Since I had paid the lorry tariff, I enjoyed the little rows that ensued, shrugging my shoulders and pointing out it was entirely their fault. Edna eventually stopped me playing this attention-attracting game and on this he was unusually sensible.

On we went, through the Pyrenees and down to southern Spain, and put the boat into the water in a marina. There we left it and drove on in a Toyota to Morocco. This time Edna had the contact, a man in Tetouan, and I left him to negotiate delivery. We bought 700 kilos. The deal was that it would be brought out to us in a fishing boat when we were ready with our boat. This was a big improvement on the original plan, my protocol of running up to the beach at night, which always caused trouble.

Back we went to Malaga, flooded the ballast tanks and puttered off under the power of the ten-horsepower outboard. Off the beach, we looked out in vain for the two marker bonfires that they had promised to light. There was no sign of them. Eventually I put Edna ashore. He was gone for a while. Shortly before dawn, he reappeared and reported they had had to call off the delivery because there were too many people around for their fisherman to be willing to go. We retired to sea and waited for the following evening, when we planned to try again.

It was an unpleasant day, choppy and windy. Finally a customs launch came alongside, took Edna on board with them, put a tow onto the yacht and took us into the port at Mdic. There the boat was searched and our passports checked. In the course of the search, it was hinted that their duties on any particular night might take them a long way down the coast if only the poor official could afford medical treatment for his daughter in France. Another £15,000 had to change hands. I had no doubt my passport check had made our purpose there clear.

Edna went and spoke to his man. One way or another, we needed more money. We had to take a bus and ferry back to Spain so that Edna could rustle up another £15,000 from a friend of his, then back we went. Two nights later, we were at the marina and then off back out to lay off from the beach, looking at two little fires winking at us a mile away.

A fishing boat loomed out of the night with no lights showing. It was hairy trying to load nearly three-quarters of a ton onto that wallowing pleasure boat and keep it stable, but we succeeded with a lot of cursing and moving boxes, first here, then there, totally unconcealed around our living space.

We staggered along very slowly up the coast to Valencia, where suspicion of boats was low. The original plan was to go all the way to Agde in France without stopping on the way, to minimise frontier issues, but that would have been too slow and nerve-wracking. What needed to be done was better done in Valencia than somewhere like Agde. We told the marina office we were only there for the day and no-one bothered us for papers. In fact we were there for three days but without leaving the marina. We had to pump out the ballast tanks, using the sink pump and a hose, and replace their contents with the great load that had been lurching around in the saloon: 700 kilos of cannabis resin.

Finally we set off along the coast, refuelled and refreshed and higher and more stable in the water. For a while things went more smoothly. When we had returned to Spain to raise the extra money, we had moved the Toyota and trailer to await our arrival at Agde in the boat. Now, on our arrival, we dragged the boat out, for all the world like tourists at the end of their season. We hitched up and set forth across France

We had only gone about twenty miles before there was a sickening lurch from behind as the steel brackets of the trailer buckled under the three-ton weight, for which it was not designed. We considered putting the boat into the Canal du Midi nearby and sailing the canals back to England but decided against it. We were running out of summer. Instead we put the boat back into the water and took the trailer to a workshop for new brackets to be made and installed.

I had noticed that Edna was always going off to be sick. He seemed to be in poor shape for someone of his age. On another occasion he left me at the workshop to go and see a pal in Barcelona. He was gone a week and I was beginning to despair when he reappeared with the Toyota, seemingly much better. He had a bandage on his stomach which he explained as the aftermath of a blood poisoning episode he had had there.

The trailer was repaired, so we again landed the boat onto it, and it held. It looked sound. We set off to Bordeaux, having lost two weeks, to join the motorway system. By now the rigid holidaying patterns of the French meant that we were no longer one of 1,000 boat trailers on the *rentrée*. Still, it felt like we had made it. We collected our ticket, went through the first *péage* without damaging the barrier, and moved out onto the huge apron that the major toll booths have on either side of them. A massive figure of a man in a blue uniform and covered in security kit stood there leaning on his motorbike. He signalled us to drive over towards him and kill the engine and for both of us to get out and show our passports.

He retired a short distance and consulted with an official in civvies. Then he returned and indicated for us to follow him with our rig. He led us off to a parking area near a building a short distance away. I still hoped we would survive and remained icy calm. Edna on the other hand sweated like a pig, turned pale and promptly had a choking fit. First they searched the car. That yielded an envelope with brown powder in it. Heroin. Edna was a junkie.

Next a German Shepherd went on board and immediately made a fuss of the flooring. I was asked a simple question which I have been asked before: Did I want to tell them what and where were the drugs on the boat? Or would I prefer them to rip the place apart looking for it? I chose the first. That night I slept on a camp bed with blankets from the boat, one hand cuffed to the radiator. Edna collapsed and was taken in an ambulance to hospital.

It took just two weeks to have us before the Tribunal in Bordeaux. On every other occasion that I have been arrested, the events that led up to it involved people informing on me. This is the only occasion on which I am convinced I was the victim of pure bad luck. This was a purely random stop which turned sour, possibly because of Edna's heroin addiction. He had not expected the excursion to last so long. Our many delays had been his undoing, because the supply of smack he had taken with him had run out. His trip to Barcelona had, for reasons I've never learnt, turned his health from poor to disastrous and maybe was what had caught their attention.

I got six years.

Aftermath

THE CENTRE PENITENTIAIRE at Gradignan, near Bordeaux, consisted of a Sixties-era pair of dreary housing blocks. Inside, the atmosphere was of a rundown, cheap hospital, with linoleum floors and concrete walls, two to a cell in bunks, French TV to drive me mad, night-time lock-up, food collected from a trolley in the corridor and eaten in the cell.

On my first night I seemed to have a cell to myself, but in the early hours a second person was inserted, and bedded below. After a while I heard a gurgling and grew uneasy. I turned the lights on to find a middle-aged man, who had cut his throat with his Bic razor. The screws arrived and bandaged his throat, took his blade and left, shouting "Pede", which means paedophile.

I hated the place. It was a big prison and I couldn't understand a word anybody said. The screws were dogmatic and formalised in their enforcement of their rules.

They were also in dispute with their government about pay and conditions and were involved in regular protests. I had nothing to do, so I watched the nightly pageant that ensued from my cell window.

19.00. Lorry arrives and drops off skip.

19.15. Van with a load of used tyres arrives. The tyres are unloaded into the skip.

19.20. About thirty screws parade round the skip. Petrol is poured over the load and set alight.

19.45. French TV van arrives with news crew. They film.

19.55. Union official steps forward to be interviewed.

20.05. Camera crew leaves

20.15. Fire engine arrives and extinguishes fire.

20.30. Lorry arrives to pick up tipper

21.30. We watch these same events, by now edited to give the impression of outraged spontaneity, on the TV in our cell.

I was used to the sergeant major ethos which lingered in the English prison system. The culture of spit and polish, inspections and barked orders were at least recognisable in their origins. Orderly institutions had the characteristics of army life. Fair enough. It was sort of patriotic to accept it.

French prison administration and its edicts seem to be rooted in a remote and obscure bureaucratic haze. We spent long periods locked up. There was little work to do. I occasionally did some English teaching. Edna worked in the kitchens. For exercise we were locked out in a yard in blistering heat for three hours. When it got cooler, I could at least master *boules*, which I got good at. To top it all, the food was revolting.

I became bolshy and withdrawn. I was angry with Edna and shunned him. The only person I spoke to was an Irishman who had run over a Moroccan in his car. Once the family came all the way to see me and we were allowed just two hours in a tiny cubicle. I stupidly insisted on appealing against my sentence, which delayed my repatriation to an English prison. Even more stupidly, I refused to go to the French language classes on offer. So I didn't learn anything, and wasted three years.

I welcomed the day when two Wandsworth screws got an away-day break to the south of France to pick me up and fly me back to the UK. They said their best gig had been Bangkok, where they got a night in a hotel. From there I went to a Cat D in Cambridge and then back to my alma mater, Ford.

My first routine on going to a new prison in England was to check out whether there was anyone I might get on with. This I achieved as follows. It was our right to read the daily newspapers in the library, and the full range was there. When the library closed, the last person out could keep his chosen paper. I kept an eye on who, apart from me, was anxious to get the *Guardian*, a sure guide in my view to who has an independent and intelligent mind.

This is how I met someone who has remained a friend. Raoul was a left-wing political refugee from Bolivia who had been living in Paris. He was only there for a few months for driving whilst disqualified. His wife Diana used to come and take us out for the day, walking in the Downs with their collie and having lunch in a village pub. I have remained friends with her, and although she has separated from Raoul we continue to have walking excursions on the Downs.

I joined a labour fatigue that bussed out to Chichester every day, where we joined an archaeological team from the Chichester Canal Trust, a group of worthy citizens. Chichester used to be the main port for supplying the Roman garrison which occupied Britain. Over the centuries the estuary had silted up and now the city is several miles inland. There is a Roman palace complex that was once on the wharves and is now beached some way away. The Victorians had cut a canal and built a pool near the walls to try to revive it, but that too had decayed and fallen in. We prisoners set about digging it out, using an excavator on a barge and our own brawn, with a view to restoring the levees, the stonework wharves and the bridges. I operated the Toytown tug that pulled the barge. We stored the rowing dinghies back at a shed at Ford and I renewed the fibreglass, varnished the oars and generally restored them. We administered the letting of the boats and selling the punters ice cream. I enjoyed it. At Easter there was an egg treasure hunt, ending with a prisoner jumping out of a hut in a bunny suit at the winning child. Unfortunately our chosen bunny was a serious alcoholic who could not resist refreshment at the nearby pub between hunts. The children reported back that the bunny was dead.

It was an academic exercise, really. A road had been built across the canal near the estuary and there were no plans to put it on a bridge, so it was really aimed at yuppie warehouse flat-living, not a revival of commercial use. It is still hoped to complete this project by opening it to the estuary, but £1.5 million was needed to unblock and re-bridge the crossing of the B-road halfway down. But it was a nice interlude for us. The students from the nearby grammar school shared their picnics and no doubt felt a frisson that we criminals seemed such normal people. For our part we could flirt with the girls.

One weekend, when the canal opened to the public, the family came down and we hired a skiff to row about and admire my works. Joyce had a son by now, and I took my grandson for a putter on the tugboat. He loved it.

Back at Ford, I got to take the train to Brighton most days to work with Arnold Rose, a chaotic curmudgeon who had a ceramics works. His workshop turned out garden pots and was quite a setup. There were five kilns to work with and he gave me a considerable degree of independence. On one occasion he went off to the south of France with his wife, leaving me in charge for a week. His business was struggling because of the competition from Asia, but he knew the system and worked it to survive. That's where the value of my free-trained labour came in, and it's why I eventually quarrelled with him when he wanted to charge me to fire some pots of my own, and left.

And so my sentence wore away. Prison is debilitating in some unexpected ways. The process of institutionalisation has been much discussed in criminology circles. One aspect is that the skills it imparts are negative ones: how to use the known rules to gain endless small advantages and make life a little more attractive than the next man's. Tools filched from the workshop, extra rations from the kitchens, tobacco pouches from the remands; it all helps while away the years.

But the other, far worse aspect of prison life is the loss of responsibility. Every moment of one's day is decided by someone else. The essentials of human life – warmth, shelter, food, a place to sleep – are all laid on by the state. The personal agency and decision-making that are the very texture of normal life outside are shelved in favour of the institution. Is it any surprise that long periods there leave one less able to cope in the outside world?

I passed another milestone in prison: I turned seventy.

When I came out, Sue and Joyce had sold up in Ibiza. Joyce had had a protracted and unhappy divorce from Lorenzo, who wouldn't let go. He besieged the court in Ibiza to keep Joyce's son and the property there. Finally it was resolved and Sue, Joyce and her son moved to a house in West Byfleet, which they deemed to be the right place for my grandson to be educated at the international school, again for the sake of the Baccalaureate. Sue had at last got Westbourne Grove off Crawshaw's creditors, the bank, and sold it.

I tried rejoining my family in their semi in West Byfleet but this only brought the emptiness of our marriage, and the depressing prospects for me in an outer London suburb, to the surface. I tried it for nine months. West Byfleet was only a temporary home for all of us, to allow Max to bed in to the international school, but it became evident that it would never work for me and I finally made the break from Sue. The resentment she had accumulated against me made a future together impossible. I had done her no good, it has to be said, and we had nothing to offer each other any more. As a result we have skipped the bitterness and remained good friends.

We all moved back to London. Care of Prisoners, a quasi-governmental charity organisation, came up trumps. They had managed to find me a one-bedroom, ground floor flat with a garden and room for my kiln and pottery studio. It was not the Kilburn warehouse I once had but it has served my purposes to this day.

You won't believe this, but it's true. I again lost all my money. I had met someone in Ford Prison, Tony Woods. I must have told him I still had some dough. He got in touch with me and explained an elaborate money-making scheme. To suck me in, he stage-managed an introduction to his wideboy partner, Jesse Richards, at his mum's grand house in Poplar. Range Rovers galore. All going to be kosher. I would run an office off Portobello, and have oversight and control of the bank accounts. In went the last of my money.

The scheme involved buying up huge quantities of scrap copper and repackaging it somehow for resale. The buyer forwarded the VAT to Customs and Excise. Our business then claimed the VAT back from

Customs and Excise as though VAT had been paid out on the purchase of the scrap. Something like that. To tell you the truth I didn't really understand it at the time, but it was explained to me as a cunning piece of perfectly legal financial wizardry which was all the rage before the credit crunch.

So most of the remnant of my inheritance, and Joyce's, went into this scheme. I was told that with a lot of leveraging, or borrowing, that they could do against my investment and that of others, we would double our money. For a while there were dazzling credits and debits to the account, and generous dividends allowed Joyce to pay for my grandson's education.

Suddenly Jesse appeared in the office. He was off in an Aston Martin to Monte Carlo, where there were some big deals in the offing in rustbelt East Europe. This meant he needed the money out of the bank account. In cash. All of it. Need I tell you any more?

He got his due in the long run and was, according to the police, murdered, although his body was never discovered. Ripping me off was child's play. But he got too cocky and applied his methods to much harder men.

I WAS eighty-one in 2015, when I completed this book. What have I been doing? Well, I lead a quiet life of genteel poverty. I survive on my pension and my housing association flat. From time to time I have conducted pottery courses, mainly for delightful ladies who want to learn and master the craft. Artistic pottery is highly competitive, with some considerable stars in the firmament. Firing and glazing clay calls for expensive equipment and a great deal of gas or electricity. At the centre of it is the gas-fired kiln, which calls for very high temperatures, up to 1,300 degrees Celsius. It is therefore capital intensive, which in a global market inclines commercial ceramics to move to India and China. Of course, studio pottery has become an art form in its own right. Bernard Leach is the godfather. He learnt his art in Japan and brought a spiritual aesthetic into our world in the inter-war years. The world is now full of skilled people making beautiful household ceramic pieces and selling them through stylish galleries in enchanting small towns. Potters like Kate Malone and Geoffrey Luff have established enviable reputations with their surreal extremes. The business is an ideal outlet for channelling the energies of skilful craftsmen operating from home. They are a hard act to compete with.

I would like to make much larger pieces with sculptural, undecorated features, echoing my history as sculptor. It's all about form and shape, not decoration. I want to lend aesthetic drama to a house or garden. It's obviously a struggle to get back on the art scene but I'm getting there. My friend Jo, to whom I am indebted for writing this memoir, has said that if the book is popular he will help me rebuild my sculpting career.

As for cannabis and sailing, all that is a long way behind me. The twentieth anniversary of the last time I moved a consignment of cannabis approaches. The only sailing I have done recently came when I was introduced to my co-writer, Jo Boothby, four years ago by someone who had been in prison with me back in 1973. He and Jo had been at the same public school. Jo had a fanciful idea that he might retire to the Mediterranean and potter about the Greek islands in a thirty-two-foot Colvic Watson. A lot of people have that idea. This friend of Jo introduced me as an experienced sailor to help get the boat from Brightlingsea, close to my childhood idyll at

Landermere, to Ramsgate, where he then lived and thence on. In due course we sailed over to St Valery, at the mouth of the Somme, where we ran aground and were stranded on the sands for a while. Then down came the masts and we entered the canal system that I knew so well. Bit by bit we moved the boat down to the Mediterranean, where a year later it ended its short life in Sète. All the places we went through had memories for me, and all the endless setbacks that beset moving around on boats were repeated – running out of fuel, grounding on riverbanks, batteries failing – but at the slow pace of our journey through France, all were of a different order to the frantic tension that any delay in my former life engendered. Yet every incident, and every place we visited, cued memories for me. I never bragged or steered the conversation in the direction of my life, it just came up because it was relevant. And that is how Jo came to think that my life might be of interest to some of the people who have lived through, or been intrigued by, my times.

It's true I occasionally suggested we sail over to Morocco. But no, I was not planning to introduce him, a barrister-at-law, to the delights of my former trade. It was purely because I would have liked to see again those beaches, the Rif mountains, and Al Hoceima, in that country I knew so well. It was not to be.

In the final reckoning, very large sums of money have passed through my hands. I had a house in Castelnau now worth £4 million, an inheritance from my father, another from my mother and a share of Morlands. Plus the vast amounts I made through drug running. Now I have nothing. I have spent more than fifteen years of my adult life in prison.

Would I have had it otherwise? Yes of course I would. But I am who I am.